Texts in Philosophy
Volume 9

Language, Knowledge, and Metaphysics
Selected Papers from the First SIFA Graduate Conference

Volume 1
Knowledge and Belief: An Introduction to the Logic of the Two Notions
Jaakko Hintikka. Prepared by Vincent F. Hendricks and John Symons

Volume 2
Probability and Inference: Essays in Honour of Henry E. Kyburg
Bill Harper and Greg Wheeler, eds

Volume 3
Monsters and Philosophy
Charles Wolfe, editor

Volume 4
Computing, Philosophy and Cognition
Lorenzo Magnani and Riccardo Dossena, editors

Volume 5
Causality and Probability in the Sciences
Federica Russo and Jon Williamson, editors

Volume 6
A Realist Philosophy of Mathematics
Gianluigi Oliveri

Volume 7
Hugh MacColl: An Overview of his Logical Work with Anthology
Shahid Rahnan and Juan Redmond

Volume 8
Bruno de Finetti. Radical Probabilist
Maria Carla Galavotti, editor

Volume 9
Language, Knowledge, and Metaphysics. Selected Papers from the First SIFA Graduate Conference
Massimiliano Carrara and Vittorio Morato, editors

Texts in Philosophy Series Editors
Vincent F. Hendricks   Vincent@ruc.dk
John Symons   jsymons@utep.edu

Language, Knowledge, and Metaphysics

Selected Papers from the First SIFA Graduate Conference

Edited by

Massimiliano Carrara

and

Vittorio Morato

© Individual authors and College Publications 2009. All rights reserved.

ISBN 978-1-904987-79-6

College Publications
Scientific Director: Dov Gabbay
Managing Director: Jane Spurr
Department of Computer Science
King's College London, Strand, London WC2R 2LS, UK

http://www.collegepublications.co.uk

Original cover design by Richard Fraser
Created by orchid creative   www.orchidcreative.co.uk
Printed by Lightning Source, Milton Keynes, UK

All rights reserved. No part of this publication may be reproduced, stored in a retrieval system or transmitted in any form, or by any means, electronic, mechanical, photocopying, recording or otherwise without prior permission, in writing, from the publisher.

Contents

Preface   vii

Contributors   ix

Section I: Language   1

1   Remarks on the Paradox of Higher-order Vagueness   3
    PABLO COBREROS

2   Betraying Davidson   23
    MARCELLO DI BELLO

3   How Similar is "Julius" to "Phlogiston"?   43
    CARLA MERINO-RAJME

4   Compositionality and Lexical Semantics   65
    DARIA MINGARDO

Section II: Knowledge   95

5   Carnapian Modal and Epistemic Arithmetic   97
    JAN HEYLEN

6   Moore, the Sceptic and Defeasible Justification   123
    DANIELE SGARAVATTI

7   Taking Externalism Seriously   147
    ASSAF SHARON AND JONATHAN YAARI

Section III: Metaphysics   165

8   An Olsonian Critique of Hitchcock   167
    BENGT AUTZEN

9   Actuality in the Garden of Forking Paths   183
    ROBERTO LOSS

10 A Linguistic Analysis of the Omnipotence Puzzle   197
    NAZIF MUHTAROGLU

11 Relative Truth and the Metaphysics of Tense   211
    GIULIANO TORRENGO

12 The Contingent *A priori*   229
    PAUL WINSTANLEY

Index   245

Preface

As a substitute for the mid-term thematic conferences traditionally organised by the Italian Society for Analytical Philosophy (SIFA), in 2007 the Society's Steering Committee proposed to further interaction among younger scholars and researchers in philosophy, both from Italy and elsewhere, by promoting the first in a series of graduate conferences.

The 12 articles published in this volume were selected from the 24 papers presented at the First SIFA Graduate Conference held in Padua in September 2007. The 24 papers were selected from more than 80 abstracts sent in response to the call for papers.

In its first edition, the aim of the Graduate Conference was to discuss topics in metaphysics, the philosophy of language, and the theory of knowledge, all construed as broadly as possible. The conference was enriched by the presence of three keynote speakers, one for each thematic area: Kevin Mulligan (University of Geneva), Paolo Leonardi (University of Bologna), and Timothy Williamson (Oxford University).

The editors would like to thank the Graduate School in Philosophy of the University of Padua and the Department of Philosophy of the University of Verona for having partially funded the conference. Special thanks go to the former institution for further financial support in the preparation of this volume.

Almost all of the Italian community of analytic philosophers has been involved in the refereeing process and the editors of the present volume would like to express their gratitude to them.

In particular, we would like to thank the members of the Scientific Commitee of the conference: Andrea Bottani (at the time, President of SIFA) and Richard Davies from the University of Bergamo, Pierdaniele Giaretta (University of Verona), Elisabetta Sacchi (San Raffaele University, Milan), and Marzia Soavi (University of Padova). Thanks also to Jane Spurr of College Publications for her valuable assistance and patience with the oddities of the Italian academic burocracy.

MASSIMILIANO CARRARA
VITTORIO MORATO

DEPARTMENT OF PHILOSOPHY
UNIVERSITY OF PADUA

Contributors

- BENGT AUTZEN is a Ph.D. student at the London School of Economics

- PABLO COBREROS is a research associate at the Department of Philosophy, University College London and Visiting Fellow at the Institute of Philosophy, School of Advanced Study, London.

- MARCELLO DI BELLO is a Ph.D. student at Stanford University.

- JAN HEYLEN is a Ph.D. student at the University of Leuven

- ROBERTO LOSS is a Ph.D. student at the University of Nottingham

- CARLA MERINO-RAJME is a Ph.D. student at Princeton University.

- DARIA MINGARDO is a Ph.D. student at the University of Eastern Piedmont.

- NAZIF MUHTAROGLU is a Ph.D. student at the University of Kentucky.

- ASSAF SHARON is a Ph.D. student at Stanford University.

- DANIELE SGARAVATTI is a Ph.D. student at the Universities of Eastern Piedmont and St. Andrews, Arché.

- GIULIANO TORRENGO received his doctorate degree from the University of Eastern Piedmont in 2007; he is now a temporary research fellow at the University of Turin.

- JONATHAN YAARI is a Ph.D. student at the Hebrew University of Jerusalem.

- PAUL WINSTANLEY is a Ph.D student at the University of Durham

Section I: Language

1

Remarks on the Paradox of Higher-order Vagueness

PABLO COBREROS

1.1 The paradox

1.1.1 A general framework

Most theories of vagueness allow for a notion of *definiteness*. In many cases, this notion can be represented formally with the aid of a possible-worlds semantics. In this kind of semantics truth-value assignments are relative to *points* in a structure; and the key feature of some theories of vagueness is that truth should be treated as relative to some parameter and *definiteness* as invariance in truth-value. An interpretation of this sort for a language with an operator for definiteness ("$\mathcal{D}$" henceforth) is an ordered triple $\langle W, R, \nu \rangle$ where W is a non-empty set of *points*, R is a relation in W and ν a function assigning truth-values to sentences at points. The definitions of "$\rightarrow$", "$\neg$" and "$\mathcal{D}$" are just like the standard definitions in modal semantics:[1]

$\nu_w(\alpha \rightarrow \beta) = 1$ iff either $\nu_w(\alpha) = 0$ or $\nu_w(\beta) = 1$
$\nu_w(\neg \alpha) = 1$ iff $\nu_w(\alpha) = 0$
$\nu_w(\mathcal{D}\alpha) = 1$ iff $\forall w'$ such that wRw' $\nu_{w'}(\alpha) = 1$

---

[1] Though this is an oversimplification, many theories of vagueness are classicist in this respect, including epistemicism, super- and sub- valuationism and some contextualist proposals. This paper is concerned with the interaction of the paradox with different notions of consequence, thus, the characterization of different theories of vagueness below will be rather superficial.

Language, Knowledge, and Metaphysics.
Massimiliano Carrara and Vittorio Morato (eds.)
College Pubblication, London, 2008.

The difference between theories at this stage concerns the informal reading of the semantics. We can read points either as epistemic alternatives (epistemicism), contexts (contextualism), precisifications (supervaluationism, subvaluationism) and perhaps something else. What concerns us here is the property of the semantics with which each theory interprets the (intuitive or philosophical) notion of truth. These are the likely options:

Definition 1 (Global truth).
A sentence φ is globally true in an interpretation $\Im$ at a point w just in case $\forall w \in W \, \nu_w(\varphi) = 1$.

Definition 2 (Local truth).
A sentence φ is locally true in an interpretation $\Im$ at a point w just in case $\nu_w(\varphi) = 1$.

Definition 3 (Stateless truth).
A sentence φ is statelessly true in an interpretation $\Im$ at a point w just in case $\exists w \in W \, \nu_w(\varphi) = 1$.[2]

Each notion of truth relates to different responses to the phenomenon of vagueness. A theory that makes use of truth-gaps to explain vagueness is *prima facie* committed to global truth, since this notion allows for failures of bivalence. In a similar way, a theory which tries to preserve classical semantics (a theory in which any interpreted sentence is true or false but not both) is likely to be committed to local truth. Finally, a theory committed to truth-value *gluts* (the same sentence, with a fixed content, can be both true and false) is committed to stateless truth. If we read logical consequence as necessary preservation of truth (something assumed now till the end of the paper) each notion of truth determines a corresponding notion of logical consequence.

Definition 4 (Global validity).
A sentence φ is a global consequence of a set of sentences Γ, written $\Gamma \vDash_g \varphi$, iff
$\forall \Im_{\langle W, \mathcal{R}, \nu \rangle}$ (if $\forall \gamma \in \Gamma \forall w \in W \; \nu_w(\gamma) = 1$ then $\forall w \in W \; \nu_w(\varphi) = 1$).

---

[2]The qualification "at a point w" in each definition is relevant just for local truth. The reason is that a sentence is globally (statelessly) true at a point just in case it is globally (statelessly) true at every point and, thus, the qualification "at a point w" is dispensable when we talk about global (stateless) truth (we might speak just about global (stateless) truth in a structure). The definitions of logical consequence for these notions omit this qualification since it is clearly redundant. In this sense global and stateless truth (and the correspondent notions of satisfaction and validity) are insensitive to the *internal* perspective characteristic of modal semantics. As we shall see, this internal perspective is an essential feature in solving the paradox of higher-order vagueness and can be recovered for global and stateless consequence in the form of regional and relative-stateless consequence.

Definition 5 (Local validity). *A sentence φ is a local consequence of a set of sentences Γ, written $\Gamma \vDash_l \varphi$, iff*
$\forall \mathfrak{J}_{\langle \mathcal{W}, \mathcal{R}, \nu \rangle} \forall w \in W$ *(if $\forall \gamma \in \Gamma$ $\nu_w(\gamma) = 1$ then $\nu_w(\varphi) = 1$).*

Definition 6 (Stateless validity).
A sentence φ is a stateless consequence of a set of sentences Γ, written $\Gamma \vDash_s \varphi$, iff
$\forall \mathfrak{J}_{\langle \mathcal{W}, \mathcal{R}, \nu \rangle}$ *(if $\forall \gamma \in \Gamma \exists w \in W$ $\nu_w(\gamma) = 1$ then $\exists w \in W$ $\nu_w(\varphi) = 1$)*

This paper explores how the paradox works for each different notion of consequence and the features of the semantics that each theory should endorse in order to solve it.

1.1.2 Fara's paradox of higher-order vagueness

Imagine a long sorites series for the predicate "tall". The first member of the series is 1.5 meters tall, the last is 2.5 meters tall, and each member of the series differs from its successor by less than a millimeter. It seems that there is no sharp transition from the members of the series of which it is true that they are tall to those of which it is true that aren't tall. The truth-gap theorist explains this fact by appealing to the existence of a borderline case in between, that is, between the members of the series of which it is true that they are tall to those of which it is true that they are not tall, there is at least an element of which it is not true that it is tall but it is not true either that it is not tall. The presence of this element avoids a sharp transition from the (truly) tall to the (truly) non-tall members of the series; and the presence of such an element is granted by the truth of the next *gap-principle*:

(GP for "F") $\mathcal{D}F(x) \to \neg \mathcal{D}\neg F(x')$,
(where "F" stands for "tall" and x' is the successor of x in the series).

As is well known, one of the hard problems of vagueness is that the seeming absence of sharp transitions cuts deeper than that. A sharp transition between the definitely tall members of the series and the non-definitely tall is as bad as (or even worse than) a sharp transition between the tall's and the non-tall's. Avoiding a boundary at the first level and positing a sharp one in the second seems to achieve no real progress. The phenomenon seems to be essentially the same ("definitely tall" seems to be vague in the same way in which "tall" is vague) and, thus, what explains this second sort of seeming absence of a sharp transition is a gap-principle, this time for "definitely tall":

(GP for "$\mathcal{D}F$") $\mathcal{DD}F(x) \to \neg\mathcal{D}\neg\mathcal{D}F(x')$.

We might use the same sort of reasons to argue for a gap-principle for each iteration of $\mathcal{D}$ to render all the gap-principles of this form:

(GP for "$\mathcal{D}^n F$") $\mathcal{D}\mathcal{D}^n F(x) \rightarrow \neg\mathcal{D}\neg\mathcal{D}^n F(x')$,[3]

The idea is that the truth of each gap-principle ensures that there is a borderline case between a member of the series that is $\mathcal{D}^n F$ and a member of the series that is $\neg\mathcal{D}^n F$, for a number n of iterations of "$\mathcal{D}$" (avoiding in this way a sharp transition between the $\mathcal{D}^n F$'s and the $\neg\mathcal{D}^n F$'s).

In her 2003 paper Delia Graff Fara argues that the truth-gap theorist cannot endorse the complete hierarchy of gap-principles for (finite) sorites series and thus cannot explain the seeming absence of sharp transitions. For the truth-gap theorist "$\mathcal{D}$" is read as an object-language expression of truth and according to Fara this commits the truth-gap theorist to the rule of $\mathcal{D}$-intro ($\varphi \vdash \mathcal{D}\varphi$) because "it seems impossible for a sentence S to be true while another sentence, 'it is true that S', that says (in effect) that it's true is not true" (Fara, 2003, p. 199-200). The problem for the truth-gap theorist is that, given $\mathcal{D}$-intro, the truth of all the gap principles is inconsistent for finite sorites series.

Take a sorites series for a predicate "F" containing m elements. The argument shows that given $\mathcal{D}$-intro, $m - 1$ gap-principles suffice to reach the contradiction. Fara's argument can be represented with the following picture:[4]

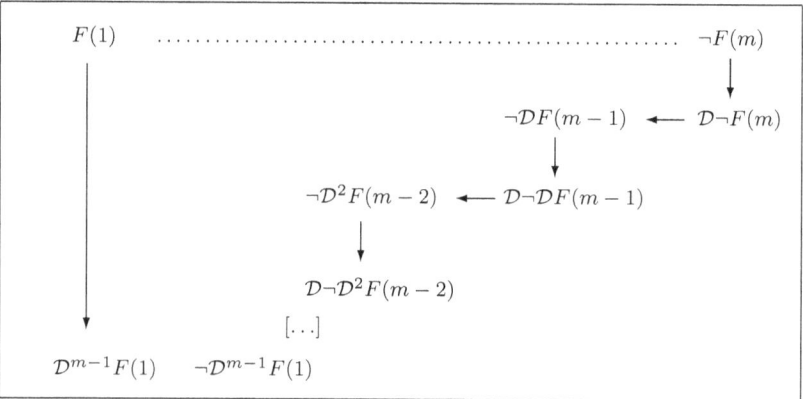

Each move downwards in the picture represents an application of $\mathcal{D}$-intro and each move leftwards an application of the relevant instance of the relevant gap-principle. After $m - 1$ moves leftwards we reach the

---

[3] Fara's argument below makes use of the contrapositive formulation of the schema: $\mathcal{D}\neg\mathcal{D}^n F(x') \rightarrow \neg\mathcal{D}\mathcal{D}^n F(x)$. These formulations are equivalent in the present framework.

[4] As Fara herself points out, her argument is based on the same idea as an argument of Wright's; see Wright (1987) and Wright (1992).

conclusion that the first member of the series is not definitely $m-1$ times tall. But by $\mathcal{D}$-intro, if the first element of the series is tall, he is tall for any iteration of "$\mathcal{D}$" (contradicting the result of our previous argument). Thus, if one is committed to $\mathcal{D}$-intro then one cannot hold the truth of all the gap-principles for any (finite) sorites series.[5]

1.1.3 The clear case constraint and definite gap-principles

This subsection presents two requirements that, *prima facie*, a theory of vagueness committed to the truth of gap-principles should meet to provide a satisfactory solution to the paradox. The first concerns what might be called the *clear case constraint*, the second the definiteness of gap-principles.

The clear case constraint. Mick Jagger is not bald. In fact, he is definitely not bald and, presumably, it is definite that he is definitely not bald. But is he definitely not bald, for any iteration of "definite"?

Definition 7 (Absolute definiteness).
A sentence φ is absolutely definite in a point w in a structure, just in case each member of $\{\mathcal{D}^n\varphi \mid n \in \omega\}$ holds in w. An object a is an absolutely definite positive case of "F" just in case "a is F" is absolutely definite; similarly, a is an absolutely definite negative case of "F" just in case "a is not F" is absolutely definite.

The idea is that a sentence is absolutely definite just in case the sentence is true for each iteration of $\mathcal{D}$. Likewise, a is an absolutely definite positive case of "F", just in case a falls under "F" for any iteration of $\mathcal{D}$. It is not completely clear whether every vague predicate has absolutely definite positive and negative cases, but it seems that we can argue for the existence of such cases for some predicates. For example, no one would count a person without a single hair on his head as not bald. It seems that our use of the predicate imposes a limit here and so, if Peter has no hair on his head, he is an absolutely definite case of "bald". If a glass contains no single drop of water it seems to be absolutely definitely not full of water and if no single drop can be added without spilling the water it seems to be absolutely definitely

---

[5] Fara (2003, p. 202) discusses and makes precise what is proved by her argument. Strictly speaking the argument does not show that there is no higher-order vagueness (the argument does not show that there is some n such that there are no sorites series in which the gap-principle for $\mathcal{D}^n F$ is true). But even though, it seems to me that the objection is compelling enough. For a start, the proof works for *any* finite sorites series: this means that no matter how comprehensive the series is, some gap-principle will be false. Secondly (and more importantly) since gap-principles characterize the approach to vagueness of theories in which borderline cases play a central role, if the paradox applies to some of these, then one has the impression that the approach itself was fundamentally wrong (at least for finite sorites series).

full. This argument is compelling under most of the informal readings of the semantics. For super- and sub- valuationism points are read as admissible precisifications (ways of making precise the language consistent with our use of it) and it seems that a precisification in which someone without a single hair is not bald is just not admissible. In a similar way, when points are read as contexts, it seems that no context allows us to count as not bald anyone without a single hair. I would say that for anyone knowing the meaning of "bald", a truth-value assignment making false the sentence "Peter is bald" (when Peter is hairless) is not an epistemic possibility, though this is perhaps a bit more controversial.[6]

If the previous remark is correct, then a sorites series might start with an absolutely definite positive case of a predicate and end with an absolutely definite negative case. As a consequence, a solution to the paradox resting on the non-absolute definiteness of the first or the last element of the series would not be fully general and, thus, it seems to miss the crux of the problem.

Definite gap-principles. The seeming absence of a sharp transition in sorites series is part of the phenomenology of vague expressions and, thus, one of the primary facts that needs to be explained by a theory of vagueness. Theories of vagueness in which the notion of *borderline case* plays a central role will find the reasons given in section 1.1.2 for the truth of gap principles (reading "definite" in the particular way of the theory) compelling. This is because the truth of gap-principles is a precise manner to characterize in an abstract form the response that these theories give to the seeming absence of sharp transitions in sorites series (in other words, the truth of gap-principles characterize the *borderline approach* to vagueness). For this reason, a theory of this sort cannot solve the paradox claiming that some gap-principle is not definite, since this would mean that, at some point, it is not definite whether the approach itself is correct (whether we can explain vagueness by means of gap-principles), jeopardizing the approach to vagueness of the theory.[7]

---

[6]In fact Williamson explicitly rejects this point in response to an objection due to Gomez-Torrente (Williamson, 2002, pp. 145-146).

[7]Williamson pointed out to me in conversation that it is not clear whether gap-principles should hold for every vague predicate. Sorensen (1985) makes use of disjunctive predicates to construct a sorites intending to show that "vague" is vague; at some point in this sorites we find predicates of which it is indefinite whether they are vague and, thus, it is indefinite as well whether gap-principles should hold for them. I concede that it might be indefinite whether gap-principles should hold for some predicates, but this is because it is vague whether they're vague and, thus, it is indefinite as well whether they deserve to be taken into account by a theory of vagueness. For the clearly vague predicates, a (borderline-based) theory of vagueness

I do not know whether the compelling character of the reasons for gap-principles entail that gap-principles are absolutely definite. But it seems to me that a satisfactory answer rules out the possibility of saying that gap-principles are not definite.

1.2 Theories, consequence and paradox

The reasons given in section 1.1.2 for the commitment to gap-principles can be generalized to theories that do not accept truth-gaps, in particular, those theories in which the notion of *borderline case* plays a central role. We have just to read "definite" in the particular way it is read in that theory. For example, for the epistemicist there is a sharp boundary between the members of the sorites that are tall to those that are not; but for the epistemicist there is no *knowable* (that is, "definite" read in epistemic terms) boundary between the talls and the non-talls (and this is supposed to explain the seeming absence of sharp transitions); likewise there is no knowable boundary between the knowably talls and the not knowably tall, etc.

Depending on the informal reading of the semantics, each theory identifies the (intuitive or philosophical) notion of *truth* with a particular notion in the semantics. Correspondingly, each theory bears a commitment to a particular notion of consequence. This section explores how the paradox interacts with each notion of consequence and aims to address the question of which features of the semantics should be endorsed by each theory to give a response to the paradox.

1.2.1 Global consequence

Supervaluationism. The supervaluationist theory (as it is standardly understood) holds that vagueness is a matter of *underdetermination* of meaning. The idea is that vague expressions can be made precise in several ways consistent with the use we make of them and so our use does not *decide* between the different ways in which expressions can be made precise. If Peter is a borderline case of the predicate "bald" then the sentence "Peter is bald" will be true for some ways of making "bald" precise but false for some others; since our use does not decide between ways of making precise the sentence has no truth-value when we attend to the complete meaning of "bald".

In the formal semantics the supervaluationist theory interprets points in a structure as *admissible precisifications* of the language, and read "$\mathcal{D}$" as an object-language expression of supertruth. The departure from standard modal semantics comes when we look at logical

---

should endorse definite gap-principles.

consequence. Supervaluationism is a truth-gap theory and, thus, supervaluationism cannot be committed to local truth since according to this notion every sentence is true or false. Thus, supervaluationism cannot be committed to local consequence either.[8] The fact that supervaluationism is a truth-gap theory is conveyed in the slogan that "truth is supertruth" (= truth in every admissible precisification) and it is usually assumed in the literature that the supervaluationist theory is committed to the global notion of consequence.[9] But if the supervaluationist is committed to global validity, then she cannot solve the paradox of higher-order vagueness (she might perhaps try to disguise the result, but cannot escape Fara's reasoning), since the reasoning used in the argument is globally valid.[10]

A way out: regional validity. The supervaluationist can escape the paradox questioning the commitment to global validity. As pointed out, if she wants to maintain that vagueness amounts to truth-value gaps, then she cannot be committed to local consequence, but she can still argue for a suitable weakening of global validity. The idea is that global truth (the notion of supertruth preserved by global validity) is too strong, since it does not allow even for just second order borderline cases.[11] For the supervaluationist truth is supertruth, but *supertruth* is itself a vague notion. The vagueness of supertruth might be captured in the semantics introducing a notion of *relative admissibility* between precisifications (in the same way modal semantics introduces relative possibility to allow for contingent necessity). The idea is that each precisification determines both a bivalent valuation of the language and a

---

[8]Varzi (2007) argues for the commitment of supervaluationism to local consequence. He acknowledges that global validity is the most natural notion of consequence in a supervaluationist framework, but he takes the option of *going local* mainly due to Fara's objection concerning higher-order vagueness. This position is rather unstable, though: either we jeopardize our commitment to truth-gaps or else we assume that validity is not a matter of preservation of truth. Neither option seems appealing for a supervaluationist. It seems to me that endorsing a suitable weakening of "supertruth" (and with it, a weakening of logical consequence) is a better alternative to solve Fara's paradox. This option is pointed out in the body of this paper.

[9]Global validity is implicitly assumed in Fine's seminal paper (Fine, 1975, p. 290). Keefe assumes global validity as well; see Keefe (2000b, p. 176) and Keefe (2000a).

[10]Cobreros (2008b) presents an adequate system of tableaux to test for global validity; this method can be used to show that the premises of the paradox are in fact inconsistent given global validity.

[11]Every sentence of the language is either globally true or not globally true anywhere in any interpretation; and so it cannot be indefinite whether a sentence is globally true. Compare with Williamson's result for S5 interpretations (Williamson, 1999, p. 134).

set of admitted precisifications. In this case, supertruth is still "truth in every admissible precisification"; but in this definition "admissible" is a relative-to-precisification notion. This makes possible for a sentence being supertrue in a precisification, and not supertrue in another precisification, in the same interpretation. When supertruth is relativized this way, the supervaluationist is committed to a notion of consequence different to either global or local validity:

Definition 8 (Regional validity).
A sentence φ is a regional consequence of a set of sentences Γ, written $\Gamma \vDash_r \varphi$ iff,
$\forall \Im_{\langle \mathcal{W}, \mathcal{R}, \nu \rangle} \forall w \in W$ *(if* $\forall \gamma \in \Gamma \ \forall w'_{\in W} \ wRw' \ \nu_{w'}(\gamma) = 1$ *then*
$\forall w'_{\in W} \ wRw' \ \nu_{w'}(\varphi) = 1)$

Informally: a sentence φ is a regional consequence of a set of sentences Γ just in case, for any interpretation and any precisification w in that interpretation, if all the γ's are true in every precisification admitted by w (that is, if all the γ's are supertrue at w in the relativized sense of "supertruth") then φ is true in every precisification admitted by w (that is, φ is supertrue at w in the relativized sense of "supertruth"). The complete hierarchy of gap-principles is regionally consistent for finite sorites series (even under the clear case constraint),[12] and so the supervaluationist might endorse all the gap-principles appealed to in the paradox if she accepts the regional notion of consequence. But to achieve this result, the supervaluationist has to accept some constraints on the admissibility relation and on the way the premises are endorsed.

According to regional validity, a set of sentences Γ is satisfiable just in case there is an interpretation with a precisification w_0 such that all the γ's take value 1 at every w_0-admitted precisification (that is Γ is satisfiable just in case there is a precisification at which every γ is supertrue, in the relativized sense of "supertrue"). It can be shown that there are interpretations with precisifications w_0 such that all the premises of Fara's argument are supertrue at w_0 for finite sorites series (in fact, this can be shown for sorites of four or more elements). But in all these interpretations some gap-principle will be false at some precisification reachable from w_0 by a finite number of R-steps. An immediate consequence of this is that to give the consistency proof in regional validity the admissibility relation R cannot be transitive. For if R is transitive, anything reachable from w_0 in a finite number of R-steps is reachable from w_0 in just one R-step and, thus, the w at which some gap-principle is false would be admitted by w_0, showing this way that gap-principles are not supertrue in w_0. Thus, if the supervaluationist

---
[12] This is shown and discussed in Cobreros (2008a).

wants to endorse all the gap-principles appealed to in Fara's argument, she needs to argue that admissibility is not transitive.

A similar remark applies to the way in which gap-principles are endorsed. The supervaluationist might accept gap-principles for finite sorites series and even that gap-principles are definite to some extent, but not that they are absolutely definite. If gap-principles were absolutely definite, a model showing regional consistency should show that there is a w_0 such that gap-principles are true at every w reachable from w_0 in any number of R-steps. But, as pointed out above, any model showing regional consistency will contain a w reachable from w_0 in a finite number of R-steps at which some gap principle is false.

Summarizing, the supervaluationist might solve the paradox endorsing regional validity, but for the solution to work, she has to justify, based on the informal reading of the semantics, that R is not transitive and that gap-principles are not absolutely definite.

1.2.2 Local consequence

Epistemicism. If Peter is a borderline case of baldness, then we do not know whether Peter is bald. For the semantic theorist this absence of knowledge is explained by an absence of anything to be known. For the epistemicist our absence of knowledge is a manifestation of ignorance: it is true or false that Peter is bald, though we do not know whether he is bald or not.

In the formal semantics points in a structure are interpreted as epistemic possibilities. Roughly, if I do not know whether Peter is bald, then the situation in which "Peter is bald" is true and the situation in which it is false are epistemic possibilities for me, since I lack a justification to tell which one corresponds to the actual situation. By contrast, if I know that Peter is mortal, then the situation in which "Peter is mortal" is false does not constitute an epistemic possibility for me. Accordingly, that φ is definite is defined as the absence of epistemic possibilities at which $\neg\varphi$. In the epistemic theory, truth is interpreted as local truth and, consequently, logical consequence is defined as local consequence.[13]

---

[13] The most well-known epistemic theory is the one defended by Williamson (in his Williamson (1994) and in a number of papers). Any epistemic theory is far more sophisticated than the sketchy comment provided in the body of this paper. For example, an epistemic theorist has to explain the source of our putative ignorance in borderline cases. Williamson provides an explanation of this sort of ignorance appealing to the presence of *margin for error principles* that are specific for vague expressions. These margin for error principles lead to a particular sort of semantics (Williamson, 1994, Ch. 8). Nevertheless, epistemic theorists are usually conservative with respect to classical logic and semantics (a *logic of vagueness* will describe

Content-contextualism. It is uncontroversial that the truth-value of a sentence might depend on the context of utterance. The sentence "I am a smart philosopher" might be false if uttered by me but true when uttered by you. Contextualism exploits this feature to explain the phenomenon of vagueness (particularly in connection to the sorites paradox). Content-contextualism holds that the content of a vague expression might vary from one context to another (say, because a variation in the relevant comparison class) and so the truth-value of a sentence might shift from one context to another. In this sort of view points in a structure are interpreted as contexts and definiteness is invariant across contexts.[14]

Content-contextualism is *prima facie* committed to local consequence. Suppose we take an argument and interpret the premises and conclusion in different contexts. The content-contextualist might reply that this procedure is defective, since in interpreting sentences in different contexts we might get different contents, and so the argument might be flawed by some equivocation. For this reason, the defender of this type of contextualism has the right to insist that truth should be necessarily preserved in each context (that is, truth is local truth).

Local-global connection. Local validity is weaker than global validity; in particular, the inference from φ to $\mathcal{D}\varphi$ is not locally valid. Moreover, under minimal conditions local validity is weaker than regional validity and, thus, an interpretation showing the regional consistency of gap-principles is an interpretation showing the local consistency of gap-principles. Nevertheless, a theorist committed to local validity should pay attention to the paradox, since there is a systematic connection between global and local validity that will enable us to reproduce the paradox in local validity under suitable conditions.

Proposition 1 (Local-global connection).
$\Gamma \vDash_g \varphi$ iff $\{\mathcal{D}^n \gamma \mid \gamma \in \Gamma, n \in \omega\} \vDash_l \varphi$.

Proof. (Right-to-left direction)

---

principles concerning our knowledge in borderline cases) and for this reason they are *prima facie* committed to local consequence, which is the *most classical* notion of consequence in the present framework.

[14] The pioneer work in contextualism goes back to Kamp (1981) in which he develops a semantics to deal with the sorites paradox. A particularity of this semantics is that each instance of the sorites induction premise is true, even when the premise itself is not. Contextualist authors typically disagree concerning the features of the semantics for vague expressions (say, wether we have to admit truth-gaps or whether we have to endorse a truth-functional semantics). Between content-contextulist theories we might encounter Tappenden (1993), Soames (1999) and Soames (2003) and Raffman (1994) and Raffman (1996).

Assume: $\Gamma \nvDash_g \varphi$. Then, there is an interpretation $\Im = \langle W, R, \nu \rangle$ where for all w and all $\gamma \in \Gamma$, $\nu_w(\gamma) = 1$ and for some w, $\nu_w(\varphi) = 0$. Name w_0 the world at which φ takes value 0. Since every γ in Γ is true everywhere in the interpretation, every γ is true at w_0 for each iteration of $\mathcal{D}$ (you will never reach a world where γ takes value 0!). Thus, world w_0 in $\Im$ shows that $\{\mathcal{D}^n \gamma \mid \gamma \in \Gamma, n \in \omega\} \nvDash_l \varphi$.

(Left-to-right direction)
Assume: $\{\mathcal{D}^n \gamma \mid \gamma \in \Gamma, n \in \omega\} \nvDash_l \varphi$. Then there is an interpretation $\Im = \langle W, R, \nu \rangle$ and a world w_0 in it such that, for every γ in Γ and any iteration of $\mathcal{D}$, $\nu_{w_0}(\mathcal{D}^n \gamma) = 1$ and $\nu_{w_0}(\varphi) = 0$. Let W' be $\{w \mid w_0 R^n w\} \cup \{w_0\}$ (w_0 plus the worlds accessible from w_0 in any number of R-steps) and R', ν' be the restrictions of R, ν to W'. We have to show a) that the interpretation $\Im' = \langle W', R', \nu' \rangle$ is still a counter-model to show $\{\mathcal{D}^n \gamma \mid \gamma \in \Gamma, n \in \omega\} \nvDash_l \varphi$ (that is, for any w' in W', $\Im$ and $\Im'$ assign the same values to sentences at w') and b) that it is in fact a counter-model showing that $\Gamma \nvDash_g \varphi$.

To show a), note first that if $w' \in W'$ then R' and R relate w' exactly to the same worlds, that is, if $w' \in W'$ then $w'R'w$ iff $w'Rw$. For if $w'R'w$ then both $w \in W'$ and $w'Rw$. On the other hand, if $w'Rw$, as $w' \in W'$, $w_0 R^m w'$ and thus $w_0 R^{m+1} w$, that is, $w \in W'$. Thus, $w'R'w$.

a) is proved by induction over the set of wff. The case for propositional variables holds by definition. The case for non-modal operators is straightforward. For $\psi = \mathcal{D}\alpha$, suppose that $w' \in W'$:

$\nu'_{w'}(\mathcal{D}\alpha) = 1$ iff $\forall w* \in W'$ such that $w'R'w*$, $\nu'_{w*}(\alpha) = 1$
iff $\forall w* \in W'$ such that $w'R'w*$, $\nu_{w*}(\alpha) = 1$ (by IH)
iff $\forall w* \in W$ such that $w'Rw*$, $\nu_{w*}(\alpha) = 1$ (by the fact noted above)

To prove b) note that w_0 has access to every world in W' (excluding, perhaps w_0 itself) in some number of R-steps. Since for every γ in Γ and every $n \in \omega$, $\nu_{w_0}(\mathcal{D}^n \gamma) = 1$, every member of Γ takes value 1 at every world in W'. On the other hand, as $\nu_{w_0}(\varphi) = 0$, there is at least one world in W' in which φ takes the value 0. Thus, $\Im'$ shows that $\Gamma \nvDash_g \varphi$. □

Given the local-global connection, we can run the paradox in local validity if, instead of the assumption of $\mathcal{D}$-intro, we assume that the premises are absolutely definite. In fact, what we need to run the paradox is just a suitable number of $\mathcal{D}$'s attached to each premise, depending on the length of the sorites series. Think again of the picture representing Fara's reasoning in subsection 1.1.2. What the rule of $\mathcal{D}$-intro adds to the proof is the *definitization* of the result of applying a gap-principle to something (the *move downwards*). Since $\mathcal{D}$ is closed under local consequence, we might get the same result if the premises are *definite enough*.

Assuming the clear case constraint, if we want to solve the paradox given local validity, we need to argue that gap-principles are not absolutely definite. On the other hand, if gap-principles are definite then R cannot be transitive, since transitivity ensures that what is definite is definitely definite. If the remark in subsection 1.1.3 about the definiteness of gap-principles is correct, then theories committed to local validity are in the same position to solve the paradox as theories committed to regional validity. Which one gives a better response to the paradox will depend on its resources to explain, based on its informal reading of the semantics, that gap-principles are not absolutely definite and that R is not transitive.[15]

1.2.3 Stateless consequence

Subvaluationism. Subvaluationism is the *dual* theory of supervaluationism. Points in a structure are read, like in the supervaluationist theory, as some sort of precisifications of the language and *definiteness* is read as invariance in truth-value across precisifications. But for the subvaluationist vagueness is a matter of *overdetermination* of meaning. If Peter is a borderline case of the predicate "bald" then the sentence "Peter is bald" is both true and false. The subvaluationist theory is clearly committed to stateless truth, and thus, committed to stateless validity.[16]

Truth-contextualism. The phenomenon of context-sensitivity is uncontroversial for some sort of expressions. A sentence might vary in truth-value across contexts due to a variation in the content expressed. Content-contextualism claims that vagueness should be understood as a particular form of context-sensitivity. Truth-contextualism is different in this respect. Both accept that the truth-value of a sentence might vary from one context to another but, whereas for the content-contextualist, a change in truth-value entails a change in content, for the truth-contextualist, there might be shifts of truth-value without change in content. The last claim is controversial. There is no worry about a sentence's having two different truth-values if it expresses two different contents (our previous example about "I am a smart philoso-

---

[15] Williamson (1994, Ch. 8) has already argued for the non-transitivity of R based on the *margin for error semantics*.

[16] The subvaluationist theory is developed by Hyde (1997). Discussion of Hyde's position can be found in Akiba (1999) and Beall and Colyvan (2001), with replies in Hyde (1999) and Hyde (2001).

pher" is enough to show this); but it is not clear at all that a sentence might have different truth-values in two different contexts if in both of them it expresses the same content. Truth-contextualism seems to endorse a particular form of relativism applied to vagueness.[17]

It seems that this sort of contextualism is committed to stateless validity. Call those contexts in which there are truth-value shifts but no shifts in content "truth-contexts" and suppose that we interpret different parts of an argument using different truth-contexts. It seems that the truth-contextualist cannot claim that there is any sort of equivocation here since a sentence's content remains the same across truth-contexts. Once the content of a sentence is fully fixed, I do not see any reason why we have to insist that what is to be preserved is truth in a point (local truth). Truth-contextualism has a paraconsistent flavour indeed, since the central claim is that the very same content can be both true and false. Where Peter is a borderline case of "bald", the sentence "Peter is bald" might be true and false in different truth-contexts. If we disagree on whether Peter is bald, we might be *really* contradicting each other and nonetheless, according to truth-contextualism, we can be both right. Whereas local validity is too strong to frame the idea that a pair of utterances expressing contradictory contents might be both true, stateless validity is weak enough.

Global-stateless connection. Every statelessly valid argument is locally valid, for if an argument is not locally valid, then there is an interpretation and a point w at which all the premises are true and the conclusion false, thus, an interpretation where the premises are statelessly true and the conclusion statelessly false. On the other hand, not every locally valid argument is statelessly valid, since $\{\varphi, \neg\varphi\} \vDash_l \bot$ but $\{\varphi, \neg\varphi\} \nvDash_s \bot$. Stateless validity can be connected to global validity. To show the connection we make use of multiple conclusions. We introduce the extension of global and stateless validity to multiple conclusions and a definition to show the connection.

Definition 9 (Global Validity: multiple conclusions).
A set of sentences Δ is a global consequence of a set of sentences Γ, written $\Gamma \vDash_g \Delta$, iff
$\forall \Im_{\langle W,\mathcal{R},\nu \rangle}$ *(if $\forall \gamma \in \Gamma \forall w \in W\ \nu_w(\gamma) = 1$ then $\exists \delta \in \Delta \forall w \in W\ \nu_w(\delta) = 1$).*

Definition 10 (Stateless validity: multiple conclusions).
A set of sentences Δ is a stateless consequence of a set of sentences Γ, written $\Gamma \vDash_s \Delta$, iff
$\forall \Im_{\langle W,\mathcal{R},\nu \rangle}$ *(if $\forall \gamma \in \Gamma \exists w \in W\ \nu_w(\gamma) = 1$ then $\exists \delta \in \Delta \exists w \in W\ \nu_w(\delta) = 1$).*

---

[17] Authors committed to the truth-contextualist view in vagueness include Fara (2000), Shapiro (2003) and (2006).

Informally read, Δ is a global consequence of Γ just in case, if all the γ's are true everywhere, then some of the δ's are true everywhere. On the other hand Δ is a stateless consequence of Γ just in case, if all the γ's are true somewhere, then some of the δ's are true somewhere.

Definition 11 (Set $\neg(\Gamma)$ generated from Γ).
Let Γ be the set of sentences $\{\gamma_1, \ldots, \gamma_n\}$. The set $\neg(\Gamma)$ generated from Γ is the result of applying to each γ_i in Γ the operator $\neg$; thus $\neg(\Gamma)$ is $\{\neg\gamma_1, \ldots, \neg\gamma_n\}$.

Stateless validity is the *dual* notion of consequence of global validity. This fact is expressed by the next proposition.

Proposition 2 (Global-stateless connection).
$\Gamma \vDash_g \Delta$ *iff* $\neg(\Delta) \vDash_s \neg(\Gamma)$.

Proof. Assume $\Gamma \vDash_g \Delta$. Then, for any interpretation if all the γ's are true everywhere, then some of the δ's are true everywhere. Contrapositively, if all the δ's are false somewhere, some of the γ's are false somewhere, that is, $\neg(\Delta) \vDash_s \neg(\Gamma)$. □

Call {Fara's} the set of premises in Fara's paradox and let $\bot = (p \wedge \neg p)$. We have that {Fara's} $\vDash_g \bot$, and by the global stateless connection, $\neg\bot \vDash_s \neg(\{$Fara's$\})$. In stateless validity, as in global validity, classically valid sentences are valid as well. This means that $\neg\bot$ is true everywhere in any interpretation and so, some of {Fara's} is false somewhere in any interpretation. If, in the spirit of the clear case constraint, we want the first and last members of the sorites to be F and not-F, respectively, everywhere in any interpretation, then some gap-principle should be false somewhere in any interpretation. For a theory committed to stateless consequence this is not that bad since "being true" means "being true somewhere" and so it does not matter very much whether some of {Fara's} is false somewhere; it might still be true somewhere else. In fact the absolute definiteness of {Fara's} is consistent for stateless validity.

Proof. There is no interpretation in which the absolute definiteness of each element in {Fara's} takes value 1 at a point. But the absolute definiteness of each element in {Fara's} might take value 1 at different (and non-connected) points, and this is what "satisfiability" means given stateless validity. For example, we might have an interpretation containing a world for each gap-principle:

$$w_1 \qquad w_2 \qquad w_3 \qquad \ldots$$

If these points do not relate to each other, we might have that the absolute definitization of the gap-principle for "F" holds in w_1, the absolute definitization of the gap-principle for "$\mathcal{D}F$" holds in w_2, etc. At each of these points, of course, the absolute definiteness of some other gap-principle will take value 0. □

Stateless validity is indeed a weak notion of consequence. The problem with the suggested proof of consistency is that there is something *incongruent* in the way the notions of truth and definiteness are treated. Truth is regarded as *truth somewhere* without restricting "somewhere" to R-related points. Since definiteness is defined as some sort of invariance in *truth*-value, "definiteness" should be defined with respect to the relevant notion of truth. Given that R plays no role in the definition of truth, it shouldn't in the definition of $\mathcal{D}$.

Definition 12 (Universal access modality).
$\nu_w(\mathcal{D}_u\varphi) = 1$ *just in case* $\forall w \nu_w(\varphi) = 1$.

It is clear that we cannot endorse the definitization of each element of {Fara's} under this notion of definiteness, since some premise must be false somewhere in any interpretation. And it is pretty unlikely that the informal reading of the semantics can justify that the premises are not definite, not even for just one iteration of the definitely-operator (see the reasons given in section 1.1.3).

A way out: relative-stateless validity. There is a clear way to address the previous objection. The theorist committed to stateless validity can argue for a strengthening of stateless truth in the same way the supervaluationist did for a weakening of global truth. Subvaluationists and truth-contextualists can argue for this on the basis of the vagueness of the notion of truth. The idea is, again, that truth should be defined as a relative-to-points notion; in other words, a sentence φ is (relative-statelessly) true at a point w just in case it is true at some R-related point w'. "$\mathcal{D}$" is then defined in the obvious way. The following definition introduces the corresponding notion of consequence.

Definition 13 (Relative-stateless validity).
A sentence φ is a relative-stateless consequence of a set of sentences Γ, written $\Gamma \vDash_{rs} \varphi$, iff
$\forall \Im_{\langle \mathcal{W}, \mathcal{R}, \nu \rangle} \forall w \in W$ *(if* $\forall \gamma \in \Gamma \exists w'_{\in W} \ wRw'; \nu_w(\gamma) = 1$ *then*
$\exists w'_{\in W} \ wRw' \ (\varphi) = 1)$.

With this notion of consequence we might still endorse the absolute definitization of {Fara's}. A proof of consistency follows from a proof of consistency for stateless consequence: take an interpretation showing consistency for the stateless consequence and add a point w_0 that bears

R to each point in W where some of {Fara's} is absolutely definite:

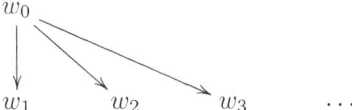

Then w_0 shows that the absolute definitization of {Fara's} is consistent for relative-stateless validity. The proof, however, needs some remarks on R.

In the first place, R cannot be symmetric. In any interpretation showing the consistency of the absolute definiteness of {Fara's} given relative-stateless validity, w_0 bears R to different points at which some of {Fara's} is absolutely definite. If R were symmetric, each of these points would bear R to w_0:

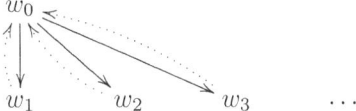

But this entails that all of {Fara's} is absolutely definite at w_0 itself, which is not possible. In the second place, R cannot be euclidean either. That R is euclidean means that if wRw' and wRw'' then $w'Rw''$. Graphically explained:

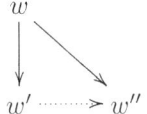

Again, to show consistency w_0 bears R to different points at which some of {Fara's} is absolutely definite. But if R were euclidean each of these points should bear R to each other:

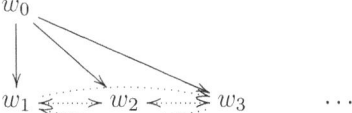

in which case the absolute definiteness of {Fara's} should be true at all these points, which is impossible.

Thus, if they want to hold the absolute definiteness of the premises of the paradox, theorists committed to stateless truth should justify, based on the particular reading of the semantics, that R is neither symmetric nor euclidean. But if the other theories can justify non-transitivity, it seems that theories committed to stateless consequence can justify that R is neither symmetric nor euclidean.

1.3 Conclusion

The paradox of higher-order vagueness was initially proposed against truth-gap theories. If these theories are committed to global validity, they cannot escape Fara's paradox. Still, truth-gap theorists can argue for a suitable weakening of global validity, namely, regional validity. If the truth-gap theorist endorses this last notion of consequence, she can solve the paradox, though she has to provide some justification for the claim that gap-principles are not absolutely definite and that the relation between points is not transitive. The paradox can be extended to cover local validity as well and in this respect, truth-gap theories are on a par with theories committed to local consequence since, plausibly enough, they also have to justify the non-absolute definiteness of the gap-principles and the non-transitivity of the relation between points.

We have considered in the third place stateless validity, a notion of consequence weaker than local validity. Endorsing (plain) stateless validity does not yield a satisfactory solution to the paradox since the notion of definiteness associated with it is too strong to endorse gap-principles even for just one *definitization*. The theorist committed to this form of consequence might reply that truth and definiteness are relative-to-point notions. Thus, for him, logical consequence is relative-stateless validity. With this notion of consequence (along with its associated notions of truth and definiteness) one might endorse the absolute definiteness of the premises in Fara's paradox. In exchange, the philosopher that favours this last notion of consequence has to justify that the relation between points is neither symmetric nor euclidean.

The question concerning which theory works out the best solution to the paradox requires attending to the informal reading of the semantics; in particular, the way in which each theory justifies the particular features of the semantics (non-transitivity, etc.) that makes possible the accommodation of gap-principles. However, if one thinks that reasons for gap-principles are highly compelling for a borderline-based theory of vagueness then there is one solution that stands out above the others. Though it might be objectionable on different grounds, relative-stateless validity allows us to endorse that gap-principles are absolutely definite and, in this sense, provides the best solution to the paradox for a borderline-based theory of vagueness.[18]

---

[18]Many thanks for comments and suggestions to Maria Cerezo, Miguel Garcia-

References

Akiba, K. 1999. On super- and subvaluationism: a classicist's reply to Hyde. *Mind* 108(432):727–732.

Beall, J. C. and M. Colyvan. 2001. Heaps of gluts and Hyde-ing the sorites. *Mind* 110(438):401–408.

Cobreros, Pablo. 2008a. Bordeline, yet not definitely so. *Unpublished* .

Cobreros, Pablo. 2008b. Supervaluationism and logical consequence: a third way. *Studia Logica (forthcoming)* .

Fara, D. G. 2000. Shifting sands: An interest-relative theory of vagueness. *Philosophical Topics*. Orignally published under the name 'Delia Graff' 28(1):45–81.

Fara, D. G. 2003. Gap principles, penumbral consequence and infinitely higher-order vagueness. In J. C. Beal, ed., *Liars and Heaps: New Essays on Paradox*, chap. 9, pages 195–221. Oxford: Oxford University Press.

Fine, K. 1975. Vagueness, truth and logic. *Synthese* 30:265–300.

Hyde, D. 1997. From heaps and gaps to heaps of gluts. *Mind* 106(424):641–660.

Hyde, D. 1999. Pleading classicism. *Mind* 108(432):733–735.

Hyde, D. 2001. A reply to Beall and Colyvan. *Mind* 110(438):409–411.

Kamp, H. 1981. The paradox of the heap. In Mönnich, U. (ed.) *Aspects of Philosophical Logic*, Dordrecht: Reidel pages 225–277.

Keefe, R. 2000a. Supervaluationism and validity. *Philosophical Topics* 28(1):93–105.

Keefe, R. 2000b. *Theories of Vagueness*. Cambridge University Press.

Raffman, D. 1994. Vagueness without paradox. *Philosophical Review* pages 41–74.

Raffman, D. 1996. Vagueness and context relativity. *Philosophical Studies* 81(2):175–192.

Shapiro, S. 2003. Vagueness and conversation. In J. C. Beall, ed., *Liars and Heaps: New Essays on Paradox*, pages 39–72. Oxford: Oxford University Press.

Shapiro, S. 2006. *Vagueness in context*. Oxford: Oxford University Press.

Soames, S. 1999. *Understanding Truth*. Oxford: Oxford University Press.

Soames, S. 2003. Higher-order vagueness for partially defined predicates. In J. C. Beal, ed., *Liars and Heaps: New Essays on Paradox*, pages 128–150. Oxford: Oxford University Press.

Valdecasas, Joshua Kassanis, Sebastiano Moruzzi, Paloma Perez-Ilzarbe and Timothy Williamson. Thanks also to the audience of the First SIFA Graduate Conference in Padua. Thanks to the Basque Government for a postdoctoral scholarship for the academic year 2008/09 (BFI07.235). This research was also funded by the research projects from the Government of Navarra (ref. 67/2006, de 29 de marzo) and the Government of Spain (ref. HUM2005-05910/FISO).

Sorensen, R. 1985. An argument for the vagueness of 'vague'. *Analysis* 45(3):134–137.

Tappenden, J. 1993. The liar and sorites paradoxes; towards a unified treatment. *Journal of Philosophy* 90(11):551–577.

Varzi, A. 2007. Supervaluationism and its logic. *Mind* 116(463):633–676.

Williamson, T. 1994. *Vagueness*. London: Routledge.

Williamson, T. 1999. On the structure of higher-order vagueness. *Mind* 108(429):127–143.

Williamson, T. 2002. Epistemicist models: Comments on gómez-torrente and graff. *Philosophy and Phenomenological Research* 64(1):143–150.

Wright, C. 1987. Further reflections on the sorites paradox. *Philosophical Topics* 15(11):227–290.

Wright, C. 1992. Is higher-order vagueness coherent? *Analysis* 52(3):129–139.

2

Betraying Davidson: A Quest for the Incommensurable[1]

MARCELLO DI BELLO

2.1 Introduction

Talks of incommensurable conceptual schemes typically allude to the following picture: There is *reality*[2] that is inaccessible *per se*, on the one hand, and there is us, or different groups of people, accessing reality by means of *conceptual schemes*, on the other. As long as schemes radically differ from each other, they will stand to one another in a relation of incommensurability. But what does it mean for two schemes to be radically different and thus be in a relation of incommensurability? And is such a relation at all intelligible to us?

Davidson (1974) has formulated an argument to the effect that incommensurability is unintelligible.[3] More precisely, his argument first provides a definition of incommensurability, and then shows that incommensurability thus defined is unintelligible. I will argue, *contra* Davidson, that his definition of incommensurability does not lend any support to the unintelligibility claim. To be sure, my attack against Davidson will be in three forms. For I will give three interpretations of his argument against incommensurability, and then provide three counter-arguments, which will have progressively weaker strength. The

---

[1] I would like to thank in particular Martin Stokhof, Michal Lukasiewicz, Sven Lauer, and Ansten Mørch Klev.

[2] Or any other controversial term one may prefer to use for what is "out there."

[3] See Davidson (1974).

first refutes the argument that emerges from the first interpretation; the second can do so with respect to the argument that emerges from the second interpretation on the basis of additional assumptions; finally, the third provides only a conjecture that the argument that emerges from the third interpretation fails.

The plan for the paper is as follows. Section 2.2 points out distinctions and inherent difficulties that are peculiar to the incommensurability debate. Section 2.3 reconstructs Davidson's definition of incommensurability. Second 2.4 contains Davidson's argument against the intelligibility of incommensurability, along with its three interpretations. Section 2.5 contains my three counter-arguments. Finally, section 2.6 concludes and points to open problems.

2.2 Preliminaries

Anyone who joins the debate about incommensurability should bear in mind certain distinctions and inherent difficulties. I would like to point out two distinctions and one difficulty, without intending to be exhaustive. The first distinction is the one between total and partial incommensurability. Intuitively, partial incommensurability holds only between restricted regions of two supposed incommensurable schemes, while total incommensurability holds between the schemes as a whole.

The second distinction is among different forms of incommensurability – for instance, semantic, methodological, and ontological incommensurability.[4] In this paper, I will be concerned with *semantic* incommensurability only. Roughly speaking, semantic incommensurability arises between languages *qua* carriers of meaning and indicates a radical meaning-difference between languages. What such a radical meaning-difference between languages is will be made more precise in the next section.[5]

Evidently, the notion of meaning is to play a crucial role for defining semantic incommensurability. It follows that the well-known difficul-

---

[4]See Sankey (1993).

[5]It is useful to contrast semantic incommensurability with ontological and methodological incommensurability. Incommensurable conceptual schemes can be taken to be languages carrying meaning, and this perspective suits the notion of semantic incommensurability. Conceptual schemes, however, can be taken to express the ontology adopted by a community of speakers. Ontology here means what is taken to exist and what not, how classifications of entities are carried out, or how the plethora of being, so to speak, is divided up. This perspective suites the notion of ontological incommensurability. Further, conceptual schemes can be taken to be scientific theories which are associated with standards and criteria concerning theory appraisal, *e.g.*, concerning what counts as evidence in favor or against the theory. This other perspective pairs with methodological incommensurability.

ties in singling out identity criteria for meaning are inherited by any attempt to define semantic incommensurability. For the sake of clarity, in the rest of the paper I will attempt to be very explicit about which assumptions about meaning I have endorsed in laying down any criteria for semantic incommensurability.

2.3 A Davidsonian definition of incommensurability

As anticipated, Davidson's argument against incommensurability is in two parts. First, a definition of incommensurability is given, and secondly incommensurability thus defined is shown to be unintelligible. This section discusses the moves made in the definitional part of the argument in which Davidson's final definition of semantic incommensurability reads: (INC-D) *Two schemes are semantically incommensurable iff (i) they fail to be intertranslatable and yet (ii) they are both true.*[6]

In what follows I will explain the significance of points (i) and (ii) of definition (INC-D). It is not my concern to defend definition (INC-D) in full, but only to elucidate it. In doing so, however, it will become apparent that (INC-D) should be slightly modified.

2.3.1 Failure of intertranslatability between languages

The definitional moves suggested by Davidson to motivate point (i) are as follows:

(M1) A conceptual scheme can be identified with a language.[7]
(M2) Untranslatability between languages is evidence for incommensurability.[8]

Move (M1) makes it precise that a linguistic-based incommensurability is at stake. As said before, the focus of this paper is semantic incommensurability, and it is natural to think of semantic incommensurability as a relation between languages *qua* carriers of meaning. If one were to deny that semantic incommensurability involves languages, one will have to deny that meaning is related to, or resides in, languages.

I did not yet say what a language should be taken to be. A language is customarily defined as the set of all well-formed sentences which can

---

[6] "And the criterion of a conceptual scheme different from our own now becomes: largely true but not translatable." (Davidson, 1978, p. 194). Note that here and in the following all quotations and page numbers are in accordance with Davidson (1978), which is a collection of of all the Davidson's papers I will refer to in this paper.

[7] "We may identify conceptual schemes with languages." See Davidson (1978, p. 185).

[8] "Can we then say that two people have different conceptual schemes if they speak languages that fail of intertranslatability?" See Davidson (1978, p. 185).

be constructed out of a given alphabet and a grammar. However, since a language is here intended to be useful for defining semantic incommensurability, in this context it cannot consist of syntactic entities only, for these must be paired with a semantics. Without any semantics in place the notion of semantic incommensurability between languages would be empty. Yet syntax and semantics are not enough to define a language, for a language is *used* by a community of speakers to communicate. Thus, here I take a language to be the set of well-formed sentences each endowed with meaning and used by a community of speakers to communicate.

Move (M2) is a natural follow-up to move (M1): If the *relata* in the relation of incommensurability are languages rather than schemes, the criterion for them to be radically different from each other, and thus incommensurable, is the failure of intertranslatability, or the non-intertranslatability, between the languages. Given the switch from schemes to languages, the failure of intertranslatability is the most obvious candidate that can function as evidence for radical meaning-difference between languages, and thus for semantic incommensurability.

To make the notion of non-intertranslatability precise, a few definitions are in order. The non-intertranslatability of two languages L and L' comes in two forms, partial and total. Languages L and L' are *partially* non-intertranslatable iff, for *some* sentences in L, a meaning-equivalent sentence in L' cannot be found, and viceversa. Languages L and L' are *totally* non-intertranslatable iff, for *all* sentences in L, no meaning-equivalent sentence in L' can be found, and viceversa. Depending on whether the failure of translatability is partial or total, incommensurability will be partial or total.[9]

2.3.2 Introducing the notion of truth

The definition of incommensurability that would result from moves (M1) and (M2) alone – *i.e.*, two languages are incommensurable iff they are non-intertranslatable – is insufficient. To see this, let us forget for a moment the switch from schemes to languages, and let us concentrate

---

[9]In the definition of (non-)intertranslatability the notion of meaning-equivalence was invoked, and yet it was left undefined. This is one of the point in the discussion about semantic incommensurability in which an appeal to different theories of meaning, and thus to different identity or equivalence criteria for meaning, can make a difference. Davidson does not make explicit which identity criteria for meaning he adopts. However, given that Davidson's account of meaning can be roughly seen as truth-conditional, for him the criterion of meaning-equivalence between sentences is likely to be truth-conditional equivalence. So, in my critique of his argument I will follow him with respect to this assumption.

on some features of conceptual schemes. Davidson makes two points about the role of conceptual schemes. First, schemes are adopted by a community of agents or speakers to categorize reality; they are about an unschemetized content which lies beyond the schemes themselves. Secondly, schemes are adopted by a community because they satisfy a certain normative requirement, *i.e.*, they fit the available evidence. But – Davidson concludes – when a scheme fits the available evidence, this means that a scheme is *true*. Now, if we grant that schemes are to be true to count as schemes, it follows that if two schemes stands in a relation of incommensurability both schemes are true.[10] So, the final definition of incommensurability will boil down to (INC-D).

However, as soon as the notion of truth is applied to languages, rather than schemes, a problem arises. In the wording of definition (INC-D), Davidson has maintained that non-intertranslatablity is evidence for incommensurability and that schemes should be true, but he has forgotten move (M1), namely that schemes can be replaced by languages. But note what happens if the contribution of (M1) enters definition (INC-D). The result would be as follows: *Two languages are semantically incommensurable iff (i) they fail to be intertranslatable and yet (ii) they are both true.* Clearly, this definition is absurd because languages cannot be true.[11]

Allegedly, Davidson had implicitly assumed that some subsets of the chosen languages, not the entire languages, are taken to be true. The main, and non trivial, problem is *which* subsets of the given languages are to be taken to be true. My suggestion is along these lines. Suppose we fix a state of the world at a certain time and place. Then, speakers of the two supposed incommensurable languages will hold true cer-

---

[10] A further argument for invoking the notion of truth is this. Let us reason for a moment in terms of scientific theories, which can be thought of as highly formalized conceptual schemes in which scientific evidence fits. Now, the incommensurability of two scientific theories presupposes that there is no available criteria to prefer one over the other. For the sake of argument, suppose the requirement of both theories/schemes being true is dropped from the definition of incommensurability. Then, we would have three cases: both theories are false; the truth-value of the theories is unknown; and one theory is true and the other is false. With respect to the first two cases, none of the theories would be even endorsed by any scientific community, because of its falsity or because of the patent lack of supporting evidence. In the third case, there would be a criteria to discriminate between the two theories, namely dismissing the false theory and retaining the true theory. In either case, incommensurability would vanish. The fact that both theories are true, thus, preserves the indecision which is required for incommensurability to obtain.

[11] Some commentators, *e.g.* Hacker (1996), go on saying that if Davidson holds that languages are true, then he has to hold that contradictions are true, which is absurd. However correct, I believe that this is a critique which is directed against the letter, but not the spirit of Davidson's argument.

tain subsets of their languages. By a Davidsonian principle of charity, the two subsets that are *taken to be true* by the two communities of speakers are regarded as simply *true*. In light of this observation, the amended version of definition (INC-D) I shall propose reads: (INC-D*) *Two languages are semantically incommensurable iff (i) they fail to be intertranslatable and yet (ii*) subsets of them are true (those subsets that are taken to be true by the communities of speakers associated with the two languages)*.

2.4 Davidson against incommensurability

Having spelled out what incommensurability is for Davidson, it is time to reconstruct his argument against it. I have said that the objective of Davidson's argument is the claim that incommensurability is unintelligible, or that such a notion cannot be made sense of. What does that mean? It is instructive to distinguish three claims:

(1) It is not possibile that incommensurability holds.
(2) Members of any community of speakers cannot coherently claim that their language is incommensurability to another.
(3) Members of our community of speakers cannot coherently claim that our language is incommensurable to another.

Preliminarily, incommensurability holds iff there exists a pair of languages (L_1, L_2) such that L_1 and L_2 stand in the relation defined by (INC-D*). So (1) is a modal claim about the *impossibility* of incommensurability, while (2) and (3) are claims about the *speakers' inability* of asserting the possibility of incommensurability. But which of these claims is the objective of Davidson's argument? I have no definitive answer to this question, so in what follows I will give three readings of the argument. One reading takes Davidsons to claim (1), the other takes him to claim (2), and yet another takes him to claim (3).

I shall begin by reconstructing the common ground of Davidson's argument, and then launch the three different readings. Incommensurability entails that two languages (or rather, some properly chosen subsets of them) are both true and yet untranslatable, by clauses (i) and (ii*) of (INC-D*). But what is truth here? Davidson makes use of Tarski's theory of truth, as he believes it to be the most natural account of what we understand by truth.[12] Tarski's theory of truth associates with each sentence φ of a language L a bi-conditional (T) of the form:

(T) φ is true iff $\overline{\varphi}$,

---

[12]Some authors have objected that Tarski's theory of truth is not as innocuous as Davidson would like it to be (see Hacker (1996)). While I believe this is certainly the case, I will not overload my critique with this observation.

where 'φ' is replaced by a name for φ and '$\overline{\varphi}$' by a translation of φ into the meta-language, such that $\overline{\varphi}$ is a translation of φ.[13]

Given this characterization of what it takes for a sentence to be true, Davidson's argument in his own words runs as follows:

> And the criterion of a conceptual scheme different from our own now becomes: largely true but not translatable. The question whether this is a useful criterion is just the question how well we understand the notion of truth, as applied to language, independent of the notion of translation. The answer is, I think, that we do not understand it independently at all. ... Since convention (T) embodies our best intuition as to how the concept of truth is used, there does not seem to be much hope for a test that a conceptual scheme is radically different from ours if that test depends on the assumption that we can divorce the notion of truth from that of translation (Davidson, 1978, p. 194).

In nutshell the argument says that, while incommensurability requires truth and translatability to *be* independent, as a matter of fact truth and translatability *are not* independent as convention (T) shows. More carefully, the *understanding* of the notion of truth is not independent of the understanding of the notion of translatability, and yet incommensurability would require the two notions to be independently understood. The argument is very brief and needs to be unpacked. In fact, depending on where the emphasis is placed – *i.e.*, on incommensurability as such, or on speakers' inability of understanding incommensurability, or on our inability of understanding incommensurability – three readings of the argument can be given, yielding claim (1), (2) and (3) respectively. I shall consider each reading in turn.

Under the *first* reading, the argument would run as follows. Recall that for languages L and L' to be incommensurable the notion of truth should be invoked. So according to the bi-conditional or convention (T), when L and L' are both true (or better, subsets of them are true), their sentences are both translatable into a common meta-language. Strictly speaking, in Tarski's theory, given two languages, there is no mention of a *common* meta-language in which truth-conditions are spelled out. However, in the case at hand, one wants to say that two languages are *both* true, so a *common* meta-language should be used, otherwise the two languages will be true under different standards. Thus, the two supposed incommensurable languages will have to be both translatable into the same meta-language. But since both languages are translatable into the same meta-language, this suggests that there must be a way to translate sentences of one language into sentences of the other

---
[13]To be precise, in the definition of the T-condition, one has to add that the syntax and semantics of the meta-language should be previously defined.

language, and viceversa, by means of the shared meta-language which would function as a common yardstick of meaning comparison that is suited to carry out the translation. In other words, the two supposed incommensurable languages must be intertranslatable. So the claim of languages/schemes being true and yet untranslatable cannot possibly hold. This shows that claim (1) holds.

The first reading implicitly assumes that the claim that languages L and L' are incommensurable would be formulated by a third-language perspective, *i.e.*, the meta-language into which both L and L' can be translated and from which both L and L' can be compared and inspected, so to speak. But the assumption of a third-language perspective is debatable. Some may hold that any incommensurability claim is formulated, or takes place, within one of the two languages which are claimed to be incommensurable. So, the *second* reading of the argument makes it explicit that:

(C) The incommensurability claim takes place within either L or L' (*i.e.*, no third language perspective is allowed).

This is reasonable in the case in which the speakers of a given language want to claim that an alien language is incommensurable to theirs.

Assumption (C) has an interesting consequence, *i.e.*, the language in which the incommensurability claim is formulated will also play the role of the meta-language. This can be easily seen. If the incommensurability claim about L and L' is localized in L, it is within L that the statement that the sentences of L and L' are true should be expressed (recall that incommensurability requires truth). So, it is by using the linguistic resources of L that convention (T) should be expressed. But convention (T) is written in the meta-language, so L is to play the role of both the object-language and the meta-language. Now, from the first reading we know that both languages L and L' must be translatable into the common metalanguage. But the meta-language in this case is L itself. Thus, L' would be translatable into L. As a result, L and L' cannot fall under (INC-D*) because point (i) is not satisfied, hence we cannot coherently claim that L and L' are incommensurable. This shows that claim (2) holds.[14]

The second reading assumes that the claim of incommensurability is made from the standpoint of *any* language. This is not incorrect, but a situation that is more closely related to us is the one in which the claim of incommensurability is formulated within our own language,

---

[14]Note that claim (2) is not that L and L' are not incommensurable, rather that whenever an incommensurability claim is being made in accordance with assumption (C), we find ourselves in a (performative) contradiction.

i.e., English. So, the *third* reading of the argument can be yielded by replacing condition (C) with the following:

(C*) The incommensurability claim takes place within English.

The argument goes very similarly to the one just given for the second reading: It is enough to replace 'L' with 'English.' Very succinctly, if the claim of incommensurability is made within English, the language L' which is claimed to be incommensurable to English will be translatable into English because English will play the role of the meta-language. Hence, claim (3) holds.

2.5 Betraying Davidson

The task is now to provide a counter-argument to the effect that the validity of the arguments leading to claim (1), (2), and (3) is undermined.[15] Three readings of Davidson's argument have been given, and thus different counter-arguments are needed, depending on the preferred reading. To refute the argument coming out of the first reading, it is enough to be able to construct an instance of (INC-D*) without generating any contradiction. Instead, to refute the argument coming out of the second reading, it is necessary to construct an instance of (INC-D*) such that, in addition, (C) is satisfied. In what follows, I will construct an instance of (INC-D*), which suffices to refute the first reading of Davidson's argument and thus claim (1). My attack against claim (2) and the second reading will be less straightforward. I will show that, under additional assumptions which Davidson should be prone to accept, claim (2) fails.

A separate consideration should be given to the argument for (3). My strategy will be to point out that, although (3) is a special case of (2), considering English instead of some other language does not make any substantial difference. Thus, if (2) fails, there is no evidence for denying that (3) would fail as well.

---

[15]There is a peripheral worry to be addressed. While Davidson's argument adopts (INC-D) as a definition, the counter-argument I shall give adopts (INC-D*) rather than (INC-D) because, as previously shown, (INC-D) needs to be slightly amended on pain of being incorrect. So a question suggests itself: is the change from (INC-D) to (INC-D*) crucial for the success of my attack against Davidson? This legitimate worry is unavoidable and cannot be fully dismissed. Yet notice that definition (INC-D) as it stands is incorrect (languages cannot be true). Hence, the adjustment from (INC-D) to (INC-D*) was an attempt to read Davidson in the most charitable way. Indeed, the doubt lingers whether a different way to amend (INC-D) would render my counter-argument ineffective, but I shall put this doubt aside.

2.5.1 Against the first reading argument

Consider two different communities of speakers endowed with two different languages.[16] Both communities are concerned with the same phenomenon (or piece of reality, uninterpreted content, etc.), namely the phenomenon of some objects being next to a given object which both communities can clearly identify and refer to by means of a proper name. Obviously the two communities will use different names, but for the present purpose it suffices to refer to such an object by the constant 'c.' The two communities also share the predicate 'next-to' (or some translation of it in the respective languages) whose meaning is the intended one.

However, the communities are not alike in that they have developed different strategies to talk about objects being next to c. One community is only able to say whether there are, or there aren't, objects next to c. The other community, instead, is more precise and can express the exact number of objects next to c, ranging from 1 to any finite number. Despite its precision, the latter community is unable to express the fact that there are 0 objects next to c, probably because such a phenomenon has never been experienced.[17]

My claim is that the languages of the two communities are incommensurable in the sense of (INC-D*). If this can be argued, an instance of incommensurability (INC-D*) can be given as a result, whereby showing that claim (1) is false. Now, recall that definition (INC-D*) is composed of two points. Point (ii*) requires certain subsets of the two languages to be true. The subsets are chosen depending on which sentences the communities of speakers hold true. To satisfy point (ii*), we may suppose that one community holds true the sentence 'there are some objects next to c' and that the other community holds true the sentence 'there are 9 objects next to c'. In addition, both sentences turn out to be true, given that there are actually 9 objects next to c. So, point (ii*) is taken care of.

Point (i) of the definition requires the two languages to be non-intertranslatable. This is probably the requirement which needs a more elaborate argument. How can one show that two languages are non-intertranslatable? To do that, I suggest to characterize the two lan-

---

[16]For expository purposes I assume their languages to be very poorly expressive. There is no problem in doing so. Definition (INC-DS*) does not restrict the choice of supposed incommensurable languages to very expressive one, although it can be debated whether a definition of incommensurability should do so.

[17]This should not come as a too big surprise, because the concept corresponding to the number zero, after all, is a rather abstract one and it is possible that communities of speakers lack it, although they can master the other numbers.

guages in a formal fashion, so that failure of intertranslatability can be argued rigorously.[18]

The language which can only express the exact number of objects next to c will be denoted by L_n, while $L_\exists$ will denote the language which can only express whether there are, or there aren't, objects next to c. The syntax and semantics of L_n and $L_\exists$ should be defined first, and subsequently their non intertranslatability can be argued.

DEFINITION 1 (Syntax). *In terms of vocabulary, languages $L_\exists$ and L_n share the constant 'c,' the variable 'x,' the two-place predicate 'next-to,' and connectives '¬' and '∨.' They differ in their vocabulary because $L_\exists$ contains the quantifier '∃' (there are...), whereas L_n contains the quantifier '$\exists_n$' (there are exactly n...).*

The well-formed formulas of L_n and $L_\exists$ can be atomic or complex. $L_\exists$ contains only one atomic formula, namely '$\exists x$: next-to(x,c).' Instead, there is an n number of atomic formulas in L_n and they are only of the shape '$\exists_n x$: next-to(x,c),' with n any natural number such that $n > 0$. Complex formulas of $L_\exists$ and L_n are built recursively using the connectives ¬ and ∨.

DEFINITION 2 (Semantics). *Let $|\ldots|_n$ and $|\ldots|_\exists$ be interpretation functions from elements of the vocabulary of L_n and $L_\exists$ to objects of an infinite domain D:*

- $|c|_n = |c|_\exists = \bar{c}$ *for a given $\bar{c} \in D$;*
- $|next\text{-}to|_n = |next\text{-}to|_\exists = \{(d, \bar{c}) \colon d \in N \subseteq D \& d \neq \bar{c}\}.$

Next, truth-conditions for formulas in $L_\exists$ and L_n can be defined as follows, where # expresses the cardinality of a set:

- $\exists x$: next-to(x,c) *is true iff* $\#\{d \in D \colon (d,\bar{c}) \in |next\text{-}to|_\exists\} \geq 1$;
- $\exists_n x$: next-to(x,c) *is true iff* $\#\{d \in D \colon (d,\bar{c}) \in |next\text{-}to|_n\} = n$, *for any n;*
- *the recursive clauses for ∨ and ¬ are standard.*

CLAIM 1. *Languages L_n and $L_\exists$ are totally non-intertranslatable, if ⊤ and ⊥ are omitted.*

Recall that two languages are totally non-intertranslatable iff for *all* sentences in L, no meaning-equivalent sentence in L' can be found, and viceversa. But what does it take for two sentences or formulas to be meaning-equivalent? Following Davidson, I will assume that two

---

[18] One could object that the formal renderings of the two languages talked by the communities is not correct. The reader may judge by herself whether or not the formal renderings I am going to propose have misrepresented the languages of the two communities.

sentences or formulas have the same meaning if they have the same truth-conditions.[19]

Preliminaries aside, the argument for claim 1 can now be given. I shall here provide only the semi-formal and intuitive ideas on the assumption that formal details can be worked out. Two sub-claims should be established: (a) for any $\varphi_\exists$, if $\varphi_\exists \in L_\exists$, then $\varphi_\exists$ cannot be translated into any $\varphi_n \in L_n$, provided $\varphi_\exists$ is not $\top$ or $\bot$; and (b) for any φ_n, if $\varphi_n \in L_n$, then φ_n cannot be translated into any $\varphi_\exists \in L_\exists$, provided φ_n is not $\top$ or $\bot$.

First, the argument for (a): Consider the formula '$\exists x : \textit{next-to}(x,c)$' in $L_\exists$. The sentence would correspond to an infinite disjunction in L_n such as '$\exists_1 x : \textit{next-to}(x,c) \vee \exists_2 x : \textit{next-to}(x,c) \vee \ldots$' However, infinite disjunctions are not allowed in L_n. Likewise, '$\neg\exists x : \textit{next-to}(x,c)$' cannot be translated into L_n, since we assumed $n > 0$. Taking disjunctive formulas in $L_\exists$ would not change much, for these will be either equivalent to some atomic or negated atomic formulas in $L_\exists$, or they will be equivalent to $\top$ or $\bot$.

Next, the argument for (b): Consider the formula '$\exists_n x : \textit{next-to}(x,c)$' in L_n. Any sentence in $L_\exists$ such as '$\exists x : \textit{next-to}(x,c)$' cannot work as a good translation. For instance consider the case there are $n+1$ objects next to w; then, '$\exists_n x : \textit{next-to}(x,c)$' would be false but '$\exists x : \textit{next-to}(x,c)$' would be true. Likewise, a negated formula such as '$\neg\exists x : \textit{next-to}(x,c)$' would not work either, as the latter is true iff 0 objects are next to c. Again, taking disjunctive formulas in L_n would not change much, for these will be either equivalent to to $\top$ or $\bot$, or they could be shown to be untranslatable by the same argument used for the atomic formulas. This establishes the total non-intertranslatability between L_n and $L_\exists$.

2.5.2 Against the second reading argument

The refutation of Davidson's argument under the first reading, and thus of claim (1), can hardly be resisted given its formal fashion. However, one may well think that the first reading is not the correct reconstruc-

---

[19]This is one of the points in the discussion about semantical incommensurability when an appeal to a theory of meaning is crucial. Davidson himself can be seen as advocating a truth-conditional account of meaning, for which formulas in L_n and $L_\exists$ are meaning-equivalent whenever one formula is true iff the other is true. I do not want to defend this assumption in full, but pointing out its plausibility should suffice. With regard to L_n and $L_\exists$, the assumption that meaning of formulas boils down to truth-conditions is reasonable on the ground that L_n and $L_\exists$ are descriptive languages composed of statements about the world. They are not composed of pieces of discourse such as commands or imperatives which are typically troublesome for a truth-conditional account of meaning.

tion of what Davidson had in mind. So let me now move to the second reading and the refutation of claim (2).

Consider, once again, languages $L_\exists$ and L_n and suppose condition (C) is satisfied, *i.e.*, the incommensurability claim takes place in, say, language $L_\exists$. I contend that speakers in $L_\exists$ can coherently claim that their language is incommensurable to L_n. Suppose that language L_n is totally alien to the speakers of $L_\exists$, or that speakers of $L_\exists$ have no idea what the speakers of L_n mean when they communicate. Further, suppose that speakers of $L_\exists$ are trying to find out a translation of L_n into their own language. This situation is that of a radical interpretation.

Given the radical interpretation scenario, I shall argue for two claims. My first claim is that speakers of $L_\exists$ are able to arrive at the conclusion that L_n is *untranslatable* into their own language. My second claim is that speakers of $L_\exists$ are able to arrive at the conclusion that sentences of L_n are true. If both claims are warranted, then speakers of $L_\exists$ can arrive at the conclusion that L_n and $L_\exists$ are incommensurable in the sense of (INC-D*). To anticipate, I must say that speakers of $L_\exists$ can only arrive at the conclusion that L_n and $L_\exists$ are *partially* incommensurable, because they can only arrive at the conclusion that L_n and $L_\exists$ are *partially* non-intertranslatable. But this is good enough to undermine Davidson's argument.

I will start by arguing for my first claim. Davidson grants that in a situation of radical interpretation we can make two assumptions. First: (A1) no matter which language we speak, we can always tell whether someone is holding a sentence true or not. Second: (A2) we can question someone by asking whether she holds a sentence true (provided the sentence belongs to the language she speaks), and we can also understand her reaction of assent or dissent. This is crucial for the process of radical interpretation to get started.[20]

Suppose now that speakers of $L_\exists$ hear speakers of L_n utter sentence φ_n. Then, speakers of $L_\exists$ will formulate an hypothesis about the meaning of φ_n by associating it with some sentence $\varphi_\exists$ in their own language $L_\exists$. The hypothesis may have the following form:

$$\varphi_n \text{ means the same as } \varphi_\exists.$$

With Davidson we may assume that speakers of $L_\exists$ have a truth-conditional theory of the sameness of meaning, hence the hypothesis will look like the following:

(H)   'φ_n' is true iff $\varphi_\exists$

---

[20] Davidson writes: "Suppose , then, that the evidence available is just that speakers of the language to be interpreted hold various sentences to be true at certain times and under specific circumstances," (Davidson, 1978, p. 135).

Speakers of $L_\exists$ can test (H) by questioning speakers of L_n. How does this work? First, speakers of $L_\exists$ have to decide whether $\varphi_\exists$ is true or not, and they can do so by knowing what $\varphi_\exists$ means and depending on the state of the world given a time and a space location. Next, they will ask whether speakers of L_n hold φ_n true or not. If they discover that there is a situation in which $\varphi_\exists$ is true but φ_n is not held true by speakers of L_n, that would show that $\varphi_\exists$ is not a good translation of φ_n.

Let us look at an example. Speakers of $L_\exists$ hear the sentence '$\exists_9 x : next\text{-}to(x,c)$' from speakers of L_n. Now, they will formulate an hypothesis and try to test it:

(H9)   '$\exists_9 x : next\text{-}to(x,c)$' is true iff $\exists x : next\text{-}to(x,c)$.

Speakers of $L_\exists$ will then consult speakers of L_n under the assumption that such a consultation is possible between speakers of L_n and $L_\exists$. Suppose that the situation is such that there are 9 objects next to c. Speakers of $L_\exists$ hold the sentence '$\exists x : next\text{-}to(x,c)$' true, and by (H9) they expect speakers of L_n to hold '$\exists_9 x : next\text{-}to(x,c)$' true. Speakers of L_n will obviously assent. This would be a first piece of evidence that '$\exists x : next\text{-}to(x,c)$' is a translation for '$\exists_9 x : next\text{-}to(x,c)$'. Now, one piece of evidence is not enough, and so speakers of $L_\exists$ will test (H9) another time, and suppose that this time the situation is such that there are 8 objects next to c instead of 9. Speakers of $L_\exists$ would still hold '$\exists x : next\text{-}to(x,c)$' true and thus by (H9) they would expect speakers of L_n to hold '$\exists x : next\text{-}to(x,c)$' true. But this time speakers of L_n will show their dissent.

From the evidence gathered, speakers $L_\exists$ will be able to conclude that the translation hypothesis (H9) is false and they will try another hypothesis. However, in general we know by claim 1 that any translation hypothesis will fail, *i.e.*, any attempt to translate '$\exists_9 x : next\text{-}to(x,c)$' into a sentence of $L_\exists$ will fail. So, suppose that speakers of $L_\exists$ can go through all the sentences in their language;[21] then, they will conclude that '$\exists_9 x : next\text{-}to(x,c)$' has no translation in their language. This will show that speakers of $L_\exists$ can arrive at the conclusion that their language is *partially* incommensurable to L_n.[22]

---

[21] After all, there are not very many sentences: $\exists x : next\text{-}to(x,c)$, $\neg \exists x : next\text{-}to(x,c)$, and the rest are tautologies and contradictions which are always translatable under a truth-conditional account of meaning, and thus are to be disregarded.

[22] A stronger conclusion could be reached, though. Speakers of $L_\exists$ wil reach the same untranslatability conclusion for any sentence they will possibly hear from speakers of L_n. So, speakers of $L_\exists$ will reach the conclusion that, *as far as they know*, any sentence in L_n cannot be translated by any sentence in $L_\exists$. Note that

This reasoning establishes my first claim, namely that speakers of $L_\exists$ can conclude that their language is not translatable (at least partially) into L_n. Yet some may object that the reasoning utilized by speakers of $L_\exists$ to reach the conclusion that $L_\exists$ and L_n are partially non-intertranslatable exceeds the expressive power of $L_\exists$ itself, so the conclusion that L_n and $L_\exists$ are untranslatable cannot be formulated into $L_\exists$ itself, nor can the reasoning leading to such a conclusion. True enough. Let us then extends $L_\exists$ in such a way that the untranslatability claim can be formulated. So, let $L_\exists^+$ be an extension of $L_\exists$ by adding: the predicate 'is true', the bi-conditional 'iff', and names to denote sentences heard from speakers of L_n. This will allow speakers of $L_\exists^+$ to formulate type (H) hypotheses. Moreover, speakers of $L_\exists^+$ will need a rule (R) of the form: *If any type (H) hypothesis of translation for a sentence φ_n in L_n encounters the dissent of speakers of L_n, then φ_n is not translatable into any sentence in $L_\exists^+$*. So, once $L_\exists$ is extended this way, it seems that we would have a scenario in which (C) is satisfied, and in which speakers of $L_\exists^+$ can coherently claim that their language is not translatable into L_n, at least partially.[23]

The second claim to be established is that speakers of $L_\exists$ can assert that languages L_n and $L_\exists$ (or better, subsets of them) are true. This is the point where Davidson's argument will start to apply. Recall: Truth is based on translatability according to Tarski's (T) convention, so any sentence that is claimed to be true by the speakers of a language will be translatable into that language. Hence, if speakers of $L_\exists$ claims that a sentence φ_n of L_n is true, that sentence will be translatable into some sentence in $L_\exists$. How can this argument be resisted? My strategy would be to undercut the very premise of the argument, namely that truth is based on translatability. I will argue that Davidson cannot consistently hold that truth is based on translatability, and at the same time hold other theses that are essential to his philosophy of language. The crucial point consists in assuming another Davidsonian thesis, *i.e.*, (A3) truth

---

this conclusion is *weaker than total* non-intertranstabality since speakers of $L_\exists$ can never be sure that the sentences their heard from speakers of L_n are alla sentences that are in L_n.

[23] There is a residual objection: The non-intertranslatablity claim was established for $L_\exists$ by using the additional expressive power of $L_\exists^+$. But what we need is to establish the non-intertranslatability claim for $L_\exists^+$ by using the expressive power of $L_\exists^+$ itself. However, I think that although $L_\exists^+$ has additional expressive power over $L_\exists$, this is of no use for finding sentences in $L_\exists^+$ that are meaning-equivalent to sentences in L_n. Observe: the sentences that are in $L_\exists^+$ but not in $L_\exists$ are type (H) hypotheses and the rule (R), but these sentences cannot serve as a translation for sentences in L_n.

precedes meaning,[24] and see that it conflicts with the claim that truth is based on translatability.[25]

It is correct to say that given a Tarski's bi-conditional, truth is based on translatability. However, Davidson has inverted the relation between translatability and truth that is encoded in Tarski's conventions (T), by inverting the relation between meaning and truth according to (A3). In Davidson, Tarski's bi-conditionals are used to deliver a theory of meaning based on truth, and not a theory of truth based on meaning. Hence, if truth precedes meaning, truth precedes translatability. My conclusion is, then, that Davidson claim that truth is based on translatability is correct if applied to Tarski (T) conventions as such, but it is not correct if applied to the way in which Davidson uses Tarski (T) conventions to deliver a theory of meaning, and not a theory of truth.[26]

More precisely, the relation between truth, meaning and translatability should be as follows. In the process of radical interpretation, one first recognizes that a sentence is held true, and also registers all cases in which that sentence is held true. Next, by the Davisonian principle of charity, one takes a sentence that is held true as simply a true sentence. Finally, one determines what the meaning of the sentence is on the basis of the circumstances in which it is (held) true. Clearly, in the process of radical interpretation one arrives at determining the meaning of a sentence that belongs to an alien language by finding a meaning-equivalent sentence into her own familiar language, or by finding a translation of the alien sentence into a sentence of her own familiar language. But notice that, in order for the whole process to get started, one has to have an independent understanding of what it takes for a sentence to be (held) true; and Davidson grants that holding a sentence true is a primitive attitude which we can all understand across languages. Under a Davidsonian standpoint, thus, there seems to be no problem in assuming that speakers of $L_\exists$ can understand and claim that some sentences of L_n are true without yet possessing a translation of these sentences into their own language.

---

[24] See in particular Davidson (1967).

[25] Assumption (A3) was also granted in the process of radical interpretation between $L_\exists$ and L_n: The attitude of holding a sentence of L_n true is recognized by the speakers of $L_\exists$ before the meaning of that sentence is reconstructed.

[26] These ideas are in line with Davidson (1973). Davidson himself writes: "In Tarski's work, T-sentences are taken to be true because the right branch of the bi-conditional is assumed to be a translation of the sentence truth conditions for which are being given ... What I propose is to reserve the direction of explanation: assuming translation, Tarski was able to define truth; the present idea is take truth as basic and to extract an account of translation or interpretation." (Davidson, 1978, p. 134).

To summarize, I have shown that speakers of $L_\exists^+$ can claim that their language is untranslatable to L_n. They can also claim that sentences of both $L_\exists^+$ and L_n are true by relying on the primitive notion of holding sentences true. As a result, speakers of $L_\exists^+$ can claim that their language is incommensurable to L_n, whence claim (2) fails.

2.5.3 Against the third reading argument

It remains to be established that claim (3) fails. More modestly, I will argue that Davidsons does not provide us with any evidence against the denial of claim (3). For claim (3) to fail, speakers of English should be able to claim that another language, call it Alien, is untranslatable into English, and moreover that sentences of English and Alien are true. Suppose speakers of English are confronted with speakers of Alien. By the same argument given for the second reading, from the attitude of holding true and by applying the principle of charity, speakers of English will be able to claim that sentences of Alien are true, although they do not know what they mean. It is significantly more difficult to show that speakers of English can claim that Alien and English are non-intertranslatable. Here I can only point out a parallelism. In the imaginary radical translation scenario, speakers of $L_\exists$ encountered speakers of L_n, and by testing several translation hypotheses (H), they could conclude that $L_\exists$ and L_n were non-intertranslatable (at least partially). Similarly, one can imagine speakers of English encountering speakers of Alien and realizing that Alien is untranslatable into English, in the same way in which speakers of $L_\exists$ realized that L_n is not translatable into $L_\exists$. This parallelism gives us the conclusion:

(E1) *Possibly*, members of our community of speakers can coherently claim that our language is not-translatable into another.

But it does give use the conclusion:

(E2) Members of our community of speakers can coherently claim that our language is not-translatable into another.

From (E1) and the fact argued before that speakers of English can claim that sentences of both English and Alien are true, this conclusion follows:

(E3) *Possibly*, members of our community of speakers can coherently claim that our language is incommensurable to another.

One can see that (E3) is not the outright denial of (3), unless (3) is read as a necessitated claim. As a result, my conclusion is that Davidson does not offer any evidence against the possibility of claim (3) failing, yet it is fair to say that I did not offer any conclusive evidence for the actual failure of (3).

2.6 Conclusion

In this paper I have reconstructed Davidson's definition of incommensurability in the form of (INC-D*). I have given three readings of his argument against incommensurability, and for each reading I have given counter-arguments showing that the argument cannot go through. With regard to the first reading, I have constructed two languages that are incommensurable according to (INC-D*). With regard to the second reading, I have shown that Davidson's argument cannot go through by assumptions (A1), (A2) and (A3). My conclusion has been weaker in the case of the second reading than in the case of the first reading. Under the latter, I could show that two given languages are incommensurable, whereby refuting claim (1). Under the former, I could show that speakers of one language can claim that their language is partially (but not totally) incommensurable to another language, whereby refuting claim (2), but only if incommensurability is taken to be partial incommensurability. In the case of the third reading, I could only offer a conjecture that claim (3) fails, in the sense that there is no available evidence to deny the failure of (3).

To conclude, I would like to address two general lines of reply that are open to Davidson. One is that languages $L_\exists$ and L_n are not natural languages, and that Davidson's argument was only about natural languages. This is a pressing worry. However, it is unclear to me how any discussion about the incommensurability between natural languages can be made precise in the first place. In particular, arguing that a natural language is non-intertranslatable into another natural language will require us to have a full account of meaning in natural languages. But this account is lacking for now. Thus, either we can circumvent the problem (but how?), or adopting toy-languages such as $L_\exists$ and L_n seems – for the time being – unavoidable, or at least convenient.

The second line of response is that languages $L_\exists$ and L_n are very poorly expressive, and that if more expressive languages were considered the incommensurability result would not be yielded. This is an interesting conjecture. For instance, it would be interesting to be able to show that, if two languages reach a certain threshold of expressive power, they will be *eo ipso* intertranslatable and thus commensurable. However, until this threshold of expressive power is spelled out precisely, I do not see any reason why very poorly expressive languages should not be considered.

References

Davidson, Donald. 1967. Truth and meaning. *Synthese* 17:304–323.

Davidson, Donald. 1973. Radical interpretation. *Dialectica* 27(3-4):313–328.

Davidson, Donald. 1974. On the very idea of a conceptual scheme. *Proceedings and Addresses of the American Philosophical Association* 47:5–20.

Davidson, Donald. 1978. *Inquiries into Truth and Interpretation*. Oxford: Clarendon Press.

Hacker, P. M. S. 1996. On davidson's idea of conceptual scheme. *The Philosophical Quarterly* 46(184):289–307.

Sankey, Howard. 1993. Kuhn's changing concept of incommensurability. *British Journal for the Philosophy of Science* 44(4):775–791.

3

How Similar is "Julius" to "Phlogiston"? Extending Evans's Notion of Descriptive Name to Names of Natural Kinds[1]

CARLA MERINO-RAJME

3.1 Introduction

If we take Gareth Evans's arguments for descriptive names as cogent, can we use them to account for the meaning and reference of theoretical terms like "electron", "Vulcan", and "phlogiston" for the period of time in which their referents, if they have such, remain unobserved? An attempt to achieve this requires, at a minimum, to extend Evans's notion of descriptive name, originally offered for grammatical proper names, to names of natural kinds. My main concern in this paper will be to show how this extension could be done. An interesting outcome is that I offer a notion of rigidity for proper names that, unlike Kripke's notion of rigid designation, can be used to account for the rigidity of empty proper names like "Vulcan". I also propose an analogous modifi-

---

[1] I thank Maite Ezcurdia for many valuable comments on previous versions of this paper. I am also indebt with Axel Barceló, Víctor Cantero, Richard Dietz, Xavier de Donato, Laura Duhau, Eduardo García, Mario Gómez-Torrente, and Ana Rosa Pérez Ransanz for their help. Earlier versions of this paper were presented at the Instituto de Investigaciones Filosóficas (UNAM) and the First SIFA Graduate Conference. I thank members of IIF-UNAM and the audience of the First SIFA Graduate Conference for their helpful comments and discussions.

cation to Gómez-Torrente's notion of essentialist predicate that can be used to account for the rigidity of empty names of natural kinds such as "phlogiston".

I start by identifying the type of terms I will be concerned with, which I dub "Referential Theoretical Terms" or "RTTs". In section II, I offer a characterization of Evans's descriptive names, as well as some of the motivations behind it. In section III, drawing an analogy to Evans's descriptive names and using Gómez-Torrente's proposed notion of rigidity for general terms, I characterize the notion of descriptive names of natural kinds. These characterizations face a challenge: while descriptive names and descriptive names for natural kinds are taken to behave rigidly, they can be referenceless or empty. Kripke's notion of rigid designator, however, cannot account for the rigidity of empty names. In section IV, I propose the notions of *e-weak rigidity* and *e-weak essentiality*, and argue that they allow us to account for the rigidity of empty descriptive names and empty descriptive names for natural kinds. Finally, in section V, I briefly discuss other problems that arise from attempting to use descriptive names to account for the meaning and reference of RTTs, and offer some suggestions on how some of them could be addressed.

3.2 Referential Theoretical Terms (RTTs)

Consider terms like "Vulcan", "Neptune", "electron", "neutrino", and "phlogiston". Terms like these are introduced through a scientific theory to refer to objects that have not been directly observed[2] at the time of their introduction.[3] Besides, it is possible that in introducing them we are mistaken so that at least some of them do not refer. Nevertheless, even if these terms have no referents, they appear to be meaningful. For example, when uttering something like "If the observations of astronomer Holden are accurate then Vulcan does not exist" or when Lavoisier uttered something like "Phlogiston does not exist", people communicate to others information about the world. Given this, we can ask whether theories of meaning and reference for these terms can be offered that account for this fact. I will focus only on the period of time in which the referents of these terms, if they exist, have not been observed (or have not been taken to be the referents of these terms), and if they do not exist, we do not know that this is the case. In other words, what is their meaning (even if empty) and how do they

---

[2] I leave aside the problem of how to understand *observation*. See note 8.

[3] The requirement that the referents have to be unobserved when the term is introduced is too strong. It suffices to claim that the referent, though observed, cannot be ostensively identified *as the referent* of the term. See note 24.

refer (when they do) for this period of time?

According to Putnam (1962), *theoretical terms* are those that are *introduced by* or *come from* a scientific theory.[4] I will use this idea to characterize what I call "Referential Theoretical Terms" or "RTT" roughly in the following way:[5]

(i) RTTs are terms first introduced through the linguistic expression of a scientific theory;[6] before the linguistic formulation of the theory was offered, these terms did not appear in natural language.[7]

(ii) RTTs are introduced to refer either to a yet unobserved[8] object or to a yet unobserved instance of a natural kind, stuff or phenomena of which no instance has been observed.[9] Terms of the first type are grammatical proper names, while terms of the second type are names of natural kinds, stuffs or phenomena.[10]

Not every theoretical term (in Putnam's sense just recalled), however, is an RTT. There are terms introduced by a scientific theory that are not used to refer to any object, like "complex current" or "ideal gas". Other terms meet (i), but are used to refer to an object that has been observed and identified as the referent of the term, and thus fail to meet (ii). Ecologists who directly observe a new species of plant and

---

[4]See Putnam (1962, p. 317).

[5]I do not intend to offer a definition for these terms, but only a characterization specific enough to allow us to recognize most of the terms we are aiming to explain.

[6]The phrase "in the linguistic expression of a scientific theory" is introduced to avoid committing the present view to a certain conception of what a scientific theory is.

[7]These terms could have appeared in natural language but only if upon introducing them within a scientific theory we are inclined to say they are cases of semantic ambiguity. For example, the name "Neptune" was first introduced as a name for the God the Seas, and after, re-introduced as a name of the planet.

[8]We will assume the view according to which we can observe macroscopic objects like cups, chairs, papers, *etc.*; with the help of a microscope, we may observe certain bacteria, cells, viruses, and several other microorganisms; with telescopes, we may observe some distant stars, planets, comets, *etc.*; with current techniques, however, we cannot observe electrons, quarks, neutrinos, *etc.*, assuming that they exist.

[9]Terms such as "water", "gold", and "tiger" are examples of names for natural kinds, while terms such as "philosopher", or "Italian" are not. I will also take terms like "electron", "phlogiston", "HIV", *etc.* as terms of natural kinds, some of which might be empty. We will not concern ourselves here with how to define a natural kind and simply understand it as a way of classifying, grouping, or ordering objects based on natural properties. I will also assume that speakers take the referents of RTTs, if there are such, to exist in the same sense in which they take chairs or tables to exist. In this sense, these terms differ from fictional names like "Santa Claus" or "Sherlock Holmes".

[10]As said in note 3, this criterion is too strong. I leave this formulation in its stronger version since this is the way in which the problem has traditionally been posed. See also 24.

baptize it will introduce a term of this type. Neither terms like "gold", "bear", or "Sun" are RTTs: though they *appear* in scientific theories, they were not firstly *introduced* by them, nor are they used to name unobserved objects. Finally, we will leave out of this discussion terms for which the nature of their referents (if seen as referential) is under severe dispute, like numbers.

3.3 Evans's descriptive names

Consider now Evans's well-known example of a descriptive name. Suppose we introduce the name "Julius" to refer to whoever was the inventor of the zip. Suppose also that we do not know who this person is, and that there are no other predicates besides "being the inventor of the zip" that we can use to link "Julius" with its referent. In addition, we do not even know if "Julius" has a referent: maybe two people invented the zip so that there is no unique inventor of it. Consider now the sentence:

(1) Julius was an Italian carpenter[11]

(1) strikes us as a meaningful sentence. If so, we can ask ourselves (keeping issues of ambiguity aside):[12] What could the meaning of (1) be when uttered by S, a competent English speaker who is aware of the way "Julius" was introduced? It seems that if "Julius" has the restrictions just imposed (and S is speaking seriously, non-ironically, non-metaphorically, *etc.*) when uttering (1), S means nothing but

(2) The inventor of the zip was an Italian carpenter.

Despite the fact that what S means by (1) is nothing but (2), "Julius" and "the inventor of the zip" are different types of expressions. In particular, "Julius" should not be seen as an abbreviation for "the inventor of the zip". Suppose "Julius" has a referent, and consider the sentences (3) and (4):

(3) Julius might have not been the inventor of the zip.

(4) Julius might have not been Julius.

While it is easy to imagine situations in which Julius was not the inventor of the zip – for instance, a situation in which Julius died before inventing anything – and thus for (3) to be true, this is not the case

---

[11]Throughout this paper, we will ignore complications having to do with tense.

[12]With this I mean the situation that arises when two different objects are both called by the same grammatical proper name (of course, the issue here is whether it is indeed the same proper name). For example, the case in which two different persons are both named "John Smith".

with (4). There are no situations in which Julius would not be identical to himself, and thus (4) is necessarily false. Furthermore, sentences like:

(5) If anyone uniquely invented the zip, Julius invented the zip.

and

(6) If anyone uniquely invented the zip, the inventor of the zip invented the zip.[13]

while both true with respect to the actual world, they can have different truth-values when considering counterfactual situations. With respect to a possible world in which someone else, different from whom actually invented the zip uniquely invents it, (5) would be false since someone other than Julius would be its unique inventor. However, with respect to this possible world, as with respect to any other, (6) is true.[14]

These examples suggest that if "Julius" is not empty,[15] then it is a rigid designator, while "the inventor of the zip" is a non-rigid designator.[16] As proposed by Kripke, an expression is a *rigid designator* if it designates one and the same object in every possible world in which the object exists,[17] and a *non-rigid designator* if this is not the case.[18]

---

[13] We are assuming a narrow scope lecture of these descriptions, as well as an attributive use of them. See footnote 27.

[14] See Kripke (1980).

[15] In section 3.5, we will see why if "Julius" is empty it cannot be a rigid designator.

[16] Though Evans does take "Julius" to be a rigid designator – as he would do for any other proper name – he prefers to use his notion of *referential expression* to account for the rigidity of proper names. The notions differ in the following way. Though all referential expressions in Evans's sense are rigid designators, the inverse is not true: for example, some definite descriptions can be rigid designators but Evans does not consider them as referential expressions. Besides, Evans's notion, compared to Kripke's notion of rigid designation, has the advantage that it can take empty descriptive names as referring expressions. Despite this, I will characterize descriptive names as rigid designators since it is difficult to see how the notion of referential expression could be extended to general terms in such a way that terms like "water" or "oxygen" are taken to be referential expressions, though excluding from this category non-rigid terms such as "Italian" or "carpenter". In this sense, the considerations made in this paper differ from Evans's. However, as mentioned before, Evans himself uses the notion of "rigid designator" to express his ideas regarding the modal behavior of descriptive names.

[17] By considering whether an expression could refer to a different object from which it in fact refers to, Kripke does not mean that the language could have been different, for example, that we could have used "Charles Chaplin" to refer to Baudelaire – something that is true. What he means is that *in the same way in which we actually use the language*, when considering a counterfactual situation, a rigid designator does not designate a different object from the one it actually designates. If we take "Charles Chaplin" as a rigid designator that actually refers to Chaplin, then Kripke's claim is that it does not refer to any object different from Chaplin in any counterfactual situation. See Kripke (1980, pp. 8–10).

[18] Kripke (1980, p. 48). In section 3.5, I will consider this notion in more detail.

But, can this be so? Can a speaker mean and understand the same by uttering (1) and (2), while one of these sentences has a rigid designator where the other has a non-rigid designator? Kripke (1980) has been taken as arguing that this cannot be the case: a pair of sentences like (1) and (2) cannot have the same meaning since their truth-values in some counterfactual situations differ.[19] This, however, seems to contradict the initial intuition that what S expresses by uttering (1) is nothing but (2). What has gone wrong?

Evans's way out is to distinguish the epistemic notion of "content"[20] from the modal notion of "proposition".[21] He takes a *content* to be akin to a Fregean thought and so answerable to epistemic considerations, whilst a proposition is a function from possible worlds to truth-values. He argues that it is perfectly coherent to claim that two sentences have the same content (that they are epistemically equivalent) but that they express different propositions (they embed differently into modal operators). The problem with the Kripkean argument, according to Evans, is that it fails to make this distinction and concludes from a difference in propositions to a difference in contents.[22] If Evans is correct, his proposal sketches a theory of meaning and reference for descriptive names that, though descriptivist, incorporates the claim that proper names are rigid designators.[23] We will not, however, be concerned with defending Evans's claims here but will assume them as correct.

Before extending Evans's ideas for descriptive names to names of natural kinds, let me clarify how I will understand the notion of "descriptive name" or "DN". Firstly, for a grammatical proper name to

---

[19] Scott Soames, in Soames (2002), for example, called this Kripkean argument "the modal argument". Evans can also be taken as interpreting Kripke in this way.

[20] Evans proposes the following as an intuitive criterion to understand his notion of "content": if two sentences *have the same content*, then what is believed by a subject who understands and accepts one of them as true is the same as what is believed by a subject who understands and accepts the other sentence as true. In this way, if two sentences *have the same content*, and a person understands both, she cannot believe what one sentence says and disbelieve what the other one says. See Evans (1979, p. 176).

[21] Evans's distinction between "content" and "proposition" may be seen as the roots of a two-dimentionalism. See Soames (2005, Ch. 6).

[22] See Evans (1979, pp. 179–180).

[23] Evans has also been interpreted as claiming that the content of a descriptive name is a rigidified description. For example, instead of taking what a speaker says by uttering (1) as (2), we could take it as saying:

(7)   The inventor of the zip *in the actual world* was an Italian carpenter.

Since a rigidified description designates, in every possible world, the object that in the actual world satisfies it, this interpretation answers the Kripkean objection by stating that both sentences have the same content and the same truth conditions with respect to every possible world (both have rigid designators).

be a DN it has to be introduced by a description and has to stand for whatever satisfies it *in the actual world*. Though for many expressions it is likely to be the case that more than one description is used to fix their references, I will follow Evans's simplifying assumption that there is only one description available for this.

Secondly, the connection between a descriptive name and a certain description will be taken as a *semantic* one. This because the description fixes the name's referent and because knowing the description and being aware of the role it plays in fixing the name's referent – knowing that the name stands for whatever satisfies the description in the actual world – is required for *understanding* the name and becoming a competent user of it. Moreover, it is precisely because of this semantic connection that the name can be taken as meaningful, or as saying something (as having a content), even if it does not refer. Thirdly, a proper name for which we can ostensively identify its referent as its referent cannot be a DN. When this happens, the tight semantic connection between the name and the description with which it was introduced is lost: someone that has been acquainted with the object and knows that it is the referent of the name can understand the name even if he ignores *this* description; many other descriptions independent from the one with which it was introduced will become available for linking the name with the referent.[24] According to Evans, what unifies all the newly available descriptions with a name is the referent, and so the semantic relation between the name and its referent, and not between the name and a certain description, becomes essential.[25]

---

[24] When this happens, the meaning and reference of the grammatical proper name are likely to be better modeled as those of any ordinary proper name introduced by description. "Julius", for example, can fail to be a DN when competent speakers are able to ostensively link it to the man that uniquely invented the zip as its referent (or through a causal chain that leads to an ostension like this). The requirement that an object cannot be ostensively linked to a DN as the referent, however, is weaker than one that stipulates that the object has to be unobserved. Julius might have been observed by many of his contemporaries, or even by the person who introduced the name as long as he does not know of this man, that he is the referent of the name. This is why it is too strong to require that the referents of RTTs have to be unobserved objects: it is only needed that the sole means of relating the term to its referent as its referent is through a certain description.

[25] Instead of establishing the reference relation as:

"Julius" refers to Julius,

that Evans takes as adequate for non-descriptive proper names, he proposes the following for descriptive names:

"Julius" refers to the inventor of the zip.

The relation of reference proposed by Evans is constructed in such a way that the name refers, in every possible world, to the object that in the actual world satisfies

Fourthly, the semantic relation between a DN and its description is *public* in the sense that every competent user of the name must know that every other competent user of it associates the name with the same description and takes it to stand for the object that satisfies this description in the actual world. Finally, as already discussed, DNs can be empty and can behave rigidly.[26]

According the above, a "descriptive name" or "DN" has the following features:

(a) **Reference:** A DN is a proper name introduced by a description (used attributively)[27] to fix its referent.
(b) **Non-acquaintance:** A DN cannot be linked to its referent, as its referent, by an ostension nor by a causal chain that leads to an ostension.
(c) **Understanding:** To understand a DN and become a competent user of it, a speaker must know that it refers to whatever satisfies in the actual world the description with which it was introduced (its reference-fixing description) and must know which description this is.[28]

---

this description and thus, behaves rigidly. See Evans (1979, pp. 164–170).

[26] One of Evans's assumptions that will not be discussed here is his use of a free logic. In his view, an atomic sentence such as (1) cannot be true (nor false) if "Julius" is empty, but, since (1) is *not true*, its negation can still be taken as false. Other differences between this logic and a classical one have to do with the laws of Existential Generalization and of Universal Elimination: since the system allows for the use of empty constants, these laws need to be restricted so as to avoid concluding from a true premise like the negation of (1) if "Julius" is empty, the false claim that something that is not an Italian carpenter exists. See Evans (1979, pp. 165–166). See also Sainsbury (2005).

[27] A description is used *attributively* if it is used to designate whatever object satisfies it. On the other hand, it is said to be used *referentially* if used to refer to some specific object even if it does not satisfy the description used to refer to it. For example, while reading a certain book I might utter

(*) The author of book X is clever

to communicate that someone is the author of book X and that she is clever. In this case, it is said that I used the description "the author of book X" attributively. Alternatively, when attending a conference and listening to a certain individual c that I take to be the author of book X, I may utter (*) to communicate that c is clever, whether or not c is, in fact, the author of book X. In this case my use of "the author of X" is said to be referential. See Donnellan (1966).

[28] DNs are not subject to some of Kripke's objections to descriptivist accounts of ordinary proper names because of requirements (a) and (c) (Soames called these Kripkean objections "semantic arguments"). Since by stipulation DNs designate whatever satisfies the description with which they are introduced, and since every competent user links the same description with the DN, it cannot be argued that the referent of the name is an object different from the one that in fact satisfies the description associated by a competent user of the name. Besides, Evans uses (c) to

(d) **Publicity:** Every competent user of a DN must associate the same description with the proper name and must know that every other competent user of it associates this description with it.
(e) **Rigidity:** Roughly, we can say that a DN is used as a rigid designator. In section 3.5, I will offer a more precise characterization of this feature.
(f) **Emptiness:** Since the semantic connection is established between a DN and its reference-fixing description and not between the DN and the referent, even if no object is the denotation in the real world of this description, the DN can be meaningful.

In what follows, I present analogous considerations for names of natural kinds.

3.4 Descriptive names for natural kinds (DNNKs)

The claim that we can account for the meaning and reference of RTTs by taking them as DNs faces the immediate objection that DNs are characterized only for proper names whilst some RTTs are names of natural kinds. Thus, a minimal requirement for further pursuing this claim is to offer an extension of DNs to names of natural kinds. The following example is intended to show that analogous motivations to the ones given for "Julius" can be offered for certain names of natural kinds.

Suppose that while doing some experiments, a pair of scientists come to believe that they have isolated a new kind of substance. The substance, the scientists think, is responsible for making bacteria B grow at a faster rate under experiment E. They introduce the name "fluxonite" to refer to it. Furthermore, suppose the scientists do not know anything else about this substance and that there are no other predicates besides "being the natural substance responsible for causing bacteria B under experiment E to increase its growth rate" that they can use to associate "fluxonite" with its referent.[29] Also, the scientists could be wrong:

---

argue against Kripke's claim (called "the epistemic argument" in Soames (2002, p. 19).) that sentences like "If something is the inventor of the zip, then Julius is the inventor of the zip" and "If something is the inventor of the zip, then the inventor of the zip is the inventor of the zip" cannot be epistemically equivalent since the second, but not the first, is known by the speaker to be true *a priori*. According to Evans, if "Julius" is a descriptive name and "the inventor of the zip" is the description with which it was introduced, then every competent user must know *a priori* that both are true.

[29] This is an oversimplification mainly because of two reasons. On the one hand, descriptions like "the substance we were isolating yesterday" or "the substance we have been working with" are also available to speakers to talk about fluxonite. On the other hand, as suggested above, in real cases it is likely to be the case that more

fluxonite might not exist.

Consider now the following sentence:

(8) Fluxonite is a potential drug for humans.

Just as in the case of (1), (8) strikes us as a meaningful sentence. It seems very plausible that if "fluxonite" has the restrictions just presented, and a speaker S is aware of this and is speaking seriously, non-ironically, non-metaphorically, *etc.*, then when uttering (8), S means nothing but

(9) The natural substance causing bacteria B under experiment E to increase its growth rate is a potential drug for humans.

Despite the fact that what S means by (8) is nothing but (9), "fluxonite" and "the natural substance causing bacteria B under experiment E to increase its growth rate", just as "Julius" and "the inventor of the zip", are different types of expressions. In particular, "fluxonite" should not be seen as an abbreviation for the description used to introduce it. Suppose "fluxonite" has a reference, and consider sentences (10) and (11):

(10) Fluxonite might have not been the natural substance causing bacteria B under experiment E to grow at a faster rate.

(11) Fluxonite might have not been fluxonite.

While it is easy to imagine situations in which fluxonite is not the substance causing these effects on B under experiment E – for example, a situation in which though fluxonite exists, B cannot metabolize it and substance R is the one responsible for the increased growth rate of B – and thus for (10) to be true, this is not the case for (11). There are no situations in which fluxonite is not fluxonite and in which (11) is therefore necessarily false.

Also, we do not seem to use "fluxonite" to say something like (12) or (13):

(12) If penicillin had been the natural substance that caused bacteria B to increase its growth rate in experiment E, penicillin would have been fluxonite.

(13) If fluxonite had not been the natural substance that caused bacteria B to increase its growth rate in experiment E, fluxonite would have not been fluxonite.[30]

---

than one description is used to introduce the name. In the last section, I will briefly consider some problems related to these.

[30] We are assuming a narrow scope lecture and an attributive use of these descriptions.

What these examples illustrate is that "fluxonite" behaves rigidly. Kripke (1980) suggested that names of natural kinds are rigid, and despite the fact that he did not offer a precise notion of rigid designation for general terms, Gómez-Torrente (2006) constructed such a notion.[31] I will use his notion of essentialist predicate to offer an initial characterization of the rigidity of descriptive names of natural kinds. In the next section, I will show how this notion can be modified to better account for empty cases of this type of expressions.

Gómez-Torrente claims that whether we believe that general terms are predicates or not, they can be used with the verb "be" of predication to form grammatical predicates. For example, with "oxygen" we can form the predicate "is oxygen" or "is a sample of oxygen"; with "horse" we can form the predicate "is a horse", *etc.*[32] It is with a feature of these predicative phrases derived from general terms and not with the general terms themselves that he constructs the notion of weak essentiality.

According to Gómez-Torrente, at an intuitive level, a predicate is essentialist if and only if the property that it expresses is a necessary property of any object that possesses it. While for weakly rigid designators it is crucial that they have the same designation in every possible world in which the designated object exists, for weakly essentialist predicates it is crucial that they apply constantly through the different possible worlds in which an object to which the predicate applies in a certain world exists. He calls this notion "weak essentialism".[33]

Weak essentiality: A predicate P is weakly essentialist iff for all worlds w and any object o, if P applies to o in w, then for all worlds w', if o exists in w' then P applies to o in w'.

For example, the predicate "is an electron" (or "is a beam of electrons") is weakly essentialist: for every world and every object, if an object is an electron in a certain world, then it is an electron in every other world in which it exists. I will not go over Gómez-Torrente's arguments for claiming that this is an adequate extension of the Kripkean notion of rigid designator for general terms; I will assume it is and

---

[31] Soames (2002) argued that an adequate extension of this notion cannot be offered. See Gómez-Torrente (2006) for some arguments against Soames's points of view.

[32] As mentioned by Gómez-Torrente, we can use this same procedure to form predicative phrases for proper names, even if these expressions are singular terms and not predicates. See Gómez-Torrente (2006, pp. 234–235).

[33] Gómez-Torrente calls this notion "weak essentialism" to distinguish it from the more fine-grained notions "persistent essentialism" and "obstinate essentialism", which he offers in analogy to Salmon's notions "obstinately rigid designator" and "persistently rigid designator". See also note 36. See Gómez-Torrente (2006, pp. 233–235).

elaborate from it.

Considering the above, it is easy to see that if we modify features (a) to (e) in the characterization offered for DNs by replacing "descriptive name" or "DN" for "descriptive name for natural kinds" or "DNNKs", "proper name" for "name of natural kind", and "rigid designator" for "weak essentialist predicate", we could offer a characterization of "descriptive names of natural kinds" or "DNNKs" analogous to the one offered for DNs and take "fluxonite" as an example of this type of expressions.

3.5 *E-weak rigidity* and *e-weak essentiality*

To see the problems that arise from attempting to use the notions *rigid designator* and *weakly essentialist predicate* to account for the rigidity of DNs and DNNKs, I will rely on the distinction between essential and accidental properties, as proposed by Kripke. This will allow me to distinguish DNs and DNNKs that are introduced by a description that fixes the reference by means of an accidental property from those that fix it by means of an essential property. The bottom line will be that while empty DNs and empty DNNKs whose reference is fixed by an essential property could be seen as weakly-rigid designators and weakly-essentialist predicates, those whose reference is fixed by means of an accidental property – which are likely to be the great majority – cannot be taken to be rigid designators or essentialist predicates, at least not without some problems in this latter case. Modified versions of these notions will be offered to account for the rigidity of these terms.

According to Kripke, an essential property is one that an object necessarily has if it exists and if it did not have it, it would not be that object. An accidental property is one that is not essential. For example, being a tall person is an accidental property: a person might have not been tall and still be that person. In contrast, being the third positive integer in the numerical line is an essential property: it is not possible for the number three not to be the third positive integer in the numerical line and still be the number three; if something is not the third positive integer in the numerical line, then that object is not number three.[34]

I will also follow Kripke in distinguishing definite descriptions that designate by means of an essential property, and those that designate by means of an accidental one. "The third positive integer in the numerical line" is an example of the first type: it is not possible for this description to designate an object other than number three. "The total number of

---

[34]See Kripke (1980, p. 63) and Kripke (1971, p. 29).

ties ever worn by Chaplin", in contrast, is an example of the second type. Suppose that the description designates the number 3, 224. We can imagine a situation in which Chaplin wore only 3, 220 ties, and thus one in which the description designates 3, 220.[35]

Using these distinctions we can classify empty DNs and empty DNNKs as follows:

(A) empty DNs introduced by a description that designates by means of an accidental property;

(B) empty DNNKs introduced by a description that designates by means of an accidental property;

(C) empty DNs introduced by a description that designates by means of an essential property;

(D) empty DNNKs introduced by a description that designates by means of an essential property.

Consider (A). We could take "Vulcan" as an example of this type of term if we consider the period of time in which the only means of linking it with its referent is through the description "the planet causing *such and such* effects on Mercury". Producing these effects is an accidental property: the planet responsible for them (if there is one) could have not produced them, for example, if it was located in a different galaxy. Suppose also, as seems to be the case, that no planet actually causes these effects, so that "Vulcan" is empty.

As we saw above, according to Kripke, an expression is a *rigid designator* if it designates the same object in every possible world in which the object exists. This notion has also been called "weakly rigid designator" to contrast it from a stronger version that stipulates that a rigid designator designates the same object even in those possible worlds in which the object does not exist[36]. According to this, it seems that for an expression to be a weakly rigid designator, it has to designate an object. Gómez-Torrente interprets Kripke in this same way. The following is a slightly modified version of his characterization of the Kripkean

---

[35] See Kripke (1980, pp. 39–45).

[36] Kripke, Kripke (1980, p. 21 and p. 49), contrasts a *weak assertion of rigidity* with a rigid designator *de jure* which "rigidly designates its referent even when we speak of counterfactual situations where that referent would not have existed"; he also calls an expression "strongly rigid" if it rigidly designates a necessary existent object. Salmon (1981) offered two more specific notions of "rigid designator" that are not weak in this sense. He proposes to call "persistently rigid" a rigid designator that does not designate any object in possible worlds in which the referent does not exist and "obstinately rigid" a rigid designator that designates an object *o* with respect to every possible world, no matter whether *o* does not exist in some of them. See Salmon (1981, pp. 33–34) and Gómez-Torrente (2006, p. 235).

notion of rigidity:[37]

Weakly rigid designator: An expression e that refers to an object o is a weakly rigid designator iff for all worlds w, if o exists in w then e designates o in w.

If "Vulcan" is empty and differs from the description used to introduce it in that the name but not the description is used to refer to a certain object in every possible world in which the object exists, then it seems plausible to claim that "Vulcan" lacks a referent in every possible world. But if this is so, according to the above definition, "Vulcan" cannot be a weakly rigid designator precisely because it does not designate any object.[38]

One might think that a modification to the Kripkean definition that could account for the rigidity of DNs like "Vulcan" may simply be as follows:

Weakly rigid designator*: An expression e that refers to an object o is a weakly rigid designator* iff if e refers to an object o, then for all worlds w, if o exists in w then e designates o in w.

This notion, however, has the problem that it takes any non-referring expression as a weakly rigid designator since for all of them the antecedent of the conditional is false. To deal with this, one might try to modify the definition so that it is *designators* and not *expressions* that are taken to be weakly rigid. Nonetheless, this raises the problem of having to say what is a designator that can account for the case in which they are empty. Though syntactic or pragmatic approaches might be a way of dealing with this, I will not explore them here but instead propose an alternative definition.[39]

But before this, let me consider another possible way out. Suppose we wanted to claim that "Vulcan" does refer to an object o with respect to every possible world in which o exists, but that the actual world is simply one in which o does not exist. If this were the case, since "Vulcan" would have a referent (at least for some possible worlds), it could be a weakly rigid designator. This claim, however, faces the following problem, first noted by Kripke (Kripke, 1980) in his observations on

---

[37] This notion differs from, Gómez-Torrente (2006, p. 235), in that it is not defined for singular terms but for expressions. In both cases, the expression or the singular term needs to designate an object to be a weakly rigid designator.

[38] Empty names like "Vulcan" could be taken as rigid designators if we stipulated that they refer with respect to every possible world to a certain arbitrary object, like the empty set. We will not assess this proposal here.

[39] As mentioned in note 16, Evans's way of characterizing "referential expressions" is not useful because it leaves out names of natural kinds.

terms like "unicorn". Since the description fixing the name's referent designates by means of an accidental property, it designates different objects with respect to different possible worlds. But then, which of these different non-actual objects does "Vulcan" constantly refer to? And how can we know which object is this?[40] In a possible world in which Pluto has a different placement in the Solar System so that it produces the required effects on Mercury, Pluto is the designation of the description; in a different possible world in which Saturn causes these effects on Mercury, Saturn is the designation of the description. Which is the object to which "Vulcan" rigidly refers to? Any answer appears to be arbitrary, and it seems preferable to claim that if no object satisfies the contingent description used to introduce "Vulcan" in the actual world, then it does not refer to any object in any counterfactual situations.

Let me now present a notion that I take to appropriately account for the rigidity of empty DNs like "Vulcan". Even if "Vulcan" is empty, we use it in such a way that *if it had referred*, it would have referred to the same object in every possible world (at least in those possible worlds in which the object exists). Moreover, for all we know, every DN, while being a DN, could be empty: since we are unable to ostensibly relate the name with its referent as its referent, we might be wrong and the object might not exist. So every intuition of the rigidity of DNs has to be compatible with the case that they are referenceless. On the other hand, definite descriptions that designate by means of a contingent property but that do not designate any object in the actual world like "the planet causing such and such effects on Mercury" do not have this property: even if the actual world had been such that this description had designated an object, the description would not designate it with respect to every other possible world. Even if in the actual world there were a planet causing such and such effects on Mercury, the description "the planet causing such and such effects on Mercury" would designate different objects in different possible worlds since in different possible worlds different objects cause these effects on Mercury.

Considering the above, I propose that the following notion roughly captures the intuition that empty DNs are rigid (@ is the actual world).

E-weak rigid designator: An expression e that for every possible world w does not designate any object is an e-rigid designator

---

[40] These two questions are analogous to Kripke's metaphysical and epistemological objections against empty names like "unicorn" or "Sherlock Holmes". See Kripke (1980, Addenda). I am not, however, suggesting that similar observations to the ones made for RTTs should be extended to fictional names. For reasons I cannot go into in this paper, I think fictional names deserve a separate treatment.

iff there is a world w' different from @ such that if w' had been actual, then the following would be true:
  (i) e would have designated an object o of w';
  (ii) for any world w'' in which o exists, e would have designated o in w'';
  (iii) for all worlds w''', e would have not designated any other object different from o in w'''.[41]

This notion has a double modality: one has to do with what is the case with respect to non-actual possible worlds and the other has to do with what is the case in non-actual worlds if a possible world different from the actual were considered as actual. The definition is rough because more clarification is required regarding this second type of modality; in particular, the modal expressions need to be replaced by non-modal expressions. However rough, I think this way of presenting the notion suffices for the present purposes and illuminates a sense in which we can take empty DNs like "Julius" or "Vulcan" as rigid.

Just as with the notion of weakly rigid designator, when considering different possible worlds here, we do not want to say that the language could have been different, in the sense, for example, that we could have used "Vulcan" to refer to a certain river or to myself.[42] The idea is to model the way in which a certain expression, as used *in a certain language*, would have referred if the actual world had been different. Keeping the semantic relation the same, an e-rigid designator is such that there is a possible world such that if it had been actual, then the e-rigid designator would have had a referent and would have referred

---

[41] Analogous extensions of these notions to Salmon's notions of persistent and obstinate rigidity are:

Persistent e-rigidity: An expression e that for every possible world w does not designate any object is a *persistent e-rigid designator* iff there is a world w' different from @ such that if w' had been actual, then the following would be true:
  (i) e would have designated an object o of w';
  (ii) for any world w'' in which o exists e would have designated o in w'';
  (iii) for all worlds w''', if o does not exist in w''', e does not designate any object (@ is the actual world).

Obstinate e-rigidity: An expression e that for every possible world w does not designate any object is an *obstinate e-rigid designator* iff there is a world w' different from @ such that if w' had been actual, then the following would be true:
  (i) e would have designated an object o of w';
  (ii) for any world w'', e would have designated o in w'' (@ is the actual world).

[42] See note 17.

to it with respect to every possible world in which this object exists. In other words, the *e*-rigid designator is such that if it had referred to an object, it would have referred to it constantly across possible worlds.

This is exactly what happens with DNs. Remember that in section 3.3 we characterized them in such a way that they have a semantic connection with the description used to introduce them. When considering counterfactual situations, the semantic connection between the DN and its description is maintained. For example, "Vulcan" is always understood as the object that in the actual world satisfies the description "the planet causing such and such effects on Mercury". If the actual world were different in such a way that an object would have caused these effects on Mercury, then this object would be the referent of "Vulcan" with respect to the actual world and with respect to every possible world in which this object exists, even if in some possible worlds it does not cause the required effects on Mercury.

Let us turn to (B) on page 55, the case in which a DNNK is introduced by a description that designates through an accidental property. "Phlogiston" could be an example of this if we focus on the period of time in which the only description associated with it and used to fix its referent is "the odorless, colorless substance contained in flammable materials that is liberated during combustion". Even if these names are empty, in section II we agreed that they are not used as abbreviations for the descriptions with which they were introduced.

Consider again the notion of weak essentiality:

Weak essentiality: A predicate P is *weakly essentialist* iff for all worlds w and any object o, if P applies to o in w, then for all worlds w', if o exists in w' then P applies to o in w'.

Even if this definition takes predicates like "is a sample of phlogiston" as weakly essentialist, this is simply because the predicate does not apply to any object, and so the antecedent of the first conditional is false and the right side of the biconditional is true. Under this definition, however, predicates like "being square-rounded" and "being odd and even" are weakly essentialist for the same reason. The notion "e-weak essentiality" is preferable because it does not commit us to take every predicate that does not have an extension with respect to every possible world as an essentialist predicate (@ is the actual world).

E-weak essentiality: A predicate P that for every possible world w does not apply to any object in w is an *e-weakly essentialist predicate* iff there is a world w' different from @ such that if w' had been actual, then the following would be true:

(i) P would have applied to at least one object of w';

(ii) for all worlds w'' and any object o, if P applies to o in w'', then for all worlds w''', if o exists in w''' then P applies to o in w'''.[43]

If "phlogiston" is empty, "being a sample of phlogiston" is an *e*-weak essentialist predicate: if a certain possible world in which a substance is liberated during combustion were actual, the predicate "being a sample of phlogiston" would have applied to this substance with respect to that world and with respect to every other possible non-actual world in which instances of this substance exist, even if with respect to these other non-actual worlds different substances were liberated from combustion. However, predicates like "being a square-circle" or "being odd and even" are not considered as *e*-weakly essentialist since they do not meet (i): no matter which possible world is actual, these predicates never apply to any object or substance with respect to any possible world.

Let us move to (C) on page 55, the case in which an empty DN is introduced by a description that designates by means of an essential property.[44] Suppose "Noman" is introduced to refer to the person who would have developed from the union of spermatozoid S and egg E, assuming that S and E actually exist but were never united and that the genetic origin is an essential property. We have two possibilities regarding this case. On the one hand, we could claim that DNs can refer to possible objects, and since in this case the description with which "Noman" is introduced designates the same object at least in

---

[43] Analogous extensions of these notions to Gómez-Torrente's notions of persistent and obstinate essentialism are:

Persistent e-essentiality: A predicate P that for every possible world w does not designate any object in w is an *e-weakly essentialist predicate* iff there is a world w' different from @ such that if w' had been actual, then the following would be true:
  (i) P would have applied to at least one object of w';
  (ii) for all worlds w'' and any object o, if P applies to o in w'', then for all worlds w''', if o exists in w''' then P applies to o in w''';
  (iii) for all worlds w'''', if o does not exist in w'''' then P does not apply to o in w'''' (@ is the actual world).

Obstinate e-essentiality: A predicate P that for every possible world w does not designate any object in w is an *e-weakly essentialist predicate* iff there is a world w' different from @ such that if w' had been actual, then the following would be true:
  (i) P would have applied to at least one object of w';
  (ii) for all worlds w'' and any object o, if P applies to o in w'', then for all worlds w''', P applies to o in w''' (@ is the actual world).

[44] This example is taken from Salmon (1981, p. 39, note 41).

every possible world in which it exists, we could say that "Noman" refers to Noman even if in the actual world Noman does not exist. Here we do not have the problem of case (A) on page 55, in which the rigidity of the DN was incompatible with the fact that many different objects in different possible worlds satisfy the description with which the DN is introduced. Under this assumption, "Noman" would have a referent, and so it could be a weakly rigid designator.[45] On the other hand, we could claim that since no actual object satisfies the description used to introduce this name, it fails to refer in every possible world. Under this assumption, "Noman" would be an e-rigid designator. I will not argue in favor of any of these options; for this discussion, it suffices to have notions of rigidity that can account for each of them.

Finally, consider (D) on page 55, the case in which an empty DNNK is introduced by a description that designates by means of an essential property. For example, assuming that the atomic number is an essential property, suppose that we introduce "TSX" to refer to the element with atomic number 533. Suppose also, that because of some accidental properties of the Earth's pressure, no element has an atomic number larger than 530. In other possible worlds in which the pressure of the Earth differs, however, there are samples of this element. In this case, just as in the case of "Noman", we have two options. We could take the predicate "is a sample of TSX" to apply to instances of the element with atomic number 533 in possible worlds in which they exist, and so take it to be a weakly essentialist predicate. On the other hand, we could claim that since no element has atomic number 533 in the actual world, the predicate does not apply to any object in any possible world. In this case, the predicate would be e-weakly essentialist. Just as with (C), it is enough for the discussion at hand to have notions of rigidity that can account for each of these alternatives.

If the considerations in this section are correct, then we need to make the following modifications in the way in which we framed "Rigidity" and "Essentiality" in the characterization of DNs and DNNKs.

Rigidity: DNs are either weakly rigid designators or e-weakly rigid designators.

Essentiality: DNNKs are either weakly essentialist predicates or e-weakly essentialist predicates.[46]

---

[45] More precisely, "Noman" would be an obstinately rigid designator.

[46] We could also characterize **Rigidity** for DNs in terms of persistent rigidity and e-persistent rigidity or obstinate rigidity and e-obstinate rigidity. Likewise, we could characterize **Essentiality** for DNNKs in terms of persistent essentiality and e-persistent essentiality or obstinate essentiality and e-obstinate essentiality. See

3.6 Further work

My attempt in this paper was to show that the fact that several RTTs are names of natural kinds does not constitute an objection for using Evans's descriptive names to account for the meaning and reference of RTTs. In particular, I showed how descriptive names could be characterized and extended to names of natural kinds. In order to do this, I offered modified (rough) notions of rigidity that could account for the rigidity of empty descriptive names and empty descriptive names of natural kinds. In this last section, I briefly consider some other problems that an attempt to use Evans's ideas to account for the meaning and reference of RTTs may encounter.

A first problem is related to **Reference** (feature (a) at page 50). Suppose, for example, that "ebola" was introduced by the description "the virus that caused the death of 100 identified subjects". Suppose also that some time later, it is discovered that one the 100 subjects is really a false positive, and that his death was due to another disease he had. If we take "ebola" as a DNNK, then it would be referenceless: no virus, in the actual world, is responsible for the death of the 100 identified subjects. It seems, however, that in a situation like this "ebola" would still be used to refer to the virus that caused the deaths of 99 of the identified subjects. A possible way of modifying **Reference** to deal with these cases could be by following Lewis's suggestion[47] that the description need not be perfectly satisfied: we might take as referent the object that comes closest to satisfying it. In the example above, though ebola does not perfectly satisfy the description with which "ebola" was introduced and thus cannot be considered as its reference, it is the one that better satisfies the description from several sufficiently close candidates. Suppose that the person who did not die from ebola died from the influenza virus. Though the influenza virus could be a sufficiently adequate imperfect satisfier of the description, the ebola virus would be a better one since it is responsible for more deaths. Lewis also proposes to take as cases of indeterminate reference those in which two or more objects either both perfectly satisfy the description or are equally good imperfect satisfiers of it and there is no stronger candidate to beat them both. In these cases, the term refers equally to both candidates.

Though insightful, I consider Lewis's suggestion to be in need of further assessment. In particular, his proposal needs to be spelled out with more detail and proved to be useful in real cases. What criteria can we use to determine whether there is no referent of a term or whether

---

notes 41 and 43.

[47]See Lewis (1984, p. 223).

an imperfect candidate is good enough to be taken as its referent? Non-question begging criteria for establishing which candidate better satisfies the description are required.

Another problem related to **Understanding** (feature (c) on page 50) arises when speakers that do not know the description used to fix the name's reference use it. For example, when a speaker S that cannot associate the description used to introduce "fluxonite" utters something like "The scientists of that lab had a hard time working with fluxonite". In this case, **Understanding** commits us to claiming that S does not understand "fluxonite" since a requirement to understand the name is to know that it refers to whatever satisfies the description with which it was introduced and to know which description this is. (Perhaps one could claim that there are different levels or types of understanding here.) However, we could still claim that though speakers like S do not properly understand "fluxonite" (or do not understand it in the same way as those who are aware of the description), they can still succeed in using it to refer to fluxonite if there is a causal-information preserving chain that links them to someone who is able to link the name with the description used to introduce it.[48]

Finally, other problems come from RTTs used to refer not only to unobserved objects, but to objects that do not yet exist, like hurricanes.[49] Salmon's approach to the analogous case of "Newman" might shed some light on cases like this.[50]

References

Davidson, Donald and Gilbert Harman, eds. 1972. *Semantics of Natural Language*. Synthese Library. Dordercht: Reidel.

Donnellan, Keith S. 1966. Reference and definite descriptions. *Philosophical Review* 77(3):281–304.

Evans, Gareth. 1979. Reference and contingency. *The Monist* 62(2):161–189. Also in Evans (1985, p. 178–213).

Evans, Gareth. 1985. *Collected Papers*. Oxford: Clarendon Press.

Gómez-Torrente, Mario. 2006. Rigidity and essentiality. *Mind* 115(458):227–260.

---

[48] See Jackson (2005, pp. 261–264) and Lewis (1997, note 22). Reimer has also noted this point with respect to descriptive names like "Julius". See Reimer (2004, p. 618).

[49] Meteorologists prepare a list of names assigned to the hurricanes that will be formed in a certain year, in order of appearance. For example, "Ana" will be the name of the first hurricane to appear in 2009 in the Caribbean region. See http://www.wmo.int/web/www/TCP/TCP-home.html.

[50] "Newman" is the name Kaplan introduced to refer to the first child to be born in the XXII century. See Salmon (1998, pp. 289–291) and Kaplan (1973).

Jackson, Frank. 2005. What are proper names for? In J. C. Marek and M. E. Reicher, eds., *Experience and Analysis*, pages 257–269. The Austrian Ludwig Wittgenstein Society, Vienna: hpt-öbv.

Kaplan, David. 1973. Bob and Carol, Ted and Alice. In Y. Hintikka, J. Moravcsik, and P. Suppes, eds., *Approaches to Natural Language*, Synthese Library, pages 490–518. Dordrecht: Reidel.

Kripke, Saul A. 1971. Identity and necessity. In M. Munitz, ed., *Identity and Individuation*, pages 135–164. New York: New York University Press.

Kripke, Saul A. 1980. *Naming and Necessity*. Cambridge MA: Harvard University Press. Originally pubblished in Davidson and Harman (1972, pp. 253–355).

Lewis, David K. 1984. Putnam's paradox. *Australasian Journal of Philosophy* 62(3):221–236.

Lewis, David K. 1997. Naming the colours. *The Australasian Journal of Philosophy* 75(3):325–342.

Putnam, Hilary. 1962. What theories are not. In E. Nagel, P. Suppes, and A. Tarski, eds., *Logic, Methodology and Philosophy of Science: Proceedings of the 1960 International Congress*, pages 240–251. Stanford CA: Stanford University Press.

Reimer, Marga. 2004. Descriptively introduced names. In M. Reimer and A. Bezuidenhout, eds., *Descriptions and Beyond*, chap. 19, pages 613–629. Oxford: Oxford University Press.

Sainsbury, Richard M. 2005. *Reference without Referents*. Oxford: Oxford University Press.

Salmon, Nathan. 1981. *Reference and Essence*. Princeton: Princeton University Press. Reprinted in 2005 by Prometheus Books.

Salmon, Nathan. 1998. Nonexistence. *Noûs* 32(3):277–422.

Soames, Scott. 2002. *Beyond Rigidity: the Unfinished Semantic Agenda of "Naming and Necessity"*. Oxford: Oxford University Press.

Soames, Scott. 2005. *Reference and Descriptions: the Case against Two-dimensionalism*. Princeton: Princeton University Press.

4
Compositionality and Lexical Semantics
DARIA MINGARDO

4.1 Introduction

The Principle of Compositionality says that the meaning of a complex expression is determined by the meanings of its constituents and by its syntactical structure. This principle is traditionally considered as one of the less negotiable principles at the basis of natural language semantics. Such a general agreement on its validity, however, does appear to fade out as soon as one tries to make its content more precise: different syntactic and semantic theories can lead to very different formulations and interpretations of it. In particular, there is no agreement on the role that such a Principle has to play in semantics itself: some authors consider it an empirical hypothesis, which has to be tested against linguistic data and speakers' intuitions; others regard it as an inference to the best explanation of the phenomena of language productivity and systematicity; others, still, think of it as a methodological assumption, charged with the task of guiding the working of syntactic and syntactic/semantic theories.

The aim of the present paper is that of providing the formulation of the Principle of Compositionality which follows from some of the assumptions of one particular branch of semantics, *i.e.* lexical semantics. More specifically, the lexical semantic theory which will be taken into consideration is N. Asher's Type Driven Theory (TDT). Combining the formalism of the typed lambda calculus with a conception of the language *à la* Pustejovsky, TDT puts itself forward as a lexical semantics sensitive to the demands of predication and context.

The paper is organized as follows. The first section offers a specification of the aim. TDT will be introduced in section 4.3, starting from the two tasks it is charged with, namely, those of determining lexical meanings and furnishing a theory of predication; tasks which, as we will see, have to be accomplished in such a way as to account for the role of context as well. Section 4.4 will try to highlight the core of TDT through a comparison with Montague's logical grammar, clearing the ground for a more detailed examination of types (section 4.5), logical forms (section 4.6), and the relation between them (subsection 4.6.1). Such work will permit us to have all the necessary elements – TDT notions of lexical and sentence meaning (subsection 4.7.1), and that of constituents (subsection 4.7.2) – to draw the conception of compositionality exploited by TDT. The formulation of the Principle of Compositionality for TDT will be given in subsection 4.7.3. Section 4.8, finally, will take into consideration the question of the consequences that such a formulation of the Principle has on TDT itself. In particular, subsection 4.8.2 will try to show how one of the major risks for TDT is that of overproductivity. The general conclusion of the paper will consist in attributing to TDT a methodological conception of the Principle of Compositionality, *contra* its traditional interpretation as an inference to the best explanation of the phenomenon of language productivity.

4.2 The aim

As anticipated above, the agreement on the validity of the Principle of Compositionality is as much widespread as it is, in facts, the disagreement on its exact formulation and on the question of its role within semantics. Throughout the paper, however, I will take as a point of reference the standard formulation of the Principle of Compositionality, which can be stated as follows:

(**PoC**) The meaning of a complex expression is determined by the meanings of its constituents and by its syntactical structure.

For example, and simplifying a little, if for "complex expression" we take the sentence:

(1)   Julius Caesar was murdered by Brutus

(**PoC**) simply says that the meaning of (1) is determined by the meanings of its constituents, *i.e.* by the meanings of the expressions "Julius Caesar", "was", "murdered", "by", and "Brutus", and by its syntactical structure. According to (**PoC**), what a competent speaker needs in order to understand a sentence is only to know the syntactical structure of the sentence and the meanings of its constituents.

The disagreement concerning the interpretation of the exact content of (**PoC**), and its theoretical role in semantics, can be traced back, first, to the differences in conceiving the notion of meaning and the interaction between meaning and syntax;[1] and, second, to the varieties of interpretations that one can give to the verb "to determine": what does it exactly mean to say that the meaning of a sentence *is determined by* the meanings of its constituents and by its syntactical structure? The debate on these and other questions is far from being settled.

Accordingly, the aim of providing a formulation of the Principle of Compositionality, starting from some of the assumptions of Asher's lexical semantics, will be reached by making explicit what Asher's theory takes the following to be:

- lexical and complex expressions meaning;
- constituents;
- relation of determination.

The variations in the interpretation of the Principle of Compositionality are attributable to the differences in the conceptions of meaning, the interface between meaning and syntax, and relation of determination. As a consequence, the aim of providing a formulation of the Principle of Compositionality, starting from some of the assumptions of TDT, can be specified as the aim of clarifying how these very notions are conceived by TDT. Most of all, what I will be looking for is the manner in which Asher conceives both lexical and complex expressions meaning, and the notion of constituents, a fundamental issue for the question of the connections between syntax and semantics. As far as the relation of determination is concerned, instead, I will be content with the usual characterization of it in terms of functions: that the meaning of a complex expression is determined by the meanings of its constituents and its structure will be taken to mean that the meaning of the complex expression is a *function* of the meanings of its constituents and its syntactical structure.

---

[1] The Principle of Compositionality requires us to know what the constituents of a complex expression consist of: it requires, in other words, a syntactic theory which specifies the part-whole relation which the Principle exploits. The choice of such a theory is not a neutral one: every hypothesis on the functioning of syntax has consequences on semantics. (**PoC**), then, can be used to choose between different syntactic and semantic hypotheses, but it can also, in turn, undergo the consequences of such choices, being reinterpreted, modified, or weakened. On these questions, however, see Gamut (1991a, pp. 140–142) or also Partee (1994).

Finally, to accomplish the task of giving a formulation of the Principle of Compositionality for TDT, we will also permit ourselves to draw some considerations about the consequences that such a formulation has on this theory, and, most of all, on the theoretical status that such a principle has within the theory itself.

4.3 The two tasks of Type Driven Theory and the role of context

N. Asher's Type Driven Theory[2] draws inspiration from Pustejovsky's Generative Lexicon.[3] Like the latter, TDT is a lexical semantics: differently from truth-conditional standard semantics, it gives prominent importance to lexical meaning, which ceases to be considered a primitive notion, to become, just as sentence meaning, a notion in demand of further clarification. The first task which Asher assigns to lexical semantics, in fact, is that of determining lexical meanings.

At the same time, the denomination of "lexical semantics" will not lead us astray. For Asher, in fact, the second task which lexical semantics must be charged with is that of providing an adequate theory of predication. It is only thanks to the predication that it is possible to completely determine the meaning of each single lexical item. Thus, there can be no inquiry into lexical meaning which does not presuppose an exam of predication, and, most of all, of the various forms in which predication is given in natural language.

Let us consider each task in a little more detail. Determining lexical meaning requires us, first of all, to decide which is the theoretical role that lexical meaning has to play. As it happens for lexical semantics in general, for Asher as well lexical meaning has to account for all the complex and systematic inferences which are supported by the lexical choice within a sentence (or a discourse).[4]

---

[2] See Asher (2006b).

[3] See Pustejovsky (1995).

[4] An important component of Asher's lexical semantics which I cannot discuss here is discourse semantics. One of the main tenets of Asher's theory is that lexical semantics and discourse semantics are closely connected, in that each one needs the other for its very existence. Asher's discourse semantics is a development of H. Kamp's DRT (Discourse Representation Theory), a theory which focuses on the semantic analysis of discourses intended as coherent sets of sentences, and which takes the basic semantic unit to be the discourse, and not the sentence. Accordingly, the meaning of a sentence is conceived in terms of the contribution which it gives to the discourse, just as traditionally happens with sub-sentential expressions, whose meaning is said to consist in their contribution to the truth conditions of the expressions in which they occur. TDT gives much space to the elaboration of the nonmonotonic, inferential relations between the parts of the discourse. Such relations will have semantic effects both on the interpretation of the sentences, and

Most importantly for the aim of this paper, lexical meaning has to be, in Asher's opinion, something that, when combined with the contributions of the other words in a sentence, yields a representation which has an interpretation sufficient to yield the truth conditional content of the sentence, *i.e.* a logical form. In other words, the lexical meanings of the words occurring in a sentence will have to combine with each other, both at a syntactic and at a semantic level, in such a way to guarantee the composition of something – a logical form – which is the ultimate bearer of truth conditional content.

Accordingly, determining the lexical meaning of a certain word W will require specifying, among other things, how W can combine with the other, syntactically related words within a sentence: namely, it will require specifying if it is the other words which function as arguments for W, or if it is W itself that plays the role of an argument for the other lexical items. This kind of statement, however, brings us directly to the core of the second task of lexical semantics, *i.e.*, the task of giving a theory of predication: predication, in facts, consists in the application of a predicate to its argument(s). In Asher's words:

> Argument structure is thus fundamentally linked to predication; when one bit of logical form functions as an argument to another, we have a predication relation between a property denoting term and its argument.[5]

Thus, in a certain sense, the task of accounting for predication acquires some priority over that of determining lexical meanings: only understanding how predication works, in fact, permits to specify how lexical meanings are determined.

The inquiry into predication implies, among other things, the recognition of the numerous, different forms in which it is used in natural language. Diverging each in its own way from ordinary predication,[6] all these forms have to be accounted for, if one wants to give an adequate characterization of lexical meanings. As an explanatory note, here it is

---

of the words they contain, and vice versa, thus substantiating the aforementioned thesis about the interaction between lexical and discourse semantics. About Kamp's semantics, see Kamp (1984); about Asher, instead, see Asher (2006b), in particular pp. 107-113.

[5] Asher (2006b, p. 2).

[6] Ordinary predication which, on the other hand, can be subdivided in various forms. For instance: predication of a VP (verb phrase) to a subject; predication of a transitive verb to an object; predication of the adjectives which act as modifiers on the NP (noun phrases), as is the case with the evaluative ones – a *rotten* violinist, a *good* rock – or with the manner adjectives – *fast* car, *slow* growth, *etc.*; finally, the predication which implies an adverbial modification, as in "Gianni walks quickly".

part of the list offered in this regard by Asher:[7]

- *copredication*:
    (2) The lunch was delicious but took forever.
    (3) The book has a purple cover and is the most intelligible introduction to category theory.
    (4) Most cities that vote democratic passed anti-smoking legislation last year.
- *coercion*:
    (5) Julie enjoyed the book.
    (6) The goat enjoyed the book.
    (7) Sabrina begun with the kitchen.
- qua *locutions*:
    (8) John as a banker makes $50K a year but as a plumber he only makes $20K a year.
- *genitive constructions*:
    (9) Kim's mother;
    (10) Kim's fish;
    (11) The girl's car.

Each one of these different forms of predication presents peculiar characteristics, which have to be brought to light on pain of not being able to assign the correct meaning to the constituents of such constructions, and, as a consequence, also to the sentences containing them:

> Each one of these forms of predication presents its own challenge for semantics and for lexical theory in particular, since lexical theory must assign to the constituent words in these constructions the right sort of meaning so as to get the right result together with the composition rules it postulates for modelling the predication itself.[8]

For example, as far as copredication is concerned, the question will be that of seeing how it allows us to access simultaneously two different but related meanings of the same lexical entry. Consider sentence (3): the properties of "having a purple cover" and of "being the most intelligible introduction to category theory" are both predicates of the same argument, "book". In spite of this fact, the first predicate selects from "book" a meaning which refers to the material aspect of the book, while the second predicate, instead, selects from it a meaning which refers to the informational aspect of the object. The meaning of the lexical entry "book", then, will have to be determined in a way that takes into account the fact that sometimes we talk about books in their

---
[7]See Asher (2006b, pp. 6-7).
[8]See Asher (2006b, p. 8).

material aspect, sometimes in their abstract, informational aspect, and sometimes, as in the phenomenon of copredication, in both aspects at the same time.

Again, consider genitive constructions,[9] in which predication consists in the application of a certain relation to the objects given by the two terms of the construction itself. What will have to be examined, in this case, is how, from time to time, the meaning of the construction is determined in favour of a particular relation between the two objects. For example, in the absence of contextual contraindications, sometimes the appropriate relation will be given directly by the NP head, as it happens in (9): "mother" is a relational noun, which already suggests the interpretation to give to "Kim's mother". Sometimes, instead, this will not be the case, as with examples (10) and (11): other hints will have to be exploited to determine the intended relation, hints which will often be given by the discourse in which the construction occurs, or, more generically, by the context in which it is uttered. Consider, for instance, (10): in the absence of a precise context, it is not possible to tell which is, exactly, the relation between Kim and the fish. But if a more precise context is given, like in:

(12) All the children were drawing fish.
(13) Kim's fish was blue.

such a relation becomes clear: Kim's fish is the fish Kim is drawing. In a different context, moreover, the relation could have been differently determined, as one of possession, for example, or one of physical proximity, and so on.

The example of the genitive constructions, then, turns out to be useful also to highlight another point of fundamental importance in TDT. More often than not, context intervenes in specifying the meaning of expressions, and this can happen even in cases in which the words at issue – or the combination of words at issue – are already endowed with a default meaning: the default interpretation of "Kim's mother", for example, takes this expression as referring to Kim's own natural mother; but in a context in which we are talking about Kim's paintings, one of which depicts a mother, "Kim's mother" will refer to that particular Kim's painting. But if this is so, for Asher a lexical semantics will have to account also for the role of the context in the determination of lexical meaning and in the functioning of predication.

---

[9]Remember that we can have predication every time an expression is adequately applied to another expression, which then represents the argument of the first one.

4.4 TDT: a comparison with Logical Grammar

In order to see how Asher's theory works, it can be useful to start drawing a comparison with Montague's logical grammar. The model which Asher chooses to represent predication, in fact, is the typed lambda calculus: the basic mechanisms of such a formalism are the same as Montague's logical grammar, from which it inherits the basic types,[10] the functional complex one,[11] and their intensional counterparts.[12] As in Montague's grammar, each predicate is translated with an appropriate lambda term, and its arguments, in turn, with other terms that saturate the lambda bound variables present in the former. Thus, both in TDT and in logical grammar, the operation of application reported below represents predication:

Application: $\lambda x \Phi[\alpha] = \Phi(\alpha/x)$.

In fact, however, Asher's system of types and of their translation in the logical language is more complex and richer than Montague's one, and, most importantly, it does reflect a different conception of it. Let us proceed in order.

In logical grammar, or at least in a certain version of it,[13] three different levels of representation are distinguished, namely:

(i) expressions;
(ii) syntactical trees;
(iii) logical expressions.

(i) is the level of natural language expressions, *i.e.* of those sequences of symbols which the grammar declares to be well-formed. If we take, for instance, sentence:

(14) Julie enjoyed the book.

we will have that (14) itself provides for such a level. (ii), instead, is the level of the syntactic-derivational analysis, usually exhibited through tree-like structures that specify both which constituent expressions are used to build the complex expression, and through which syntactic rules they are gradually combined. Leaving out details, in the case of (14) we will have something like:[14]

---

[10]The type e, *i.e.* the type of expressions which refer to entities, and the type t, *i.e.* the type of expressions which refer to truth-values, namely the type of sentences.

[11]The type $<a, b>$, *i.e.* the type of those expressions which, when applied to an expression of type a, give as result an expression of type b.

[12]Where $<s, a>$ will be the type of an expression which refers to functions from possible worlds to entities of type a.

[13]The version provided in Montague (1973).

[14]Capital letters indicate the category which the expression belongs to; "r" followed by a subscript, instead, indicates the syntactic rule exploited to obtain the

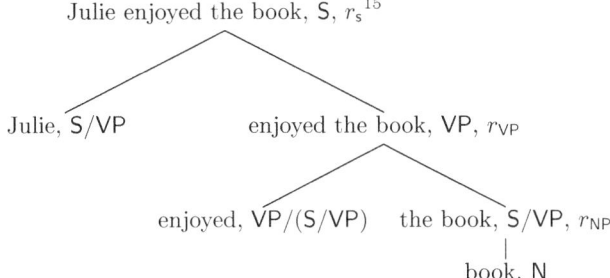

(iii), finally, is the level of the translation of the syntactic tree in the logical language, *i.e.* in the language of the intensional theory of types. In short, the translation proceeds as follows. First, an appropriate logical type is assigned to each expression which occupies a node in the tree: "enjoyed the book", for example, will be of type $<e,t>$. Second, these logical types get combined according to translation rules which correspond to the rules of syntactical concatenation: if the syntactical rules operate on two or more expressions to produce a new, complex one, the translation rules will have to define this new complex expression in terms of the translation of each constituent expression.

One important thing to notice is that once the syntactic-derivational analysis of a sentence is given, then the meaning of the sentence is also given: each constituent and each step of syntactical construction receives a translation in the language of types which brings with itself the meaning of every expression, both simple and complex. For instance, and simplifying, the assignment of the type $<s,<e,t>>$ to a predicate P says that the intension of the predicate consists in a function from possible worlds to sets of individuals, those individuals that, in each possible world, have the property indicated by P. Moreover, it says that the extension or denotation of P in a world w is a set of individuals, those individuals that, in the world w, have the property P. Most of all, what has to be noticed is that the reason why the syntactical analysis is able to determine the meaning of the sentence consists in the fact that such analysis provides for the disambiguation of the sen-

---

corresponding expression. In the case of the whole sentence "Julie enjoyed the book", S indicates the membership to the category of sentences, and r_S the syntactic rule which has to be followed to obtain the sentence from the combination of the proper noun "Julie" (of category S/VP) with the verbal phrase "enjoyed the book" (of category VP).

[15] The notation used here follows that used by Asher. He exploits a bidirectional category grammar, where: (i) if α belongs to category A and β to category A/B, then $\alpha\beta$ belongs to category B; (ii) if α belongs to category A/B and β to category B, then $\alpha\beta$ belongs to category A.

tence: every ambiguous sentence has as many different syntactical trees as possible interpretations, and the formal translation doesn't work on the starting expression, but only on the expression syntactically analysed.

Let us see Asher's case now. He doesn't spend much time on syntactical considerations, but it seems legitimate to affirm that he adopts a category grammar very similar to the one used by Montague. What is different, with respect to Montague's logical grammar, is the presence of an intermediate level between the syntax of an expression and its translation in the formal language, with a consequent modification in the conception of the latter. In fact, while in Montague the levels of representation are three (expressions, syntactical trees, logical forms), in Asher they become four:

(i) natural language expressions;
(ii) syntactic trees;
(iii) types;
(iv) logical forms.

The first two levels, those of expressions and syntactic trees, correspond exactly those fixed by Montague. Differences, however, emerge starting from the third level, the one of types, and the parallelism with Montague's grammar breaks up. To begin with, instead of admitting only the basic types e and t, and the functional ones, Asher multiplies types up to the point of assuming that each distinct lexical root gives rise to a different type:

> [...] *distinct word roots* that may undergo nominalization, verbalization or adjectivization have *distinct types*.[16]

I will devote the next paragraphs, then, to examining in detail Asher's conception of the two remaining levels, the level of types and the level of logical forms.

4.5 Types

For Asher, types are concepts. In spite of the fact that he begins by declaring that they are only similar to concepts, in the course of the text he constantly treats types as such. This conflict between statements is never solved, and somewhat compromises the clarity of the whole theory. Be that as it may, however, exactly like concepts types have a hierarchical organization, which is exploited by Asher to make types play

---

[16] Asher (2006b, p. 20), italics mine.

[...] the fine grained roles that philosophers require of concepts.[17]

Take, for example, what in an extensional fragment *à la* Montague is the type of expressions which refer to entities, *i.e.* the basic type e. For Asher such a type, far from being a basic type, includes varieties of sub-types that articulate it and that, from time to time, specify it: e will include, for example, sub-types as PHYSICAL OBJECT, CONTAINER, APPLE, PERSON, INFORMATIONAL OBJECT, HEAVENLY BODY, and so on. Such sub-types are, moreover, hierarchically organized: the type PHYSICAL OBJECT, for example, will be at the same time a sub-type of the type of entities, e, and a type which itself includes other sub-types, for instance HEAVENLY BODY; this latter, besides being a sub-type of e and of PHYSICAL OBJECT, will include for instance HESPERUS as a sub-type; and so on.[18] The sub-typing relation plays a central role in Asher's theory: its richness and its hierarchical structure permit us to account for the various forms of predication, and, at the same time, for the context-sensitivity of predication itself.

Asher says that types are "at the hearth of a theory of predication".[19] Their task is that of guiding, and checking, the predication and the construction of the logical form:[20]

> They represent enough content to guide predication and the construction of logical form in the linguistic system.[21]

Let us try to clarify the point. As has been reported above, the operation of application lacks the condition on types. Such an operation, in fact, can succeed only on condition that the type of the bound variable x is equal to the type of the term α:

Type Restricted Application: $\lambda x \phi[\alpha] = \phi(\alpha/x)$, on condition that $\text{type}(x) = \text{type}(\alpha)$; otherwise, $\lambda x \phi[\alpha]$ undefined.

In other words, the argument to which the lambda term is applied has to be of an appropriate type; otherwise, the predication will be blocked[22] or semantically infelicitous. It is in this sense, then, that the

---

[17] Asher (2006b, p. 19).

[18] Henceforth, I will follow Asher in indicating types with capital letters. In this way, while "Hesperus" will denote the term, HESPERUS will denote the corresponding type.

[19] Asher (2006b, p. 23).

[20] As you will remember, the logical form of a sentence is, for Asher, a representation which has an interpretation sufficient to yield truth conditions for the sentence itself.

[21] Asher (2006b, p. 24).

[22] The predication is blocked when the types of the lambda term and of the argument cannot be combined: in such a case, in fact, the expression $\lambda x \phi[\alpha]$ is not well-formed.

system of types guides and checks predication: it permits us to understand if the predication is allowed, and, in case of a positive answer, if it is semantically felicitous or not. Consider, for example, the following sentences:

(15) That person has an interesting idea about Freud.
(16) That person contains an interesting idea about Freud.

Unlike sentence (15), (16) seems not to work. It is somehow, as said above, semantically infelicitous: people are not the kind of things which can contain information (or at least not literally, but Asher says nothing on the subject). The explanation of such infelicity, for Asher, lies in the fact the type of the argument doesn't coincide with the type required by the predicate for its arguments, namely in the fact that the predication at issue violates the application condition on types:[23] the predicate "to contain" would require, in the subject position, an appropriate argument, *i.e.* an argument of the type of a "physical container or container of information", while what in fact it is given to it in (16) is "that person":

> (1a) [here: (16)] involves a misuse of the language, because contain requires for its subject argument either a physical container or a container of information, and persons are not of the type information containers – that's just to say that they don't contain information the way books, journal articles, pamphlets and the like do.[24]

Such statements can seem odd. In what sense, in fact, could the reason of the mismatch between the type of the predicate and the type of the argument which is given to it, consist in the fact that people are not of the type of a "physical container", or of a "container of information"? It is at this point, then, that the sub-typing relation comes into play: the type PERSON is a sub-type neither of the type PHYSICAL CONTAINER nor of the type CONTAINER OF INFORMATION. The sub-types inherit the characteristics of the types which they are subordinate to. In order for the predication to fail, then, it will be sufficient to have an argument of a type different from the one required by the predicate with which it combines, where for "different" it is to be intended either a type different from the one required or a type not included in the set

---

[23] The idea that a phrase or a sentence can be semantically infelicitous was already adopted by Pustejovsky, who talks, in this regard, of semanticality and semantic well-formedness: "I will introduce a notion of semanticality analogous to the view of grammaticality, but ranging over semantic expressions rather than syntactic structures. Semanticality refers to the semantic well-formedness of expressions in a grammar." Pustejovsky (1995, p. 40).
[24] Asher (2006b, p. 4).

of sub-types governed by the required type. Consider now the following passage, which may perhaps better clarify the point:

> [...] if we have a predicate P that requires the relevant argument to be occupied by something of the type PHYSICAL-OBJECT, then the predication $P(x)$ should succeed if x has the type HESPERUS.[25]

If a predicate P requires that its own argument is of type PHYSICAL OBJECT, and if the argument to which it is applied is of type HESPERUS, the predication will be felicitous: Hesperus is, in fact, a physical object, and so HESPERUS will be a sub-type of PHYSICAL OBJECT. More specifically, we will have the following hierarchy:

> HESPERUS, PHOSPHORUS $\sqsubseteq$ HEAVENLY-BODY $\sqsubseteq$ PHYSICAL OBJECT $\sqsubseteq$ e

where e is the usual type of entity, and $\sqsubseteq$ stands for the relation of inclusion between types, *i.e.* the sub-typing relation. Such a relation, moreover, doesn't concern only the type e, but also every other type: for instance, if APPLE is a sub-type of e, RED is a sub-type of the functional type of predicates $< a, b >$ (namely, the type of expressions which, applied to expressions of type e, yield expressions of type t), and RED(APPLE) is a sub-type of type t. This allows a sharp distinction between the types associated to propositions, as can be seen from the fact that, for Asher, the following predications identify each as a different sub-type of type t:

> a. RED(APPLE); b. RED(SWEATER); c. RED(MEAT)

Hence, propositions, which Asher identifies with sets of "possible worlds or with an appropriate dynamic meaning", *à la* Kamp, are each to be associated with a specific sub-type of t; to the point that, if I label the individual concept of the apple that at this moment is in front of me with $APPLE_1$, the predication $RED(APPLE_1)$ will be a sub-type of t different from RED(APPLE).

4.5.1 Dot Types and Dependent Types

For Asher, however, it is not only a matter of splitting up classical types in hierarchies of sub-types. In order to account for the different forms of predication, in fact, he adds to the (Montagovian) system of types also the following new complex types, different from the classical, functional one:

- *dot-types* (• types), used to account for copredication;
- *associating types* ($\otimes$ types), used to account for associated types;
- *dependent types*, used to represent types which are determined by other types in the predicative context;

---

[25] Asher (2006b, p. 19).

- *dynamic types*, used to account for presuppositions, or, more generally, for pre- and post-lexical conditions.

It is not possible to examine such types one by one. Leaving out technicalities, I will just illustrate the two which Asher most focuses on, namely dot types and dependent types. Dot types are used to account for the phenomenon of copredication.

Consider, then, the following sentence:

(17) The book weighs five pounds and is an interesting story.

(17) is a case of copredication, in that it contains two predicates with incompatible conditions on types, *i.e.* "weighs five pounds", and "is an interesting story": the first requires an argument of type PHYSICAL OBJECT, the second, instead, an argument of type INFORMATIONAL OBJECT. What happens, however, is that they are both applied to the same argument, *i.e.* "book". We said that the problem with copredication is that of determining the meaning of "book" in a way which can account for the duplicity of aspect with which such a term enters copredication. In this case, then, we will have to find, for "book", a type apt to contemporarily satisfy the type constraints of both predicates. This type is, for Asher, a dot type: a complex type which consists in the two sub-types PHYSICAL OBJECT • INFORMATIONAL OBJECT, namely

> [...] a type with a "dual" nature – two alternative conceptualizations, if you will.[26]

The intuitive idea behind dot types is that of conceiving of them as the type of expressions which refer to objects of the form $\alpha \bullet \beta$ (dot objects), *i.e.* objects having two aspects, the aspect of being α and the aspect of being β, and of treating the predication of a property no longer as predication to an object, but to an aspect of the object:

> Predication typically involves the attribution of a property to an object considered under a certain conceptualization, aspect or trope.[27]

In this way, what happens in copredication is that different properties are attributed not to the same object, but to different aspects of the same object.[28]

---

[26] Asher (2006b, p. 19).
[27] Asher (2006b, p. 53).
[28] Dot types, like all the other types introduced by *TDT*, have remarkable consequences at the ontological level, which, however, it is not possible to examine here. Just to give an example, for Asher, dot types correspond to what in the real world are dot objects: the dot object "lunch", for instance, under a certain aspect is completely an event, and under a certain other aspect, instead, is completely food, and so, a concrete object. To account for such a duplicity of aspect, Asher adopts a (not so clear) theory which he labels as "property multi-ism". See Asher (2006b,

Now, the dependent types. A dependent type ϵ matches the type α of an object with the type of object, usually an event, conventionally associated with objects of type α. This allows us to treat, for example, cases of coercion like the ones triggered by verbs as "enjoy", or by the so-called aspectual verbs, like "begin", "start" and "finish". Consider, again, sentence (14).[29] The standard reading of this sentence will consist in (18), namely in

(18) Julie enjoyed reading the book.

The dependent type ϵ matches the type of the term "book", a dot type $P \bullet I$ (PHYSICAL OBJECT $\bullet$ INFORMATIONAL OBJECT), with the type of event conventionally associated with it, namely READING. This latter type, then, will be represented through the formula $\epsilon(a_1, a_2)$, where a_1 stands for the first argument of the dependent type, and a_2 for the second one: as READING types an event, the first argument will be the Agent (Julie, in this case), and the second will be the Object (the book). This association, moreover, will be rendered explicit at the level of types through an associating type $\otimes$, so that the final type of "book" will be something like BOOK $\otimes$ ϵ (JULIE, BOOK), or, better $(P \bullet I) \otimes \epsilon$(HUMAN, $P \bullet I$).

4.5.2 The context-sensitivity of types

Another fundamental difference with Montague's logical grammar is given by the fact that Asher's theory is a *context-sensitive* theory of types. Types represent the device that Asher uses to account for the contextual dependence of meaning. While in Montague's grammar we have that each single lexical item is associated with a type once for all, depending on the syntactical category it belongs to, in Asher's theory types are assigned to single words in an elastic, mobile manner, depending on the demands of predication and context. Asher's theory, in fact, allows type shifting, where the shift can be commanded both by the linguistic and by the extralinguistic context.

Consider again sentence (14). We said that the standard interpretation for this sentence is plausibly (18), according to which Julie enjoyed reading the book, so that the final type for "book" is $(P \bullet I) \otimes \epsilon$(HUMAN, $P \bullet I$). But suppose now we are given a context in which it is known that Julie is a writer: in this case, the interpretation of (14) will be something as

(19) Julie enjoyed writing the book.

---

pp. 53–69).
[29]See p. 72.

This interpretation will be given through a different typing of the term "book", *i.e.* something like $(P \bullet I) \otimes \epsilon (\text{AUTHOR}, P \bullet I)$: what happens, in this case, is that the context intervenes to block the default reading of (14) in favour of an interpretation, (19), which selects from the type HUMAN a more specific sub-type, namely the type AUTHOR. Now suppose, instead, that sentence (14) is uttered in a (non-fictional) context in which it is clear that Julie is a goat. The most immediate interpretation for (14) will probably be the following:

(20) Julie *enjoyed* eating the book.

In this case, as in the previous ones, the context will be responsible for the type shifting which allows for the relevant interpretation, making the type of "book" change from $(P \bullet I) \otimes \epsilon \, (\text{HUMAN}, P \bullet I)$ to $(P \bullet I) \otimes \epsilon \, (\text{GOAT}, P \bullet I)$.

4.6 Logical forms

After types, the fourth level of representation in Asher's system is constituted by logical forms. For Asher, the logical form of a sentence is a representation which has an interpretation sufficient to yield the truth conditions for the sentence itself. As only the interpreted logical form can be the bearer of the truth conditional content, moreover, we will have that the notion of meaning has to be applied *in primis* to the (interpreted) logical form of a sentence, and only indirectly to the natural language sentence itself.

This way of talking about the meaning of a sentence can legitimately raise the question of the relationship between types and logical forms: what do their respective roles exactly consist in, and in which way, if any, are they related? For Asher, formalism of types and formula for logical forms do indeed play different roles in the theory: types furnish the cognitive component of meaning; logical forms, instead, the externalist component. Asher, in fact, affirms that:

> If the types are concepts, then these are to be distinguished from the logical forms themselves that denote features of the real world, properties and individuals. The role of type formalism and logical forms are different. Types and their adjustment are at the heart of a theory of predication, while the logical forms are the soul of a theory of word meaning. Types are at best a partial guide to the semantic value of a word and certainly don't suffice to exhaust their contents; as we know from the many externalist arguments in the philosophy of mind and the philosophy of language, concepts, our internal mental reflection of real world properties and things don't suffice to determine denotations or intensions. [...] Since concepts are, if anything is, "in the head", it follows that types, as they are concepts, cannot by themselves play

the role of logical forms whose semantics incorporate the externalist elements isolated by Kripke *et al.* Nevertheless, concepts as types play a role in semantics. They represent enough content to guide predication and the construction of logical form, which is an internal matter, something that speakers do "in their heads." Thus, we appear to need both types and logical form, but they need to be distinguished.[30]

Types, as they are concepts, are not sufficient to determine the denotation of the words which they are associated with. The denotation can be given only through the logical form, and its corresponding model-theoretic interpretation. Types, and their combining into predication, constitute only a guide to the construction of the logical form, which remains the only component responsible for the assignment of truth conditions to the sentence which it represents. Strictly speaking, then, it is possible to talk of meaning only in the externalist sense, relatively to the denotation of the logical form and of the terms which go into its composition.

4.6.1 The relation between types and logical forms

In spite of their difference, however, types and logical form do remain closely linked. Between them there is a close correspondence, to the point that the relations between types will reflect analytical implications between the logical forms they correspond to, and that every change at the level of types will induce a corresponding effect at the level of the logical form. Such effects will be registered at the level of logical form through what Asher calls transfer rules:

> Given that I will use rules to change complex types when predications demand it, I will also argue, in virtue of the type formula correspondence, that these rules for introducing or exploiting complex types will affect logical form. As part of the analysis of predication then, I will introduce transfer rules that tell us what are the effects of a type shift on the logical forms of the terms in predication.[31]

Thus, only logical forms can receive an interpretation in model-theoretical, truth-conditional terms. Nonetheless, such forms are not, so to speak, directly supplied by the syntactical structure of the sentence (together with the appropriate rules of translation), but depend instead on what happens at the level of types, namely, at the level of the linguistic-conceptual elaboration operated by the competent speaker on the sentence itself and its constituents. Consider, once again, sentence (14). As already said, in a standard context this sentence is interpreted as (18). In a context in which it is known that Julie is a writer, instead,

---

[30] Asher (2006b, p. 23).
[31] Asher (2006b, p. 15).

it can be interpreted as (19).

The expressions "reading" and "writing" do not appear as syntactical constituents in the starting sentence, which in both cases is (14). They emerge only at the level of the typing process: "enjoy" is a predicate which requires as its own argument a type of event that, not being signalled in the sentence (14), it is given to it in the process of typing through a modification of the type "book" (type shift). And, most of all, the logical form of (14) is constructed not starting from the syntactical analysis of (14), but from the sentence typing process: in the case of (14) interpreted as (18), the transfer rules will register in the logical form READ as constituent; in the case of (14) interpreted as (19), instead, they will register WRITE. In order to produce a logical form, hence, the syntactical information will have to be supplemented, where necessary, with the typing operations on the expressions. Asher writes:

> [...] the operations on types, though simple, have important effects on logical form, sometimes introducing new variables and new material in the lambda terms to be combined and thus into logical form. Our rules are [...] ampliative with respect to logical form: they add content.[32]

Transfer rules, then, are ampliative, they add material. The constituents "reading" or "writing" are not present in the syntactical tree of sentence (14), but they are inserted in the logical form by the transfer rules, which reflect changes and operations that went through at the level of types.

4.7 The Principle of Compositionality in TDT

4.7.1 Lexical and Sentence meaning

What has been said so far about types, logical forms, and the relationship between them, has already provided all the necessary hints to understand what, in Asher's theory, the notion of lexical and sentence meaning does consist in.

Let us begin with sentence meaning. Although, strictly speaking, we can talk about the meaning of the sentence only in an externalist sense, referring, namely, to the denotation of the interpreted logical form, the construction of the logical form would not even be possible without the typing process which goes on at the cognitive level. Sentence meaning, thus, will be given by two components, (1) the typing process and (2) the (interpreted) logical form, closely linked together by transfer rules. For example, as far as the sentence meaning of (14) is concerned, the typing process is given by (21), where (21a) represents the lambda term corresponding to sentence (14) and (21b) represents the typing context

---
[32] Asher (2006b, pp. 104-105).

(*i.e.* the context which specifies the types to be assigned and used in the typing process of the sentence itself), and the interpreted logical form is represented by (22), obtained from (21) through transfer rules:

(21a) $\lambda \mathcal{P} \lambda u \mathcal{P}(\lambda v \, \text{enjoy}(u,v) \wedge Ag(v) = u)[\lambda P \exists x (\text{book}(x) \wedge P[x])]$

(21b) $c = < \mathcal{P} : (\epsilon(a_1, a_2) \to t) \to t,$
$v : \epsilon(a_1, a_2),$
$x : (p \bullet i) \otimes (\epsilon(a_1, a_2)) \Rightarrow y : (p \bullet i) \otimes \epsilon(a_1, a_2),$
$x : \epsilon(a_1, a_2), \, x : \text{READ} >$

(22) $\lambda u \lambda e \exists x \exists y \, (\text{book}(y) \wedge (\text{read}(x, u, y) \wedge \text{enjoy}(e, u, x)), \, c$

As far as (21) is concerned, we have that the verb "enjoy" requires, as its own argument, an event, which is represented by the variable v, to which the dependent type $\epsilon(a_1, a_2)$ is assigned. This induces a coercion on the term "book", and this coercion gives rise to a change on the type assignment to the variable x: from the dot type $(p \bullet i)$, we obtain the dependent type $\epsilon(a_1, a_2)$, *i.e.* READ, an event defined through the two parameters a_1 (the agent of the event) and a_2 (the object, namely the book). Notice that "enjoy" becomes a one place, third order predicate (something as "liked by Julie"). Applied to a second order predicate, $\lambda P \exists x (\text{book}(x) \wedge P[x])$, it yields an expression of type t, the type of sentences.

As far as (22) is concerned, instead, we have that c stands for the typing context, u for the agent, e for the event represented by "enjoy", x for the activity of reading, and y for the object denoted by "book". What is important to notice, here, is that the transfer rules are responsible for the emerging, in the logical form, of the effects of the type changes at the linguistic-conceptual level.

Now, lexical meaning. As you will remember, for Asher a lexical semantics has to specify the "lexical resources used to build the logical forms",[33] where for lexical resource he generically intends something that, when combined with the contribution of the other words in a well-formed sentence, yields a logical form. The fact that Asher also maintains that types, as we saw above, "represent enough content to guide [...] the construction of logical form" could let one think that such lexical resources are represented by types, and that it is the combination of the types associated with each word within a sentence that gives, in the end, the logical form of the sentence itself. It could be thought, in other words, that there is coincidence between types and lexical

---

[33] Asher (2006b, p. 2).

meanings. Asher himself, after all, often uses the term "lexical meaning" while talking about the type or types associated with an expression.

In some passages, however, the intention of distinguishing lexical meaning from the expression type clearly emerges. Intention, on the other hand, is already clear from the distinction of the roles which types and logical forms have to play within TDT. The expression type constitutes only a part of the lexical meaning, or "a partial guide to it",[34] but it doesn't exhaust it: what lacks, in fact, is the denotation of the term. The lexical meaning of a word, thus, will have to bring with itself both the information about the type to be associated with the expression, and the information about its denotation. In other words, for Asher, each lexical entry has to contain two pieces of semantic information, namely: (i) a lambda term, with the corresponding model-theoretic interpretation, and (ii) a typing context: for each term t, the corresponding typing context determines a type assignment to every sub-term of t, *i.e.*, to its constituents. For example, the complete lexical entry for "book" will consist in

(23) $\lambda v \text{book}(v), < v : P \bullet I >$

where the variable v ranges over objects which have both a physical aspect and an informational aspect, as specified in the type $< v : P \bullet I >$ assigned by the typing context, which we can indicate with c. In this way, the task of keeping track of the effects of the context on the meaning of the single entries, and through them, on that of sentences, is entrusted to that part of semantic information, inscribed in each single entry, which is the typing context. For each term occurring in a given sentence, in other words, the typing context will indicate what types will have to be assigned to the variables and constants which compose the term itself, where such an indication will vary according to the variations in the demands of predication which are commanded by the context itself.

The fact that the typing context is placed among the semantic information of a term coheres with the general framework of the theory, but it could legitimately raise more than one doubt. First, it is not clear whether Asher intends the typing context only as linguistic and/or extralinguistic context, or only as the effects of the context on the type to be assigned to the expression, or both. And second, most of all, it is not clear how these kinds of information can be expected to be fully semantic. Even if the typing context were to limit itself to registering the effects of the context on the content of the word, as it is maybe more reasonable to think, we would still have a content whose determi-

---

[34] Asher (2006b, p. 23).

nation remains at the mercy of a context which can vary indefinitely. Asher doesn't claim that the meaning of a word is something underdetermined, which is, in a second moment, determined by the context, leaving such a second stage, so to speak, out of the semantic level; he locates both the underdetermination, and the process and the result of the contextual determination within the semantic content of the word.

4.7.2 The constituents: a comparison with logical grammar

What we finally need in order to give a formulation of the *TDT* Principle of Compositionality is to make precise the notion of constituents which it exploits. In this case as well, a comparison with Montague's logical grammar seems useful. Logical grammar employs a "strict" compositionality: to each step of syntactical construction there corresponds a step of semantic construction.[35] This implies that there are no syntactical constituents which do not receive a translation in the formal language, or, again, that there are no nodes in the syntactical tree which do not receive an interpretation. In Gamut's words:

> Every sentence, no matter how complex, is the result of a systematic construction process which builds it up step by step, and in which every step can receive a semantic interpretation.[36]

In logical grammar, then, the constituents of which (**PoC**) talks about are to be identified with the syntactical constituents of the complex expression.

In Asher's theory, instead, the parallelism between syntax and semantics is broken: transfer rules are ampliative, and not only in the sense of adding variables, but also in the sense of changing the meaning of the terms which occur in the sentence: the construction of the logical form of (14), for example, requires that, essentially, the meaning of "enjoyed the book" is modified in that one of "enjoyed reading the book". But then, in Asher's theory, the constituents of the logical form may not coincide with the constituents we find at the syntactic level.

4.7.3 The Principle of Compositionality in *TDT*

As Asher himself states, *TDT* is a two-stage compositional theory: in the first stage we will have the process of the information packaging, *i.e.* of the assemblage of types; in the second stage, instead, we will have

---

[35] (**PoC**) is not equivalent to strict compositionality. It is possible to conceive of compositional languages, in fact, in which the meaning assignments are not strictly parallel to syntax. Strict compositionality implies (**PoC**), but it requires something more, namely the parallelism between syntax and semantics. See Szabò (2000, pp. 6–14).

[36] Gamut (1991a, vol. 2, pp. 4–5).

that the transfer rules provide the construction of the logical form, *i.e.* the level of the informational content built from the contributes of the relevant lexical resources.

The TDT process of meaning composition, then, will be more complex than in theories which only require an operation of application of the lambda term to his argument(s). By adding complex types different from the classical ones, Asher's semantics requires new rules for the composition of such types, and most of all it renders the composition of the logical form dependent upon the assignments and modifications given at the level of types. Namely, it is the types assigned to the variables in each lambda term which determine how this term can combine with the other terms in the composition of the logical form. The logical form, hence, can be obtained only indirectly, passing through the information packaging process, which is accomplished at a cognitive level.

If this is so, the meaning of a complex expression in TDT is determined not by the meaning of its constituents and by its immediate syntactic structure, but rather by the meaning of the constituents of the logical form and by the way these constituents are combined, where, in turn, the constituents of the logical form are determined, via transfer rules, by the typing process. In other words, the Principle of Compositionality exploited by TDT can be stated as follows:

(**PoC**$_{TDT}$) The meaning of a complex expression is determined by the meanings of the constituents of its logical form, and by the manner in which such constituents are combined; in turn, the constituents of the logical form are determined, via transfer rules, by the types assigned to the complex expression through the typing process, and their mode of combination corresponds to the mode of combination of the corresponding types.

What remains to be done, now, is consider what kind of consequences this formulation of the principle has on Asher's theory and, last but not least, what kind of theoretical role (**PoC**$_{TDT}$) can be said to play in it.

4.8 Consequences of PoC$_{TDT}$

4.8.1 Safety with respect to contextualist objections

The assignment of types to an expression keeps constant track of the demands of predication and of the context in which the expression is uttered. Contrarily to what happens in logical grammar, where each syntactic category is associated with a single semantic type, and compositionality is conceived as strict, in TDT each expression is associated with a whole class of types. And this is so because the types provided by TDT are sensitive to the context, a context which Asher seems to conceive of as both linguistic and extralinguistic: in the first case we have to do with the relevant linguistic unit in which the expression occurs (a complex expression, a sentence, a discourse); in the second case, instead, with the concrete situation in which the expression is uttered. As a consequence, the notion of compositionality called into play by TDT will have to obey itself to a certain context-sensitiveness. Talking about the linguistic kind of context, for example, Asher writes:

> [...] we need at least a notion of composition on which combining the meanings of two words may result in a change to those meanings themselves. That is, we need at the very least a context-sensitive notion of composition, which is not what we find in the standard theory of composition found, *e.g.*, in Montague Grammar. [...] What earlier theories lacked was an account of how the "composition" of new information in [linguistic] context could in fact alter the information as well as elements in the [linguistic] context in ways not predictable within a framework countenancing only operations like application of functions to arguments or merge.[37]

To compose the meaning of a sentence like (14) implies changing the meaning of "book" in something like "reading the book", because of the presence of a predicate, "enjoy", which requires an event as its own argument: combining the meaning of two words can result, Asher affirms, in a change in meaning of the words themselves. It is the linguistic context of "book", then, which determines the meaning of the word itself.

Now, the role which Asher assigns to the context – both linguistic and extralinguistic – doesn't seem to menace (**PoC**). Asher inscribes the effects of the context within each single constituent of the complex expression: each single word in a sentence brings with itself two pieces of semantic information, the lambda term and the typing context. It is this latter which signals the type to be assigned to the word, which enters in the composition of the sentence meaning only after it has been modelled by the context. And as long as the context acts only at the level of each single constituent of a complex expression, (**PoC**) is safe: (**PoC**), in fact, requires that the meaning of a complex expression is determined by the meaning of its constituents and by its syntactical structure, but it leaves quite complete freedom on the ways in which the meaning of the single constituents are determined. (**PoC**) concerns the determination of the meaning of the complex expressions, not of the simple ones, which

---
[37] Asher (2006a, pp. 1–2).

could well depend upon the context for the determination of their own meaning. If we leave aside the above mentioned difficulty about Asher's intention to inscribe the effects of such context in the semantics of the expression,[38] then the role of context in TDT doesn't seem to create particular problems for compositionality. It is not a problem, namely, if in interpreting the sentence:

(24) Lizzie enjoyed the rock.

we have to resort to the help of context: the context intervenes only in specifying the meaning of "the rock" (for example, in the sense of climbing the rock), meaning which, once specified, will enter the process of sentence meaning composition together with the meanings of other constituents.

Context could menace (**PoC**) only if it acted at the level of sentence meaning. (**PoC**) says that the meaning of a complex expression is determined by the meanings of its constituents and by its structure, and by nothing else: if it came out that the determination of such meaning depends also upon the intervention of the context, (**PoC**) would be falsified. It is what C. Travis tries to show through his famous example of the painted leaves. Imagine a context in which Pia paints a russet leaf green. Referring to the leaf, Pia utters:

(25) The leaf is green.

(25) will be true, Travis maintains, if uttered as an answer to a photographer who is looking for a green subject; false, instead, as an answer to a botanist who is classifying leaves. But if this is so, Travis argues, the meaning of the constituents and the syntactical structure of the sentence are not sufficient in determining the meaning of the sentence, and (**PoC**) has to be abandoned. Asher doesn't take into consideration cases like this, but I think that the kind of solution he would offer would go in the same direction as before, *i.e.* of a context which intervenes only at the level of the single constituents, and not of the whole sentence; a solution which is proposed, on the other hand, also by authors foreigner to lexical semantics.[39] A hint in this sense is represented by the fact that he considers RED(APPLE), RED(SHIRT), RED(MEAT) as different propositional sub-types, in that

> [...] the predications here are distinct. When we predicate a colour of an apple, we predicate it typically of the skin, whereas a red shirt doesn't have a skin. It is the object that is designated as red. Finally

---

[38] See section 4.7.1, p. 82.
[39] For example, Szabò (2000); for a comparison between the different solutions to this problem see also Predelli (2005, pp. 357–360).

red meat refers to a type of meat, which may not be at all red after cooking. This leads to a finegrained conception of propositional types, and we can also think now of propositional types as having parameters that can be replaced by variables.[40]

The example of the red meat seems to be very close to that of the painted leaf: after cooking the meat, the sentence:

(26) The meat is red.

will be true if uttered as an answer to somebody who wants information on the kind of meat; false, if what is in question is its actual colour. In this regard, Asher assumes propositional types provided with parameters: parameters which say, in the case of the leaf, which is the relevant surface of the leaf in a certain context, or, in the case of the meat, if "red" is to be taken as pertaining to the kind of meat, or to its actual colour.

It is possible to affirm, then, that the role of context in the determination of the meaning of expressions doesn't threaten (**PoC**). The lexical meaning constantly depends on the context, and TDT type composition logic is conceived in such a way as to formalize this very dependence, without this being a problem for the compositionality of meaning.

4.8.2 Overproductivity

There remains a last consideration to make on the notion of compositionality in Asher's theory, a consideration, on the other hand, not unconnected to the role of the context in the determination of meaning. We just said that the context doesn't menace (**PoC**), in that its effects are confined at the lexical level, and (**PoC**) allows for freedom in the modalities of determination of the meaning of constituents. The problem is that such freedom, as exploited by TDT, could end up being excessive, giving rise to a phenomenon of overproductivity. Asher is aware of the problem, and talking about the operations on types he writes:

> Some of these processes may be grammatically determined, say by suffixes as in English. But others may not be overtly marked in the grammar or may come about just because of clashes in predication. Such arrows must be constrained and linguistically motivated if the whole system is to not collapse. If arbitrary type transformations are allowed, then compositionality becomes trivial and the type hierarchy becomes meaningless.[41]

---

[40] Asher (2006b, p. 21).
[41] Asher (2006b, p. 50).

In other words, the problem is that, once syntactically ill-formed expressions are excluded, every complex expression which is somehow interpretable against a certain context will be, in any case, endowed with a meaning compositionally obtained. I will try to clarify the point through some examples. Consider then the following sentences:

(27) Mary read the book.
(28) John read the rumour about his ex-wife.
(29) Mary read the subway wall.

For Asher, the predicate "read" requires that its argument is of a dot type, *i.e.* a complex type formed in this way: PHYSICAL OBJECT • INFORMATIONAL OBJECT. If the argument does not, in fact, correspond to the required type, where possible we will have a phenomenon of coercion of the predicate on its argument, whose type will be changed in the appropriate one. This is what happens in the examples (28) and (29). In Asher's words:

> One can hear rumours and spread rumours, which one cannot do with books (even if you are listening to a book on tape); on the other hand, one can't see or look at rumours whereas one can see or look at a book. On the other hand, one can see a subway wall or look at it, without getting any informational content. However, in (82b,c)[42] the arguments of read change their meaning. [...] One explanation for this phenomenon is that read coerces its arguments into objects of the same type as book. For both (82b) and (82c) the predicate coerces its complement to the appropriate type, that of informational object with physical manifestation. In each of these cases, there is a "missing element" to the complex type: for (82b) the coercion effects the introduction of the physical manifestation to the otherwise informational type; for (82c) the coercion results in the introduction of an informational component to an otherwise merely physical type.[43]

On the basis of coercion, then, both arguments undergo a change in meaning: both are associated with the dot type PHYSICAL OBJECT • INFORMATIONAL OBJECT, for this is what is required by the verb "read". The logical form, moreover, will undergo modifications parallel to this type shift. But consider now the following sentences:

(30) Mary reads the cards.
(31) Mary reads the future.
(32) Mary reads the coffee grounds.
(33) Mary reads the lips.

---

[42] (82b) = (28), (82c) = (29).
[43] Asher (2006b, pp. 67–68).

(34) Mary reads the fear in Tom's eyes.
(35) The ancients read the sky and the birds' flight.

According to what Asher affirms in the passage just quoted, and analogously to what happens in sentences (28) and (29), we will have to say that (30)–(35) are all examples of coercion of the predicate "read" on its own argument. If one is willing to say that, *via* coercion, rumour can acquire a physical aspect and a subway-wall an informational one, there is no reason to deny such a possibility also to cards, lips, future, fear, coffee grounds, sky, and bird flight. Maybe "fear" and "future" can seem slightly different cases, after all the fear is not properly what Mary reads, but what Mary concludes reading Tom's eyes, and the future, similarly, is what Mary draws by reading the cards or the coffee grounds. But then, a different treatment should be reserved also to "rumor", a thing that doesn't happen anyway. Consider, finally, the following sentences:

(36) The children read the elephant.
(37) John reads the pavement.
(38) The sailor reads the sea.

The elephant, the pavement and the sea are not, typically, things that one can read. But by adding some contextual details each of the sentences (36)–(38) can receive an interpretation, which will imply, not differently from all the sentences considered so far, a coercion of the predicate on its own argument. Following Asher, there is no reason why we cannot do this; even the subway-wall and the rumour about the ex-wife are not, typically, things that one can read. There is something intuitively not literal in saying that the children read the elephant or that the sailor read the sea, but the same can be asserted for sentences like (28) and (29). But then, it (16)[44], Asher claims that the predication doesn't work, and that if (16) can nonetheless convey something, it is only through a re-interpretation:

> The reason in such a theory why some predications involve misuses of words, don't work or require reinterpretation, is because the types of the arguments don't match the types required by the predicates for its argument places. (1a)[45] involves a misuse of the language, because contain requires for its subject argument either a physical container or a container of information, and persons are not of the type information containers [...].[46]

---

[44] See p. 76.
[45] (16) in the text.
[46] Asher (2006b, p. 4).

What does "re-interpreation" mean? If the processes we exploit in understanding (28) and (29) are the same as the ones required for the interpretation of sentences (30)–(35), and for the reasons seen above also of (36)–(38), why would (16) have to be an example of misuse? What I'm trying to say, in substance, is that in TDT a real semantic constraint on the application of the rules of introduction and exploitation of the complex types doesn't exist, and that, in principle, every sentence semantically "strange" can gain, *via* coercion for example, the appropriate adjustment of the argument type. This may not be a problem by itself: maybe it is just exploiting mechanisms of this kind that we are able to interpret even the hardest metaphors. The problem, rather, is that each transformation at the level of types gives rise to changes at the level of the logical form: dot types, for instance, induce the introduction of a new variable in the logical form. But then, first, also sentences like (36)–(38) and (16) will receive a truth-conditional interpretation, loosing an already weak notion of the difference between literal and non-literal language; and, second, the truth conditions so obtained will be not so much truth conditions for the sentence, but rather truth conditions which pertain to the final interpretation of the sentence itself, or, we can say, to the utterance of the sentence. In this way, however, the risk of overproductivity is always round the corner – all sentences, even the anomalous or non literal-ones, would be semantically interpretable, and they would be interpretable, most of all, according to a Principle of Compositionality which appears emptied of its own explicative function.

4.9 Conclusions

The exam of Asher's theory has highlighted how, for him, the meaning of a complex expression is determined not by the meaning of its immediate constituents and by its immediate syntactical structure, but by the meaning of the constituents of its logical form, and by the way in which such constituents are combined. We have seen, moreover, that the constituents of the logical form result from the transfer, at the level of the logical form itself, of the types associated with the expression, and the mode in which they combine with each other reflects the mode of composition of the corresponding types. Assembled in this way, the logical form finally receives a truth-conditional interpretation, and furnishes in this manner also the externalist component of the sentence meaning.

Moreover, the extreme context-sensitivity of types constantly shows his effects on the logical form, without this representing a menace to the compositionality of meaning: the effects of the context, conceived as both linguistic and extralinguistic, are inserted at the level of the single constituents (of the logical form), and not at the level of the whole sentence. Nonetheless, it is this very extreme context-sensitivity, plus the thesis according to which every variation at the level of types induces a corresponding variation in the logical form (the ultimate bearer of truth conditions), that lead to a compositionality which, in fact, applies not to the starting sentence, but rather to the cognitively elaborated sentence. In other words, the meaning of the sentence, given in terms of truth conditions, is something that belongs not to the sentence itself but only to the sentence as uttered in a precise context which triggers the elaboration at the level of types. The truth conditions are assigned, we could say, not to the sentence but to the utterance: what is being evaluated in (14) is not the sentence "Julie enjoyed the book", but rather "Julie enjoyed reading the book", or "Julie enjoyed writing the book", depending on the context.

If things are so, however, the distinction between literal and non-literal language, already difficult to delineate, appears to be at risk. Not that this represents, by itself, an insurmountable problem: after all, there are theoretical positions devoted just to denying the legitimacy or the utility of such a distinction. What is by no means clear, however, is the difference between cases of syntactically well-formed sentences in which the predication results not working, and cases in which, instead, this doesn't happen; even in the first cases, in fact, there will be some mechanisms that intervene in fixing the matters, allowing for the assemblage of the logical form, and so, for the compositional interpretation.

For these reasons, I think we can affirm that the Principle of Compositionality in Asher's theory is used not as an empirical hypothesis which has to be tested through the linguistic data, or as an inference to the best explanation, but as a methodological assumption which constantly guides the setting of the type theory, and, as a consequence, the combination of the constituents in the logical form. Such a conception of (**PoC**), though legitimate, does seem however to be very far from the original motivations which pushed the formulation of the principle itself, *i.e.* the need of accounting for the phenomena of productivity and systematicity of language.

References

Asher, Nicholas. 2006a. Lecture notes. Graduate Program University of Verona.

Asher, Nicholas. 2006b. A type driven theory of predication and lexical and

discourse meaning. Draft.
Gamut, L.T.F. 1991a. *Intensional Logic and Logical Grammar*. Chicago: The University of Chicago Press. Volume II of Gamut (1991b).
Gamut, L.T.F. 1991b. *Logic, Language and Meaning*. Chicago: The University of Chicago Press.
Gleitman, Lila R. and Liberman Mark, eds. 1994. *An Invitation to Cognitive Science*. Cambridge MA: The MIT Press.
Kamp, Hans. 1984. A theory of truth and semantic interpretation. In J. Groenendijk, T. Janssen, and M. Stokhof, eds., *Truth, Interpretation and Information*, pages 277–322. Dordrecht: Foris Publications.
Montague, Richard. 1973. The proper treatment of quantification in English. In J. Hintikka, J. Moravcsik, and P. Suppes, eds., *Approaches to Natural Language*, pages 221–242. Reidel: Dordrecht. Reprinted in (Richard, 1974, pp. 247–270).
Partee, Barbara. 1994. Lexical semantic and compositionality. In L. Gleitman and L. M., eds., *Language*, pages 311–360. Cambridge MA: The MIT Press. Volume I of Gleitman and Mark (1994).
Predelli, Stefano. 2005. Painted leaves, context, and semantic analysis. *Linguistics and Philosophy* 28(3):351–374.
Pustejovsky, James. 1995. *The Generative Lexicon*. A Bradford Book. Cambridge MA: The MIT Press.
Richard, Montague. 1974. *Formal Philosophy*. New Haven: Yale University Press.
Szabò, Zoltan Gendler. 2000. *Problems of Compositionality*. Studies in Philosophy. New York: Garland Publishing.

Section II: Knowledge

5

Carnapian Modal and Epistemic Arithmetic[1]

JAN HEYLEN

The subject of the first section is Carnapian modal logic. One of the things I will do there is to prove that certain description principles, viz. the "self-predication principles", i.e. the principles according to which a descriptive term satisfies its own descriptive condition, are theorems and that others are not. The second section will be devoted to Carnapian modal arithmetic. I will prove that, if the arithmetical theory contains the standard weak principle of induction, modal truth collapses to truth. Then I will propose a different formulation of Carnapian modal arithmetic and establish that it is free of collapse. Noteworthy is that one can retain the standard strong principle of induction. I will occupy myself in the third section with Carnapian epistemic logic and arithmetic. Here too it is claimed that the standard weak principle of induction is invalid and that the alternative principle *is* valid. In the fourth and last section I will get back to the self-predication principles and I will point to some of the consequences if one adds them to Carnapian Epistemic arithmetic. The interaction of self-predication

---

[1] An earlier version of this paper was presented at the First SIFA Graduate Conference (Padua, 11-12 September 2007). A later version was presented at a seminar organised by the CLAP (University of Leuven). The final version was presented at the Sixth ESAP Conference (Krakau, 21-26 August 2008). Research for this paper was supported by a grant of the Fund for Scientific research –Flanders, which is gratefully acknowledged. I would like to thank the audiences at those events for their comments. Thanks especially to Leon Horsten for his many comments on the series of papers leading up to and including this paper.

Language, Knowledge, and Metaphysics.
Massimiliano Carrara and Vittorio Morato (eds.)
College Pubblication, London, 2008.

principles and the strong principle of induction results in a collapse of *de re* knowability.

5.1 Carnapian logic

First, I will say a few words about the language and quite a few more words on the formal and informal interpretation of the language. Next, I will then briefly sketch the theory and discuss the formal and informal soundness of the principles. Finally, I will prove and disprove a few description principles.

5.1.1 The language and its interpretation

The non-logical terminology of $\mathcal{L}$ consists of a set of individual constants, $\mathcal{C}_\mathcal{L}$, a distinguished constant $c^* \in \mathcal{C}_\mathcal{L}$, a set of functions, $\mathcal{F}_\mathcal{L}$, and a set of predicates, $\mathcal{P}_\mathcal{L}$. Sofar the only unusual feature is c^*. Its role and importance will become clearer later.

The set of well-formed terms and formulas can be defined recursively as follows:

Definition 1. *For all $c_i \in \mathcal{C}_\mathcal{L}$, c_i is a well-formed term; if $t_1, \ldots, t_n$ are well-formed terms and if $f_i^n \in \mathcal{F}_\mathcal{L}$, then $f_i^n(t_1, \ldots, t_n)$ is a well-formed term; if ϕ is a well-formed formula, then $\iota x \phi$ is a well-formed term; if $t_1, \ldots, t_n$ and if $P^n \in \mathcal{R}_\mathcal{L}$, then $t_i = t_j$ (with $1 \leq i \leq j \leq n$) and $P^n(t_1, \ldots, t_n)$ are well-formed formulas; if ϕ, ψ are well-formed formulas, then $\neg \phi, \phi \wedge \psi, \phi \vee \psi, \phi \rightarrow \psi, \phi \leftrightarrow \psi, \Box \phi$ are well-formed formulas; if ϕ is a formula with, then $\forall x \phi$ and $\exists x \phi$ are well-formed formulas; nothing else is a well-formed term or formula.*

The set of closed terms, $\mathcal{T}_\mathcal{L}$, contains all well-formed terms in which no variable is free. The set of closed formulas, $\mathcal{S}_\mathcal{L}$, contains all well-formed formulas in which no variable is free.

An unusual feature of the above definition is that the iota-operator is conceived as a term-forming operator and not as a formula-forming operator. In this respect the ι-operator differs from the quantifier $\forall$. Both operate on a formula ϕ, but the first transforms ϕ in an term, whereas the latter transforms ϕ in a new formula. On an alternative conception the iota-operator should also be a formula-forming operator. On that line of approach descriptions are like quantifiers. $(\iota x \phi(x))(\psi(x))$ should be read as: "concerning the ϕ, ψ". Russell's theory of descriptions was in a way a mixture of the term approach on the one hand and the quantifier approach on the other hand, since he allowed descriptions as quasi-terms but defined away formulas with descriptions occurring in them as complex quantified formulas.

Usually one gives separate definitions of the set of well-formed terms on the one hand and the set of well-formed formulas. The choice for descriptions as terms blocks this approach however, for the separate definitions would then be circular, since one step in the definition of the well-formed terms requires a well-defined set of well-formed formulas (viz. the recursive step in which ι-terms are introduced), while one step in the definition of well-formed formulas requires that one has a well-defined set of well-formed terms (viz. the basic step in which the atomic formulas are listed as well-formed formulas). By giving one recursive definition for both the well-formed terms as the well-formed formulas one avoids circularity. First, one builds all description-free well-formed terms. Next, one uses these building blocks to build all description-free well-formed terms. Then one can build the description terms the descriptive condition of which does not contain other description terms. Subsequently one can use those description terms to construct the well-formed formulas which contain at most the description terms which are already defined, and so on.

It was already pointed out that the set of well-formed terms and the set of well-formed formulas have to be defined simultaneously. As a consequence, the interpretation of the terms and formulas also need to be given in one definition:

Definition 2. *A model is a quintuple $\langle W, @, D, d^*, I \rangle$ where W and D are non-empty sets, $@ \in W$, $d^* \in D$ and I is a function defined as follows: if $c \in \mathcal{C}_\mathcal{L}$, then $I(c) \in D$; $I(c^*) = d^*$; if $P \in \mathcal{P}_\mathcal{L}$, then for all $w \in W$, $I(P, w) \subset D^n$. Let i be a function from W to D and let a be a function such that, if x is a variable, $a(x) = i$ for some i. Let $a[i/x]$ be a function differing from a at most in mapping i to x. Then let $V_\mathcal{M}$ be a function defined as follows: if x is a variabele, $V_\mathcal{M}(x, w, a) = (a(x))(w)$; if $c \in \mathcal{C}_\mathcal{L}$, $V_\mathcal{M}(c, w, a) = I(c)$; if $P^n \in \mathcal{P}_\mathcal{L}$, $V_\mathcal{M}(P(t_1, \ldots, t_n), w, a) = T$ iff $\langle V_\mathcal{M}(t_1, w, a), \ldots, V_\mathcal{M}(t_n, w, a) \rangle \in I(P, w)$; $V_\mathcal{M}(t_1 = t_n, w, a) = T$ iff $V_\mathcal{M}(t_1, w, a) = V_\mathcal{M}(t_2, w, a)$; the clauses for $\neg$ and $\rightarrow$ are as can be expected; $V_\mathcal{M}(\forall x \phi, w, a) = T$ iff $V_\mathcal{M}(\phi, w, a[i/x]) = T$ for every i; $V_\mathcal{M}(\Box \phi, w, a) = T$ iff $V_\mathcal{M}(\phi, w', a) = T$ for every $w' \in W$; $V_\mathcal{M}(\iota x \phi, w, a) = d$ if*

1. *for some i, $V_\mathcal{M}(\phi, w, a[i/x]) = T$ and*
2. *for every i, if $V_\mathcal{M}(\phi, w, a[i/x]) = T$, then $i(w) = d$*

$V_\mathcal{M}(\iota x \phi, w, a) = d^*$ *otherwise.*

If ϕ is closed, then $V_\mathcal{M}(\phi, w) = V_\mathcal{M}(\phi, w, a)$. Finally, let $V_\mathcal{M}(\phi) = V_M(\phi, @)$. The above formal interpretation of $\mathcal{L}$ was given by Kremer (1997, p. 632-64).

5.1.2 The theory and its soundness

Carnapian modal logic, **C**, is the combination of first-order logic, the modal system **S5** and some characteristic principles regarding identity and descriptions. In the paper I will make use of a weaker theory, $\mathbf{C_T}$, which is exactly like **C**, except for the fact that it comprises the modal system **T** instead of **S5**. The sole motivation for doing so is, of course, that the weaker the theory, the stronger the proof of the theoremhood of a certain formula.

First-order logic is well-known, and need not be described in full detail here. Suffice it to say that the quantifier principles are the following:[2]

∀**E** If $\Gamma \vdash \forall x \phi$, $\Gamma \vdash \phi[x|t]$, provided that t is free for x in ϕ.

∀**I** If $\Gamma \vdash \phi$ and x does not occur free in any member of Γ, then $\Gamma \vdash \forall x \phi$.

Modal system **T** consists of two rules:[3]

□**E** If $\Gamma \vdash \Box \phi$, then $\Gamma \vdash \phi$

□**I-T** If $\Gamma \vdash \phi$, then $(\Box)\Gamma \vdash \Box \phi$, with $(\Box)\Gamma = \{\Box \psi | \psi \in \Gamma\}$

The identity principles are somewhat deviant. There are two elimination rules for identity rather than one.[4]

=**E** If $\Gamma_1 \vdash t_1 = t_2$ and if $\Gamma_2 \vdash \phi$ with no occurrences of $\Box$ in ϕ, then $\Gamma_1, \Gamma_2 \vdash \phi'$ where ϕ' is obtained from ϕ by replacing zero or more occurrences of t_1 with t_2, provided that no bound variables are replaced, and if t_2 is a variable, then all of its substituted occurrences are free.

□ =**E** If $\Gamma_1 \vdash \Box t_1 = t_2$ and if $\Gamma_2 \vdash \phi$, then $\Gamma_1, \Gamma_2 \vdash \phi'$ where ϕ' is obtained from ϕ by replacing zero or more occurrences of t_1 with t_2, provided that no bound variables are replaced, and if t_2 is a variable, then all of its substituted occurrences are free.

The deviancy lies in the fact that =**E** is usually taken be holding of *all* well-formed formulas, not merely of all the box-free well-formed formulas. For the latter □ =**E** is needed. The only I would like to note here is that it is a good thing that =**E** is restricted to non-modal formulas. It is well-known that, if $\forall x \Box x = x$ is a theorem, which it is in $\mathbf{C_T}$, and if one has the unrestricted =**E**-rule, then one can prove that $\forall x (x = y \rightarrow \Box x = y)$. This formula will play a role later on. So

---

[2] See Shapiro (Fall 2007, section 3).
[3] See G. Hughes (1996, p. 214 and p. 216).
[4] For =**E** see Shapiro (Fall 2007, section 3).

the elimination rule for identity is deviant, but the introduction rule for identity on the other hand is non-deviant.

=I $\Gamma \vdash t = t$, where t is any term.

When formulating the rules for descriptions, it will be convenient to use the following abbreviatory definition:

Definition 3. $!\phi(t) =_{df} \phi(t) \land \forall y (\phi(y) \to y = t)$

The introduction and elimination rules for descriptions can then be formulated as follows:

ιI If $\Gamma \vdash \psi(\iota x \phi(x))$, then $\Gamma \vdash \exists x (!\phi(x) \land \psi(x)) \lor (\neg \exists x !\phi(x) \land \psi(c^*))$.

ιE If $\Gamma \vdash \exists x (!\phi(x) \land \psi(x)) \lor (\neg \exists x !\phi(x) \land \psi(c^*))$, then $\Gamma \vdash \psi(\iota x \phi(x))$.

These rules are the natural translation of a contextual definition given by Kremer (1997, p. 631) as an improvement on the definition given by Carnap himself and an earlier improvement given by Marti (1994). I will not go into the whys. There is a very important restriction on the last contextual definition: descriptions should always be assigned the smallest possible scope. E.g., if ψ is of the form $\Box \varphi$ and if φ is a atomic well-formed formula, then the definiens of $\Box \varphi (\iota x \phi(x))$ is the following:

$$\Box (\exists x (!\phi(x) \land \varphi(x)) \lor (\neg \exists x !\phi(x) \land \varphi(c^*)))$$

This concludes the description of the theory.

Both **C** and **C$_T$** are sound under the Kremer interpretation, as the reader can verify for him or herself. If I had added a reflexive accessibility relation to the models, one would get a class of models which validate **C$_T$** but not **C**. I have not done so, however, since the more encompassing models are, the stronger the proof of the non-theoremhood of a certain formula.

5.1.3 Self-predication principles

It is intuitively true that, if there is one president of France, then the president of France is a president (of France). Let us call this description principle the self-predication principle. So it is a good thing that the following is a theorem of **C$_T$**:

Theorem 1. $\vdash_{\mathbf{C_T}} \exists x !\phi(x) \to \phi(\iota x \phi(x))$ *for all box-free* ϕ

Proof. Assume that $\exists x !\phi(x)$. Suppose that $!\phi(t)$ for some term t, i.e. suppose that $\phi(t) \land \forall y (\phi(y) \to y = t)$. By =I and ∧I one can infer from the previous that $\phi(t) \land \forall y (\phi(y) \to y = t) \land t = t$. Next, by ∃I one may infer that $\exists x (\phi(x) \land \forall y (\phi(y) \to y = x) \land x = t)$. Application of ∨I delivers one then the definiens of $t = \iota x \phi(x)$ and, therefore, also the definiendum. If ϕ is box-free, one may use =E to infer from

$t = \iota x \phi(x)$ and $\phi(t)$ that $\phi(\iota x \phi(x))$. Finally, it follows by $\exists \mathbf{E}$ from $\exists x! \phi(x)$ that $\phi(\iota x \phi(x))$. □

The above self-predication principle is restricted to non-modal well-formed formulas. One might wonder if it is possible to generalize the self-predication principle to all well-formed formulas, be they non-modal or modal. The answer is that it is not possible.

Theorem 2. *There is a modal well-formed formula ϕ and a model of* **C** *in which $\exists x! \phi(x)$ is true but $\phi(\iota x \phi(x))$ is not true.*

Proof. Let us take $\Box F(x)$ as an example of a modal well-formed formula and consider the following model: $D = \{d_1, d_2, d^*\}$; $W = \{@, w_1\}$; R is a total two-place relation on W; $I(F, @) = \{d_1\}$; $I(F, w_1) = \{d_1, d_2\}$. Next, consider the following individual concept: $i_1 : w \mapsto d_1$.

Clearly, $i_1(w') \in I(F, w')$ for all $w' \in W$. It follows that

$V_{\mathcal{M}}(\Box F(x), @, a[i_1/x]) = T$.

Next thing to verify is that for all i', if $V_{\mathcal{M}}(\Box F(y), @, a[i'/y]) = T$, then $i'(@) = i_1(@) = d_1$. There are three cases to be considered. First, if $i'(@) = d_1$, then the consequent is true and, therefore, the conditional is true. Second, if $i'(@) = d_2$, then $V_{\mathcal{M}}(\Box F(y), @, a[i'/y]) = F$, since it is not the case that $d_2 \in I(F, @)$ and since R is a total relation on W. Third, if $i'(@) = d^*$, then $V_{\mathcal{M}}(\Box F(y), @, a[i'/y]) = F$, for the same reason as in the previous case. In conclusion, $V_{\mathcal{M}}(\exists x! \Box F(x), @, a) = T$.

This leaves us with checking that $V_{\mathcal{M}}(\Box F(\iota x \Box F(x)), @, a) = F$. The latter is false if and only if $V_{\mathcal{M}}(\iota x \Box F(x), @, a) \in I(F, @)$, and $V_{\mathcal{M}}(\iota x \Box F(x), w_1, a) \in I(F, w_1)$. The first condition is fulfilled, since $d_1 \in \{d_1\}$. The latter condition is satisfied if and only if either for some i, $V_{\mathcal{M}}(\Box F(x), w, a[i/x]) = T$, and for every i, if $V_{\mathcal{M}}(\Box F(x), w_1, a[i/x]) = T$, then $i(w_1) = d_k$ with $k \in \{1, 2\}$, and $d_k \in I(F, w_1)$, or $d^* \in I(F, w_1)$. Let us consider the disjuncts in order of presentation. Next to the earlier introduced i_1 there are only three other individual concepts: $i_2 =_{df} i_2(@) = d_1$; $i_2(w_1) = d_2$; $i_3 =_{df} i_3(@) = d_2$; $i_3(w_1) = d_1$; $i_4 =_{df} w \mapsto d_2$. The last two individual concepts will not do, since $V_{\mathcal{M}}(\Box F(x), w_1, a[i_l/x]) = F$ with $l \in \{3, 4\}$, because it is not the case that $d_2 \in I(F, @)$. The first two individual concepts can pass this barrier however. But the fact that they denote two different individuals in w_1 barrs them from taking the last hurdle. So the first disjunct can be dismissed. This leaves us with the second disjunct. Since it is not the case that $d^* \in I(F, w_1)$, one may dismiss the second disjunct too. Therefore the second condition is not satisfied and $V_{\mathcal{M}}(\Box F(\iota x \Box F(x)), @, a) = F$ is consequently true. □

So the self-predication principle cannot be generalized to all well-formed formulas while at the same time retaining soundness in $\mathbf{C_T}$-models. But one might ask, what if considers weaker self-predication principles which hold for all well-formed formulas nonetheless? One possibility is that the antecedent of the self-predication principle ought not to be merely true but also necessarily true. Unfortunately, this is no good either.

Theorem 3. *There is a modal well-formed formula ϕ and there is a $\mathbf{C}$-model in which $\Box\exists x!\phi(x)$ is true but $\phi(\iota x\phi(x))$ is not true.*

Proof. Take $F(x) \wedge \neg\Box F(x)$ as an example of a modal well-formed formula and consider the following model: $D = \{d_1, d_2, d^*\}$; R is a total reflexive two-place relation on D; $W = \{@, w_1\}$; $I(F, @) = \{d_1\}$; $I(F, w_2) = \{d_2\}$. The model makes it true that

$$V_{\mathcal{M}}(\Box\exists x!(F(x) \wedge \neg\Box F(x)), @, a).$$

Indeed, one has both $V_{\mathcal{M}}(\exists x!(F(x) \wedge \neg\Box F(x)), @, a) = T$ (take $i_i : w \mapsto d_1$) and $V_{\mathcal{M}}(\exists x!(F(x) \wedge \neg\Box F(x)), w_1, a) = T$ (take $i_i : w \mapsto d_2$). But

$V_{\mathcal{M}}(F(\iota x(F(x) \wedge \neg\Box F(x))) \wedge \neg\Box F(\iota x(F(x) \wedge \neg\Box F(x))), @, a) = F.$

Suppose that the latter is false. Then

$$V_{\mathcal{M}}(\neg\Box F(\iota x(F(x) \wedge \neg\Box F(x))), @, a) = T,$$

which is the case if and only if it is not the case that

$$V_{\mathcal{M}}(\iota x(F(x) \wedge \neg\Box F(x)), w', a) \in I(F, w')$$

for some $w' \in W$. Since there there are two worlds, there are two cases to be considered. First, note that $V_{\mathcal{M}}(\iota x(F(x) \wedge \neg\Box F(x)), @, a) = i_1(@) = d_1$. This is partly due to the fact that $V_{\mathcal{M}}(F(x), @, a[i_1/x]) = T$, which can only be the case if $i_1(@) \in I(F, @)$ or, equivalently, $V_{\mathcal{M}}(\iota x(F(x) \wedge \neg\Box F(x)), @, a) \in I(F, @)$. Second, the case of w_1 is completely analogous. So, contrary to our assumption,

$V_{\mathcal{M}}(F(\iota x(F(x) \wedge \neg\Box F(x))) \wedge \neg\Box F(\iota x(F(x) \wedge \neg\Box F(x))), @, a) = F$

is true. □

Another possibility is to commute the box operator and the existential quantifier in the previous self-predication principle. This is a good move, since the resulting self-predication principle *is* provable in $\mathbf{C_T}$ *and* it holds for all well-formed formulas.

Theorem 4. $\vdash_{\mathbf{C_T}} \exists x\Box!\phi(x) \rightarrow \phi(\iota x\phi(x))$ *for all ϕ.*

Proof. Assume that $\exists x \Box !\phi(x)$. Suppose that $\Box !\phi(t)$ for some term t, i.e. suppose that $\Box (\phi(t) \land \forall y (\phi(y) \to y = t))$. By $=$**I**, $\Box$-**T** and $\land$**I** one can infer from the previous that $\Box (\phi(t) \land \forall y (\phi(y) \to y = t)) \land \Box t = t$. It is a theorem of $\mathbf{C_T}$ that $(\Box \psi \land \Box \varphi) \to \Box (\psi \land \varphi)$. Consequently, one may derive that $\Box (\phi(t) \land \forall y (\phi(y) \to y = t) \land t = t)$. Since it is a theorem of $\mathbf{C_T}$ that $\Box \psi(t) \to \Box \exists x \psi(x)$, one may infer that $\Box \exists x (\phi(x) \land \forall y (\phi(y) \to y = x) \land x = t)$. Application of $\lor$**I** delivers one then the definiens of $\Box t = \iota x \phi(x)$ and, therefore, also the definiendum. One may use $\Box =$**E** to infer from $\Box t = \iota x \phi(x)$ and $\phi(t)$ that $\phi(\iota x \phi(x))$. Finally, it follows by $\exists$**E** from $\exists x \Box !\phi(x)$ that $\phi(\iota x \phi(x))$. □

Summing up, in this section I have discussed four description, all of which fall for obvious reasons in the category of what I have dubbed "self-predication" principles. The principles were in order of presentation:

(1) $\exists x !\phi(x) \to \phi(\iota x \phi(x))$ for all non-modal ϕ
(2) $\exists x !\phi(x) \to \phi(\iota x \phi(x))$ for all ϕ
(3) $\Box \exists x !\phi(x) \to \phi(\iota x \phi(x))$ for all ϕ
(4) $\exists x \Box !\phi(x) \to \phi(\iota x \phi(x))$ for all ϕ

The first and last are provable in $\mathbf{C_T}$, whereas the second and third are not. The above description principles will play a big role in the discussion to come.

In this section I have covered Carnapian modal logic. In the next section, I will take a dive into the subject of Carnapian modal arithmetic.

5.2 Carnapian Modal arithmetic

The subject of this section is the combination of the earlier introduced $\mathbf{C_T}$ on the one hand and arithmetic on the other hand. I will first look at the extension of $\mathbf{C_T}$ with the principles of elementary arithmetic, $\mathbf{Q}$. Then I will turn to a further extension, namely the theory which results by adding the principles of induction. Call it $\mathbf{C_T PA}$. The main part of this section is devoted to a proof of the statement that there is a collapse of modality into truth in $\mathbf{C_T PA}$. I will analyze the result and provide a remedy.

The language of arithmetic, $\mathcal{L}^*$, consists of the individual constant **0**, the one-place function **s**, the two-place functions $+$, $\cdot$ and the two-place relation $<$. The standard interpretation of the language assigns the number zero to **0**, the successor function to **s**, the addition function to $+$, the multiplication function to $\cdot$, and the less-than relation to $<$.

The theory of elementary arithmetic, **Q**, consists of the axioms which describe the deductive behaviour of the forementioned individual, function and relation terms.

If one conjoins Carnapian logic with elementary arithmetic one gets Carnapian modal arithmetic, $\mathbf{C_TQ}$. The language of $\mathbf{C_TQ}$ contains $\mathcal{L}^* \cup \{\Box, \iota\}$. A standard model of $\mathcal{L}^* \cup \{\Box, \iota\}$ is a quintuple $\langle W, @, D, d^*, I \rangle$ as before, except for the following: $D = \mathbb{N}$ (with $\mathbb{N}$ the set of natural numbers), $d^* = n^*$ for some $n^* \in \mathbb{N}$, $I(\mathbf{0}) = 0$ (with 0 the number zero), $I(\mathbf{s}) = s$ (with s the successor function), $I(+) = +$ (with $+$ the addition function), $I(\times) = \times$ (with $\times$ the multiplication function) and with $I(<) = <$ (with $<$ the smaller than relation).

One could extend $\mathbf{C_TQ}$ by adding one of the principles of induction. The following are respectively the weak and the strong principle of induction.[5]

(5a) $\qquad (\phi(\mathbf{0}) \land \forall x (\phi(x) \to \phi(\mathbf{s}(x)))) \to \forall x \phi(x)$

(5b) $\qquad \forall x (\forall y (y < x \to \phi(y)) \to \phi(x)) \to \forall x \phi(x)$

When $\phi \in \mathcal{L}^*$ and when **Q** is the background theory, then the so-called "weak" principle of induction is deductively stronger than the so-called "strong" principle of deduction, since the weak principle of induction implies the strong principle of induction and since the strong principle of induction implies the weak principle of induction only if one assumes $\forall x (x = \mathbf{0} \lor \exists y (x = \mathbf{s}y))$, which is by the way also a consequence of the principle of weak induction. There are multiple textbook proofs of these deductive relations.[6] The reason for calling the deductively weaker principle the "strong" principle lies in the fact that the antecedent of the principle is stronger than is the antecedent of the deductively stronger principle. This can easily be seen from the fact that, given $\forall x (x = \mathbf{0} \lor \exists y (x = \mathbf{s}y))$, the antecedent of (5b) is equivalent to:

$$\phi(\mathbf{0}) \land \forall x (\forall y (y < \mathbf{s}(x) \to \phi(y)) \to \phi(\mathbf{s}(x)))$$

The second conjunct says in effect that one can deduce $\phi(\mathbf{s}(x))$ if one has $\phi(\mathbf{0})$, $\phi(\mathbf{s0})$, ..., $\phi(x)$. According to the second conjunct of the antecedent of (5a) it suffices to have $\phi(x)$. When $\phi \in \mathcal{L}^* \cup \{\Box\}$ and when $\mathbf{C_TQ}$ is the background theory, one must take care not to use the classical substitution principle in the proof, but it can be done.

I should note that the principle of strong induction (5b) is provably equivalent to the so-called "least number principle":

(6) $\qquad \exists x \phi(x) \to \exists x (\phi(x) \land \forall y (y < x \to \neg \phi(x)))$

---

[5]The displayed formulas should be prefixed by as many universal quantifiers as there are free variables in ϕ, but for sake of brevity, I will suppress them.

[6]See e.g. Boolos et al. (2003, p. 212-214) for the relevant proofs.

This principle will play an important in the next section.

It is usual to refer to $\mathbf{Q} \cup \{(5a)\}$ as "Peano Arithmetic" (**PA**) and therefore it is appropriate to call $\mathbf{C_T Q} \cup \{(5a)\}$ "Carnapian Peano Arithmetic" (**CPA**). I will now prove a lemma which will allow me to deduce that $\mathbf{C_T PA}$ collapses into **PA**.

Lemma 1. $\vdash_{\mathbf{C_T PA}} \forall x \, (\Box x = \mathbf{0} \vee \exists y \Box \, (x = \mathbf{s}(y)))$

Proof. First, one needs to prove that:

(7) $\qquad\qquad\qquad \Box \mathbf{0} = \mathbf{0} \vee \exists y \Box \, (\mathbf{s}(y) = \mathbf{0})$

But this is easy, since it follows from $=$**I** and $\Box$-**T**.

Second, one needs to establish that:

(8)
$\forall x \, ((\Box x = \mathbf{0} \vee \exists y \Box \, (\mathbf{s}(y) = x)) \rightarrow (\Box \mathbf{s}(x) = \mathbf{0} \vee \exists y \Box \, (\mathbf{s}(y) = \mathbf{s}(x))))$

Assume that:
$$\Box t = \mathbf{0} \vee \exists y \Box \, (\mathbf{s}(y) = t)$$
We have to consider two cases. First, consider the case in which:
$$\Box t = \mathbf{0}$$
It is an instance of $=$**E** that $\forall x \forall y \, (x = y \rightarrow \mathbf{s}(x) = \mathbf{s}(y))$ and, consequently, it is by successive application of $\forall$**E** and $\Box$-**T** it is also a theorem that $\Box t = \mathbf{0} \rightarrow \Box \mathbf{s}(t) = \mathbf{s}(\mathbf{0})$. It therefore follows from $\Box t = \mathbf{0}$ that $\Box \mathbf{s}(t) = \mathbf{s}(\mathbf{0})$. Existential generalization allows one then to conclude that $\exists y \, (\Box \mathbf{s}(t) = \mathbf{s}(y))$. Second, consider the case in which:
$$\exists y \Box \, (\mathbf{s}(y) = t)$$
Suppose that there is some term t' such that $\Box \, (\mathbf{s}(t') = t)$. From this one can derive by reasoning analogous to the above reasoning that $\Box \mathbf{s}(\mathbf{s}(t')) = \mathbf{s}(t)$. One can apply existential generalization once more, the result being $\exists y \Box \, (\mathbf{s}(y) = \mathbf{s}(t))$. There is no mentioning of t' anymore, so the latter existentially quantified formula follows from the former existentially quantified formula. So both cases lead one to conclude that $\exists y \Box \, (\mathbf{s}(y) = \mathbf{s}(t))$. Hence, $\Box \mathbf{s}(t) = \mathbf{0} \vee \exists y \Box \, (\mathbf{s}(y) = \mathbf{s}(t))$. This conclusion was reached for some arbitrary t. So one may apply universal generalization. This concludes the proof of (8).

The lemma follows then by modus ponens from (5a) and the conjunction of (7) and (8). $\qquad\square$

Corollary 1. $\vdash_{\mathbf{C_T PA}} \forall x \forall y \, (x = y \rightarrow \Box x = y)$

Proof. First, one needs to prove the induction base:

(9) $\qquad\qquad\qquad \forall y \, (\mathbf{0} = y \rightarrow \Box \mathbf{0} = y)$

So assume that $\mathbf{0} = t$ for some term t. Since it is an axiom of $\mathbf{Q}$ that $\neg \exists y\, (\mathbf{s}(y) = \mathbf{0})$ and since it is by $=\mathbf{E}$ a consequence of the axiom and $\mathbf{0} = t$ that $\neg \exists y\, (\mathbf{s}(y) = t)$, it follows by the contraposition of $\Box \mathbf{E}$ that $\neg \exists y \Box\, (\mathbf{s}(y) = t)$. On the basis of lemma 1 one may conclude that $\Box t = \mathbf{0}$. It is a tautological consequence that $\mathbf{0} = t \to \Box t = \mathbf{0}$. Finally, universal generalization delivers us (9).

Second, one needs to prove the induction step:

(10) $\quad \forall x\, (\forall y\, (x = y \to \Box x = y) \to \forall y\, (\mathbf{s}(x) = y \to \Box \mathbf{s}(x) = y))$

Assume that $\forall y\, (t = y \to \Box t = y) \wedge \mathbf{s}(t) = t'$, for some terms t and t'. From the conjunct $\mathbf{s}(t) = t'$ and from the $\mathbf{Q}$-axiom $\neg \exists y\, (\mathbf{s}(y) = \mathbf{0})$, it follows by $=\mathbf{E}$ that $t' \neq \mathbf{0}$. Therefore it holds that $\neg \Box t' = \mathbf{0}$, from which by lemma 1 one can derive that $\exists y \Box\, (\mathbf{s}(y) = t')$. Now suppose that $\Box\, (\mathbf{s}(t'') = t')$, for some term t''. It is a consequence of the second conjunct, $\Box \mathbf{E}$ and $\mathbf{s}(t) = t'$ that $\mathbf{s}(t) = \mathbf{s}(t'')$. The $\mathbf{Q}$-axiom $\forall x \forall y\, (\mathbf{s}(x) = \mathbf{s}(y) \to x = y)$ guarantees then that $t = t''$. From here it follows by $\forall y\, (t = y \to \Box t = y)$ that $\Box t = t'''$. This allows one to use ($\Box =\mathbf{E}$) in order to derive $\Box \mathbf{s}(t) = t'$. Finally, (10) follows from $\to \mathbf{I}$, exportation and $\forall \mathbf{I}$.

The corollary follows from (9) and (10) by (5a). $\square$

Corollary 1 has tremendous importance, since it effectively reinstates the classical substitution principle in power. A very disturbing consequence of this is the collapse of **CPA** into **PA**.

Theorem 5 (Føllesdal). $\forall x \forall y\, (x = y \to \Box x = y) \vdash_{\mathbf{C_T}} (\phi \wedge \Box\, (z \neq c^*)) \to \Box \phi$

Proof. Føllesdal (2004, p. 70) $\square$

Corollary 2. $\vdash_{\mathbf{C_T PA}} \phi \to \Box \phi$

Proof. Take $\mathbf{s}(c^*)$ for z. It is a theorem of $\mathbf{C_T Q}$ that $\forall x \Box\, (x \neq \mathbf{s}(x))$ $\square$

Is this result relevant? Most philosophers are convinced of the necessity of arithmetical truths, so they will prima facie not be bothered by the above result. Recall however that the language *contained* $\mathcal{L}^* \cup \{\Box, \iota\}$ but is *not identical* to it. To be more precise, the language also contains predicates and relations other than $<$. Among these predicates and relations there might be predicates contingently satisfied by numbers. But more importantly, one should not automatically assume that the box operator should be read as a necessity operator. For instance, in the next section we will look at a system which contains **S4**. The **S4**-laws can be seen as epistemic principles. Since **S4** contains **T**, the collapse result holds also for $\mathbf{C_{S4}PA}$. And it is far more controversial to claim that it is all right for epistemic modalities to collapse into truth.

So Carnapian Peano Arithmetic is in a bad shape. Now I turn to a diagnosis. First, I will prove that the standard weak principle of induction is invalid. Then I will propose an alternative weak principle of induction. This alternative principle will be proved to be valid. Next, I will show that there is no collapse of modality into truth if one extends $\mathbf{C_T Q}$ with the alternative principle of induction. Finally, as a bonus I will show that one can retain the standard least number principle.

As stated above, the standard weak principle of induction is invalid.

Theorem 6. *There is a standard model of $\mathbf{CQ}$ in which (5a) is not true.*

Proof. Consider any standard model of $\mathbf{CQ}$ with W containing at least two possible worlds and with R a total relation on W. Let ϕ be the following well-formed formula:

$$\Box x = \mathbf{0} \vee \exists y \Box x = \mathbf{s}(y)$$

One can then show that:

1. $V_{\mathcal{M}}(\phi(\mathbf{0}) \wedge \forall x (\phi(x) \to \phi(\mathbf{s}(x))), a) = T$;
2. $V_{\mathcal{M}}(\forall x \phi(x), a) = F$.

The first statement is true if only if both conjuncts are true.

Consider the first conjunct. $V_{\mathcal{M}}(\Box \mathbf{0} = \mathbf{0} \vee \exists y \Box \mathbf{0} = \mathbf{s}(y), a) = T$. It suffices that one of the disjuncts is true. Now $V_{\mathcal{M}}(\Box \mathbf{0} = \mathbf{0}, a) = T$ if and only if $V_{\mathcal{M}}(\mathbf{0} = \mathbf{0}, w, a) = T$ in all words $w \in W$, which at its turn is true if and only if $I(\mathbf{0}) = I(\mathbf{0})$. The latter holds in any model, so one of the disjuncts of the first conjunct is true and, ergo, the first conjunct is true.

Consider the second conjunct.

$V_{\mathcal{M}}(\forall x ((\Box x = \mathbf{0} \vee \exists y \Box x = \mathbf{s}(y))) \to (\Box \mathbf{s}(x) = \mathbf{0} \vee \exists y \Box \mathbf{s}(x) = \mathbf{s}(y)), a) = T$

The above is true if and only if for all i, if $i(w) = 0$ for all $w \in W$ or there is a i' such that $i(w) = V(\mathbf{s}(y), w, a[i'/y])$ for all $w \in W$, then $V_{\mathcal{M}}(\mathbf{s}(x), w, a[i/x]) = 0$ for all $w \in W$ or there is a i' such that $V_{\mathcal{M}}(\mathbf{s}(x), w, a[i/x]) = V(\mathbf{s}(y), w, a[i'/y])$ for all $w \in W$. Assume that the antecedent holds. Furthermore, suppose that the first disjunct holds. Then $V_{\mathcal{M}}(\mathbf{s}(x), w, a[i/x]) = 1$ for all $w \in W$. Consequently, there is a i' such that $V_{\mathcal{M}}(\mathbf{s}(x), w, a[i/x]) = V(\mathbf{s}(y), w, a[i'/y])$ for all $w \in W$. Indeed, take $i' : w \mapsto 0$. If one disjunct of the consequent is true, then the consequent itself is also true. Next, suppose that the second disjunct holds. Then there is a i' such that $i(w) = V(\mathbf{s}(y), w, a[i'/y])$

for all $w \in W$. Hence there is a i' such that $V_\mathcal{M}(\mathbf{s}(x), w, a[i/x]) = V(\mathbf{s}(\mathbf{s}(y)), w, a[i'/y])$ for all $w \in W$. Now if $V_\mathcal{M}(\mathbf{s}(y), w, a[i'/y]) = n$, let $i'' : w \mapsto n$. Then there is a i'' such that $V_\mathcal{M}(\mathbf{s}(x), w, a[i/x]) = V(\mathbf{s}(y), w, a[i'/y])$ for all $w \in W$. Again, if one disjunct of the consequent is true, then the consequent itself is also true. Moreover, if the consequent follows from either of the disjuncts of the antecedent, then it follows from the disjunction too. Thus the second conjunct is also true.

The second statement is true if and only if there is an i such that $i(w') \neq 0$ for some world $w' \in W$ and for all i' there is some world w'' such that $i(w'') \neq V(\mathbf{s}(y), w'', a[i'/y])$. Let $i(w') = 1$ and $i(w'') = 0$. Clearly, $i(w') = 1 \neq 0$. Moreover, $i(w'') = 0 \neq V(\mathbf{s}(y), w'', a[i'/y])$, whatever i' may assign to y in w''.

This concludes the proof. □

The interesting thing about the above proof is not only that it shows that the standard weak principle of induction is invalid, but also that that induction principle fails precisely in the case in which it was used in the proof of theorem 1, which was essential in the larger proof of the collapse result.

If the standard weak principle of induction is invalid, then one should wonder if there is a valid induction principle which can replace it. Recall that (5a) was supposed to hold for all $\phi \in \mathcal{L}$. Therefore the substitution principle ($\Box =\mathbf{E}$) is relevant. This teaches us that the antecedent of (5a) is equivalent to the following:

(11) $\quad \forall x (\Box x = \mathbf{0} \to \phi(x)) \land \forall x (\forall y (\Box y = x \to \phi(y))$
$$\to \forall y (\Box y = \mathbf{s}(x) \to \phi(y)))$$

A similar point can be made about the antecedent of (5b), which is equivalent to:

(12) $\quad \forall x (\forall y (y < x \to \phi(y)) \to \forall y (\Box y = x \to \phi(y)))$

Now the idea is to change the antecedent of the weak induction principle as follows:

(13) $\quad \forall x (x = \mathbf{0} \to \phi(x)) \land \forall x (\forall y (y = x \to \phi(y))$
$$\to \forall y (y = \mathbf{s}x \to \phi(y)))$$

In a similar vein the antecedent of (5b) could then be rewritten as follows.

(14) $\quad \forall x \left(\forall y \left(y < x \to \phi \left(y \right) \right) \to \forall y \left(y = x \to \phi \left(y \right) \right) \right)$

The latter is provably equivalent to:

(15) $\quad \exists x \left(\exists y \left(x = y \wedge \phi \left(y \right) \right) \wedge \forall y \left(y < x \to \neg \phi \left(y \right) \right) \right)$

Whether this is a good idea depends, first, on whether (13) (call it **W-INDa**) is a valid principle, second, whether one manages to block the proof of the collapse result, and, third, whether modalities do not collapse in $\mathbf{CQ} \cup \{\mathbf{W - INDa}\}$ (call this theory **CMA**). I can be short about the second requirement. The proof of corollary 2 is blocked, since one cannot prove that $\forall x \left(x = \mathbf{0} \to \Box x = \mathbf{0} \right)$, as is needed to prove theorem 1. The other requirements are also met, as is proved below.

Theorem 7. *W-INDa is valid.*

Proof. The proof is by induction on the complexity of ϕ. I will restrict myself to the case in which $\phi = \Box \psi$. One can prove that the theorem holds in this case by reductio ad absurdum. So assume that: $V_{\mathcal{M}} \left(\left(13 \right), @a \right) = T$, and $V_{\mathcal{M}} \left(\forall x \phi \left(x \right), @, a \right) = F$. The second statement is true if and only if $V_{\mathcal{M}} \left(\psi \left(x \right), w', a[i'/x] \right) = F$ for some i' and some $w' \in W$. By definition $V_{\mathcal{M}} \left(x, @, a[i'/x] \right) \in \mathbb{N}$. Suppose that $V_{\mathcal{M}} \left(x, @, a[i'/x] \right) = n$ for some $n \in \mathbb{N}$. Moreover, the first statement makes it true that for all i'', if $V_{\mathcal{M}} \left(x, @, a[i''/x] \right) = n$, then $V \left(\phi \left(x \right), w'', a[i''/x] \right)$ for all $w'' \in W$. So it is also true that if $V_{\mathcal{M}} \left(x, @, a[i'/x] \right) = n$, then $V \left(\phi \left(x \right), w', a[i'/x] \right) = T$. The consequent is false. Hence, $i' \left(@ \right) \neq n$, contrary to the assumption. But n was arbitrary. Consequently, it is not the case that $V_{\mathcal{M}} \left(x, @, a[i'/x] \right) \in \mathbb{N}$. Contradiction. □

Theorem 8. *There is a standard model of **CQ** in which some well-formed ϕ is true but $\Box \phi$ is not.*

Proof. Consider the following model: $D = \mathbb{N}$; $W = \{@, w\}$; R is a total relation on W; $I \left(P, @ \right) = \{2\}$; $I \left(P, @ \right) = \{3\}$; the standard assignments to the arithmetical vocabulary (see above). The following two claims hold then: $V_{\mathcal{M}} \left(P \left(\mathbf{s} \left(\mathbf{s} \left(\mathbf{0} \right) \right) \right), @, a \right) = T$ and, hence, $V_{\mathcal{M}} \left(P \left(\mathbf{s} \left(\mathbf{s} \left(\mathbf{0} \right) \right) \right) \right) = T$; $V_{\mathcal{M}} \left(P \left(\mathbf{s} \left(\mathbf{s} \left(\mathbf{0} \right) \right) \right), w, a \right) = F$ and, therefore, $V_{\mathcal{M}} \left(\Box P \left(\mathbf{s} \left(\mathbf{s} \left(\mathbf{0} \right) \right) \right), @, a \right) = F$, and, hence, $V_{\mathcal{M}} \left(\Box P \left(\mathbf{s} \left(\mathbf{s} \left(\mathbf{0} \right) \right) \right) \right) = F$. □

It was argued that it is a good move to replace the antecedent of the standard weak principle of induction by (13). One could wonder at this point whether one should also replace the antecedent of the standard strong principle of induction by (14) or, equivalently, replace the consequent of the standard least number principle by (15). The answer is negative. Once one has **W** − **INDa**, one also has the standard strong principle of induction.

Theorem 9. **W** − **INDa** $\vdash_{\mathbf{C_T}}$ (6)

Proof. Take the proof of (5a) ⊢ (6) in Boolos et al. (2003, p. 213-214). There it is assumed that $\neg \exists x \, (\phi(x) \wedge \forall y \, (y < x \to \neg \phi(y)))$. Then one can prove that $\forall x \neg \exists y \, (y < x \wedge \phi(y))$. The proof is by induction. At this point one should replace (5a) with (13) → $\forall x \phi(x)$. It is easy to check that $\forall x \, (x = \mathbf{0} \to \neg \exists y \, (y < x \wedge \phi(y)))$ is true for the same reason that $\neg \exists y \, (y < \mathbf{0} \wedge \phi(y))$ is true. Next, one needs to show that

$$\forall x (\forall z (z = x \to \neg \exists y (y < z \wedge \phi(y)))$$
$$\to \forall z (z = \mathbf{s}(x) \to \neg \exists y (y < z \wedge \phi(y))))$$

The proof is by reductio ad absurdum. So suppose that for some term t, $\forall z \, (z = t \to \neg \exists y \, (y < z \wedge \phi(y)))$, for some term t', $t' = \mathbf{s}(t)$, and for some term t'', $t'' < t'$ and $\phi(t'')$. Then $t'' < \mathbf{s}(t)$. Hence, by an axiom of arithmetic, $t'' = t$ or $t'' < t$. Suppose the latter. It follows by ∃**I** that $\exists y \, (y < t \wedge \phi(y))$. The first of the reductio assumptions and =**E** imply that $\neg \exists y \, (y < t \wedge \phi(y))$. So one must drop that option. Suppose then that $t'' = t \wedge \phi(t'')$. It follows from the first conjunct that $\neg \exists y \, (y < t'' \wedge \phi(y))$. One may then infer on the basis of ∧**I** and ∃**I** that $\exists x \, (\phi(x) \wedge \forall y \, (y < x \to \neg \phi(y)))$, contradicting the very first assumption of the proof. The remainder of the proof is exactly as in Boolos et al. (2003, p. 214). □

This concludes the discussion of Carnapian modal arithmetic. Next on the agenda is Carnapian epistemic arithmetic.

5.3 Carnapian Epistemic Logic and Arithmetic

Horsten (2005) described and used Carnapian Epistemic Arithmetic (henceforth **CEA**) in an interesting and fruitful manner. I will very briefly write about the language of **CEA**, its informal and informal interpretation, the theory and its consistency.

In his paper Horsten starts with second-order languages, whereas in this paper I started with first-order languages. In order not to complicate things, I will stick to the first-order fragment of his theory. Moreover, in this section I will ignore descriptions. The informal interpretation of the box operator is as follows:

> The operator □ will be interpreted as "It can be established in the actual world by person K that", "It is verifiable in the actual world by person K that", or "It can be shown in the actual world by person

K that". Here the person K, our nondescript epistemic agent, will be kept fixed throughout. Horsten (2005, p. 233-234)

About the formal interpretation he says the following:

> A model $\mathcal{M}$ for a Carnapian language $\mathcal{L}_C$ is determined by a universe of objects $\mathcal{D}$, a collection of presentations (of objects, sets, relations) taken from a language $\mathcal{L}$, a collection of sentences S of this language $\mathcal{L}$, and assignments to expressions of $\mathcal{L}_C$. The elements of S make up the extension of $\Box$ in $\mathcal{M}$: the elements of S are the sentences the truth of which our epistemic agent K is able to establish. Truth in a model, validity, consequence are then defined on the basis of such a notion of models for Carnapian languages. Horsten (2005, p. 234)

Horsten freely admits that there is more formal work to be done here. But the basic idea is more or less clear. If $\exists x \Box F(x)$ is true, then there is a presentation p_o of an object o such that $F(p_0)$ is in S. A presentation p_o should be presumably be thought of as a closed term of some sort.

The common feature of the formal interpretation intended by Horsten and the Carnap-Kremer interpretation consists in what Kripke dubbed "Carnapian double think". In the Carnap-Kremer interpretation variables range over individual concepts, i.e. functions from the domain to possible worlds. But if a formula does not contain box operators, then only the values of the individual concepts at a given world, viz. the objects, count. In the Horsten interpretation variables range over presentations of objects when they are in the scope of a box operator and they range over the objects themselves when they are embedded in non-epistemic contexts.

Carnapian epistemic logic is just like $\mathbf{C_T}$, except that $\Box$-$\mathbf{T}$ is replaced by:

$\Box$**I-S4**   If $(\Box)\Gamma \vdash \phi$, then $(\Box)\Gamma \vdash \Box\phi$.

Call the theory which is exactly like $\mathbf{C_T}$, except that $\Box\mathbf{I}$-$\mathbf{T}$ is replaced by $\Box\mathbf{I}$-$\mathbf{S4}$, $\mathbf{C_{S4}}$. $\mathbf{C_{S4}}$ encompasses $\mathbf{C_T}$. Horsten proved the consistency of $\mathbf{C_{S4}}$ by making use of the eraser translation. Of course, the Carnapian models used in the previous sections of this paper will do just fine for a soundness proof and thus for a consistency proof. The only thing which needs to be taken care for is that the relation R should not merely be a reflexive two-place relation but also a transitive reflexive two-place relation. Obviously, since there is not a full-detailed formal interpretation of the lines sketched by Horsten, there cannot be a soudness nor a completeness proof with the models intended by him.

As for informal soundness, there are arguments to be found in the literature that the sentential part of $\mathbf{C_{S4}}$ (call it $\mathbf{S4}$) it is indeed the correct logic for something like demonstrability.[7] It should be noted that it is desirable to restrict =**E** to non-modal formulas, so as to avoid the provability of $\forall x \forall y\, (x = y \rightarrow \Box x = y)$, since the latter is informally incorrect given the intended reading and given its instantiability with description terms.

The combination of $\mathbf{C_{S4}}$ with **PA** is called $\mathbf{C_{S4}PA}$. One might ask oneself the question whether the standard weak principle of induction is valid in the Horsten interpretation. This is a pressing question, since the reasoning developed in section 5.2 can be repeated here to demonstrate that the standard weak principle of arithmetic leads to a collapse of the notion of provability or verifiability into truth. Interestingly, Horsten makes the following comment about the relevant principle of induction:

> It should be noted that the full second-order principle of mathematical induction is not intuitively valid in the Carnapian setting. The antecedent of the induction axiom is satisfied by a property Θ if Θ holds of the numerals 0, S0, SS0, ...But for the consequent to be valid Θ must hold not only for these standard numerals, but for *all* presentations of natural numbers. In response to this difficulty, one may want to restrict universal quantifier in the consequent of the induction axiom to the *standard Peano numerals*. (Horsten, 2005, p. 256)

This is a problem which is analogous to the one we encountered before: the antecedent of the induction principle says that $\phi(x)$ holds of all the natural numbers, but the consequent says that $\phi(x)$ holds of all the individual concepts. Horsten could have opted for a solution analogous to the one given in the previous section. Indeed, under his interpretation (13) says that ϕ is true of all number denoting terms, which are of course all the terms, not only the standard numerals or the terms which provably codenote with the standard numerals. But instead he opted for a different solution. Rather than making the range of the x in the $\phi(x)$ of the antecedent of the induction principle less restrictive, he suggests to restricting the range of the x in the $\phi(x)$ more restrictive. In a first-order setting one could achieve this by replacing the consequent $\forall x \phi(x)$ by $\forall x \exists y\, (x = y \wedge \phi(y))$.[8] Let us call the resulting alternative principle of weak induction **W-INDc**. Note that **W-INDc** also allows for a proof of (6). This is good, since Horsten argues that (6) should be valid under his interpretation.[9] Not only do **W-INDa** and **W-INDc** seem to be equally valid and equally good for proving the least number principle, they also both block the collapse argument expounded in section 5.2. So I lack a reason to prefer

---

[7]See Burgess (1999).
[8]This was pointed out to me in private communication with Horsten.
[9]See Horsten (2008).

W-INDa to W-INDc.

In the next section we will see what happens if one adds self-predication principles to Carnapian Epistemic Arithmetic.

5.4 Descriptions in Carnapian Epistemic Arithmetic

In subsection 5.1.3 I discussed self-predication principles. One might ask oneself if one of the previously discussed self-predication principles are valid under the Horsten interpretation, if there are any. If the descriptive condition is non-epistemic, then what the restricted self-prediction principle (2) says is that, if there is some object such that the descriptive condition ϕ is uniquely satisfied by it, then the descriptive condition is also satisfied by the object denoted by the description term. This seems to be all right. If the descriptive condition is epistemic, then what the unrestricted self-prediction principle (2) says is that, if there is some closed term t such that the descriptive condition ϕ is satisfied by t and such that all terms t' which satisfy the descriptive condition are codenoting with t, then the descriptive condition ϕ is also satisfied by the description term $\iota x \phi$ itself. Of course, t need not have been $\iota x \phi$, so there does not seem to be a necessary connection between the antecedent and the consequent. So perhaps the unrestricted self-predication principle is not valid either in Carnapian Epistemic Arithmetic. But pending a formal Horsten interpretation it is perhaps safer to take a look at some of the consequences of the self-predication principles. If there are some consequences, e.g. collapse results, which show that the principles must be informally unsound, then we have an additional reason to drop them.

One interesting set of consequences from the above point of view can be derived using the following lemma:

Lemma 2.

$$\vdash_{\mathbf{CQ}} \exists x (\phi(x) \wedge \forall y (y < x \rightarrow \neg \phi(y)))$$
$$\rightarrow \exists x! (\phi(x) \wedge \forall y (y < x \rightarrow \neg \phi(y)))$$

Proof. Left as an excercise for the reader. □

The self-predication principle (1) which is restricted to non-modal/non-epistemic well-formed formulas has the following consequence:

Theorem 10. $\vdash_{\mathbf{C_T Q} \cup \{(1),(6)\}} \square \exists x \phi(x) \rightarrow \exists x \square \phi(x)$ *for all non-modal* ϕ

Proof. Assume first that $\exists x \phi(x)$. The least-number principle (6) allows one to infer $\exists x (\phi(x) \wedge \forall y (y < x \rightarrow \neg \phi(y)))$ from $\exists x \phi(x)$. Lemma

2 guarantees then that $\exists x! \left(\phi\left(x\right) \land \forall y \left(y < x \to \neg\phi\left(y\right)\right)\right)$. Let us abbreviate $\phi\left(x\right) \land \forall y \left(y < x \to \neg\phi\left(y\right)\right)$ with $\psi\left(x\right)$. One may use (1) to prove that $\psi\left(\iota x \psi\left(x\right)\right)$. Subsequently, one may put $\land \mathbf{E}$ to work to derive $\phi\left(\iota x \psi\left(x\right)\right)$. By $\Box\mathbf{I}\text{-}\mathbf{T}$ one can derive $\Box\phi\left(\iota x \psi\left(x\right)\right)$ from $\Box\exists x \phi\left(x\right)$. All that leaves to be done then, is to apply $\exists \mathbf{I}$ to the latter, the result being a proof of $\exists \Box \phi\left(x\right)$ from the assumption that $\Box\exists\phi\left(x\right)$. □

Analogous theorems involving the unrestricted self-predication principle (2) and one of the weaker unrestricted self-predication principles, (3), can be proved analogously.

Theorem 11. $\vdash_{\mathbf{C_T Q} \cup \{(2),(6)\}} \Box\exists x\phi\left(x\right) \to \exists x\Box\phi\left(x\right)$ *for all* ϕ

Theorem 12. $\vdash_{\mathbf{C_{s4} Q} \cup \{(3),(6)\}} \Box\exists x\phi\left(x\right) \to \exists x\Box\phi\left(x\right)$ *for all* ϕ

Obviously, no such theorem can be proved with (4) as the sole self-predication principle.

The formula featuring in the above theorems is sometimes called the converse Ghilardi formula. It is not valid under the Kremer interpretation. Shapiro pointed out its invalidity to Marti. He noted, more specifically, that if there is more than one object in the universe, then $\Box\exists x \left(x \neq c \land \Diamond\neg x \neq c\right)$ is true but $\exists x \Box \left(x \neq c \land \Diamond\neg x \neq c\right)$ is not. It is no coincidence that this counterexample has the same form as my counterexample to (3). However, as I stressed above, as long as there is no formal Horsten interpretation, we should look at other means of judging the soundness of the principle involved.

The proofs of the above theorems can be easily adapted to proofs for the Barcan formula:[10]

Theorem 13. $\vdash_{\mathbf{C_T Q} \cup \{(1),(6)\}} \Diamond\exists x\phi\left(x\right) \to \exists x\Diamond\phi\left(x\right)$ *for all non-modal* ϕ

Theorem 14. $\vdash_{\mathbf{C_T Q} \cup \{(2),(6)\}} \Diamond\exists x\phi\left(x\right) \to \exists x\Diamond\phi\left(x\right)$ *for all* ϕ

Theorem 15. $\vdash_{\mathbf{C_{s4} Q} \cup \{(3),(6)\}} \Diamond\exists x\phi\left(x\right) \to \exists x\Diamond\phi\left(x\right)$ *for all* ϕ

This has the prima facie devastating consequence that *de re* verifiability collapses into *de dicto* verifiability, since $\exists x \Box \phi\left(x\right) \to \Diamond\exists x\phi\left(x\right)$ and $\Box\forall x\phi\left(x\right) \to \forall x\Box\phi\left(x\right)$ are theorems too.

Ackerman (1979) gave an argument which is in important respects similar to the the kernel of the proof of theorem 10, and she thought that the argument is invalid. I will expand her argument so as to make the relevancy of it more apparent. Suppose that someone believes that there are perfect numbers, i.e. numbers which are equal to the sum of their proper divisors. Then that someone believes that there is a

---

[10]I would like to thank Horsten for directing my attention to this fact.

least perfect number, which is of course unique, and therefore he or she believes that the least perfect number is the least perfect number. It follows then by existential generalization that there is a number of which he or she believes that it is the least perfect number. But, she added, that conclusion is wrong. It does not need to be the case that he or she believes of the number six, which happens to be the least perfect number, that it is the least perfect number. In her eyes the argument allowed an unacceptable transition from a *de dicto* statement to a *de re* statement. Her preferred solution was to restrict existential generalization to standard numerals. Ackerman's argument is interesting, but perhaps not very persuasive, since belief is not closed under logic, as is witnessed by the notorious inconsistency and incoherence of people's beliefs. Belief is just too liable to all sorts of intrinsic and extrinsic factors: failing memories, limited intelligence, lack of time, inadequate training, political correctness, and so on. In contrast, absolute provability is closed under first-order logic. Thus instead of following Ackerman's lead by sacrifizing the unrestricted principle of existential generalization, one could just as well or even better deny the closure of belief under modus ponens.

But whatever the merits of her argument are, it is under the Horsten interpretation of the variables and quantifiers very questionable to see $\exists x \Box \phi (x)$ as an expression of a *de re* epistemic (or in her case, doxastic) attitude towards numbers. The standard syntactic definition of a *de re* formula stipulates that a formula is *de re* if and only if there is a free variable occurring in the scope of a modal operator. Under this definition $\exists x \Box \phi (x)$ is *de re*. But the definition is correct only given the interpretation of variables as ranging over objects (even) when the variables occur in the scope of a modal operator. In the Horsten interpretation variables ranges not only over objects but also over closed terms denoting those objects, and when the variables occur in the scope of a modal operator the terms are the values assigned to the variables. Thus what $\exists x \Box \phi (x)$ says is that there is some closed, denoting term t such that it is absolutely provable that $\phi (t)$. Moreover, if one scrutinizes the proof of theorem 10, it should be apparent that what is actually proved is that there is a denoting closed *descriptive* term, $\iota x \psi (x)$, such that is absolutely provable that $\phi (\iota x \psi (x))$. It is central to the broadly Carnapian approach to epistemic logic that the coreferentiality of a descriptive term and some other denoting closed term does not in general entail the provability of the coreferentiality statement. To sum up, it is doubtful whether $\exists x \Box \phi (x)$ expresses *de re* absolute provability, since: (i) the value of x is not an object, but a term; and (ii) its value is not merely a term, but a descriptive term, which need not be epistemically transparant.

As for Ackerman's solution to the problem, namely to restrict the quanfifier principles to standard numerals rather than all terms, it should be noted that although it is indeed possible to restrict the quantifier principles to description-free terms, there are alternatives. For instance, one could refuse to manipulate the quantifier principles and adopt (4) as the sole self-predication principle when the well-formed formula involved is epistemic.

Theorem 11 has an interesting consequence:

Corollary 3. $\vdash_{\mathbf{C_T Q} \cup \{(2),(6)\}} \neg \Box \exists x \, (\phi(x) \wedge \neg \Box \phi(x))$

Proof. Suppose that $\Box \exists x \, (\phi(x) \wedge \neg \Box \phi(x))$. By theorem 3 it follows that $\exists x \Box \, (\phi(x) \wedge \neg \Box \phi(x))$. By $\Box$**I-T**, one may conclude that $\Box \, (\psi \wedge \varphi)$ $\vdash \Box \psi$ from $\psi \wedge \varphi \vdash \psi$, and the latter is easily proved from the rule of assumptions and $\wedge$**E**. So we also have $\exists x \, (\Box \phi(x) \wedge \Box \neg \Box \phi(x))$. Applying $\Box$**E** leads straight to the contradictory $\exists x \, (\Box \phi(x) \wedge \neg \Box \phi(x))$. □

Again, similar corollaries can be derived given the other self-predication principles, if the background epistemic logic is strong enough. Corollary 3 has been proven by Horsten (2005, p. 238) with the difference that he did not prove theorem 11 but rather gave a direct proof of the above result. In the same paper he concluded from this that (2) is unsound.

For further discussion of this it is convenient to replace the unitary knowability operator $\Box$ by a complex operator $\Diamond K$, with $\Diamond$ the possibility operator and K the knowledge operator. Let us call the language with the unitary knowability operator $\mathcal{L}_\Box$ and the other language $\mathcal{L}_{\Diamond K}$. The **S4**-logic could then be replaced by a logic in which every occurence of $\Box$ in a **S4**-theorem is replaced by an occurrence of $\Diamond K$, plus the following purely epistemic principles:

FACT $K\phi \to \phi$

DIST $K \, (\phi \wedge \psi) \to (K\phi \wedge K\psi)$

It will be convenient to use the following abbreviatory definitions:

Definition 4. $\phi^*(x) =_{df} \phi(x) \wedge \neg K \phi(x)$

Definition 5. $\phi^{**}(x) =_{df} \phi^*(x) \wedge \neg \Diamond \phi^*(x) \wedge \forall y \, (y < x \to \neg \phi^*(y))$

In this logic the following lemma holds:

Lemma 3. $\Diamond K \forall x \neg \Diamond K \phi^*(x)$

Proof. Suppose for a reductio that $\Diamond K \phi^*(t)$, for some arbitrary t. Use **DIST** to deduce $\Diamond \, (K\phi(t) \wedge K \neg K \phi(x))$. Then use **FACT** to deduce the contradictory $\Diamond\left(K\phi\left(t\right)\wedge\neg K\phi\left(x\right)\right)$. Finally, use universal generalization and the fact that $\Diamond K$ is closed under theoremhood. □

The above lemma can be put to good use in the proof of the following theorem:

Theorem 16. $\vdash_{(2),(6)} \neg\Diamond K\exists x\left(\phi\left(x\right)\wedge\neg K\phi\left(x\right)\right)$

Proof. Assume for a reductio that $\Diamond K\exists x\phi^{*}\left(x\right)$. Use the lemma and the distributivity of $\Diamond K$ over material implication to get

$$\Diamond K\exists x\left(\phi^{*}\left(x\right)\wedge\neg\Diamond K\phi^{*}\left(x\right)\right).$$

Next, use (6) and the same $\Diamond K$-rule to get $\Diamond K\exists x!\phi^{**}\left(x\right)$. Application of (2) yiels $\phi^{**}\left(\iota x\phi^{**}\left(x\right)\right)$, which entails $\Diamond K\phi^{*}\left(\iota x\phi^{**}\left(x\right)\right)$. Reasoning analogous to the reasoning in the proof of the lemma leads then to a contradiction. □

In proof I make use of the distributivity of $\Diamond K$ over material implication. However, it is possible to give a counterexample to that modal-epistemic principle: (16) and (17) could both be true, whereas (18) cannot be.[11]

(16) $\Diamond KK\left(\mathbf{0}=\mathbf{0}\right)$

(17) $\Diamond K\neg K\left(\mathbf{0}=\mathbf{0}\right)$

(18) $\Diamond K\left(K\left(\mathbf{0}=\mathbf{0}\right)\wedge\neg K\left(\mathbf{0}=\mathbf{0}\right)\right)$

Note that it is crucial for both the counterexample and for the proof of the theorem that the complex operator $\Diamond K$ may be split up in the simple operators $\Diamond$ and K. So one line of response to the above argument against (2) is restricting it to formulas in which every K is preceded by a $\Diamond$.[12] It is supposed to be non ad hoc, since the move is also needed to prevent counterexamples to other principles of the epistemic logic, e.g. the distributivity of $\Diamond K$.[13]

If a collapse of *de re* into *de dicto* verifiability already worries certain people, then a collapse of verifiability into truth will worry many more. As far as I can see, there is no way to prove such a collapse on the basis of the self-predication principles alone. But it can be done, if the following rule also belongs to the system:

$\iota\mathbf{E}$ If $\Gamma\vdash\iota x\phi\left(x\right)\neq c^{*}$, then $\Gamma\vdash\exists x!\phi\left(x\right)$.

---

[11] See Horsten (2008). He also gave a more complicated counterexample to the principle in higher-order settings in his Horsten (2000, p. 50-51).

[12] This was suggested by Horsten (2008).

[13] See Horsten (2008).

When taken as primitive rules the self-predication principles are in a way description introduction rules. Normally one should then also have description elimination rules. The above rule falls within that latter category. It is a valid rule under the Kremer interpretation. With the unrestricted self-predication principle and the above rule one can then prove the following theorem.

Theorem 17. *(2), $\iota \mathbf{E} \vdash (\phi \wedge \exists z \Box z \neq c^*) \to \Box \phi$ for all closed well-formed formulas ϕ*

Proof. Suppose that $\phi \wedge \exists z \Box z \neq c^*$, for any closed ϕ. By $=$**I** and $\wedge$**I** one may infer from $\Box t \neq c^*$ that $\Box t \neq c^* \wedge t = t$. By $\exists$**I**, $\wedge$**I**, and the fact that ϕ is closed, it follows that

$$\exists z \, (\phi \wedge \exists x \, (\Box z \neq c^* \wedge z = x))$$

Ergo, the above follows by $\exists$**E** from $\phi \wedge \exists z \Box z \neq c^*$. Clearly, the latter entails that

$$\exists z! \, (\phi \wedge \exists x \, (\Box z \neq c^* \wedge z = x))$$

For suppose not. Then there is some y such that it inter alia satisfies $y = x$ but also $y \neq z$. But since $z = x$ is also given, this is a violation of transitivity of identity. So the condition for deriving

$$\phi \wedge \exists x (\Box \iota z (\phi \wedge \exists x (\Box z \neq c^* \wedge z = x)) \neq c^*$$
$$\wedge \iota z (\phi \wedge \exists x (\Box z \neq c^* \wedge z = x)) = x)$$

on the basis of (2) is fulfilled. From the fact that x is not free for quantification in

$$\Box \iota z \, (\phi \wedge \exists x \, (\Box z \neq c^* \wedge z = x)) \neq c^*$$

one can infer by $\wedge$**E** and $\exists$**E** that

$$\Box \iota z \, (\phi \wedge \exists x \, (\Box z \neq c^* \wedge z = x)) \neq c^*$$

The combination of ι**E**, $\Box$**I**, and the last displayed formula gives one:

$$\Box \exists z! \, (\phi \wedge \exists x \, (\Box z \neq c^* \wedge z = x))$$

$\square$

Corollary 4. *(2), $\iota \mathbf{E}$, $\mathbf{Q} \vdash \phi \to \Box \phi$*

There are of course ways to avoid a collapse. One way would be to drop (2) and adopt either (3) or (4) for the cases in which the descriptive conditions are epistemic, or even adopt no other self-predication principle than (1). Adopting (4) has already been considered as a solution for avoiding a collapse of *de re* into *de dicto* verifiability. Another possibility is to tinker with the elimination rule for descriptions. In Horsten (2005, p. 238) the following description rule is considered as the only primitive rule for descriptions: from $\exists x!\phi(x)$, infer $\forall y\,(y = \iota x\phi(x) \leftrightarrow !\phi(y))$.[14] It is easy to see that the rule in question implies (2), but at the same time there is no collapse forthcoming from the combination of (2) with the derived elimination rule (if $\Gamma \vdash \exists x!\phi(x) \wedge \iota x\phi(x) = t$, then $\Gamma \vdash !\phi(t)$).

Summing up, adopting the unrestricted self-predication principle (2) leads to a collapse of *de re* into *de dicto* demonstrability or verifiability and, if one adopts certain elimination rules for descriptions, one even gets a collapse of demonstrability or verifiability into truth. While the first result need not be a bad result given the Horsten interpretation, the second result certainly is. Both kinds of collapse can be avoided if only (4) is countenanced as a sound self-predication principle for the cases in which the descriptive condition is epistemic.

5.5 Conclusion

In this paper I have discussed deductive systems formulated within languages containing an intensional operator ($\Box$) and a term-forming operator (ι). I have looked at two interpretations of the languages, one by Kremer and one by Horsten. The latter is intended to be a suitable interpretation for a reading of the box operator as a demonstrability or verifiability operator. Both formal interpretations are labelled 'Carnapian'. In the Kremer interpretation variables range over individual concepts if they are within the range of the intensional operator, whereas in the Horsten interpretation variables range over individual closed terms in those circumstances. Interestingly, one cannot add one of those logics to Peano arithmetic without getting a collapse of validity or demonstrability into truth. There is however an alternative formulation of arithmetic possible which can be safely combined with any of the mentioned logics. I also looked at certain description principles, which I dubbed 'self-predication' principles. Several among them were proved to be invalid under the Kremer interpretation. Matters were less clear if one reads them under the lights of the Horsten interpretation. At the very least one should take care in selecting a suitable elimination rule for descriptions, for otherwise one can derive the collapse of demonstrability or verifiability into truth, given some self-predication principle and the least number principle. More importantly, self-predication principles in combination with strong induction lead to a collapse of *de re* into *de dicto* verifiability. Within an arithmetical context this leads

---

[14] Actually there is a omission in the rule considered there: the exclamation mark preceding $!\phi(y)$ was left out. Alternatively, the exclamation mark could have been left out, but then the biconditional should have been an ordinary conditional.

to an interesting conclusion about the limits of verifiability. The way to make progress at this point is to develop Horsten interpretations in full detail.

References

Ackerman, Diana. 1979. De Re propositional attitudes toward integers. In R. Shahan and C. Swoyer, eds., *Essays on the Philosophy of W. V. Quine*, pages 145–153. Norman OK: University of Oklahoma Press.

Boolos, George S., John P. Burgess, and Richard C. Jeffrey. 2003. *Computability and Logic*. New York: Cambridge University Press, 4th edn.

Burgess, John P. 1999. Which modal logic is the right one? *Notre Dame Journal of Formal Logic* 40(1):81–93.

Föllesdal, Dagfinn. 2004. *Referential Opacity and Modal Logic*. London: Routledge.

G. Hughes, M. Cresswell. 1996. *A New Introduction to Modal Logic*. Routledge.

Horsten, Leon. 2000. Models for the logic of possible proofs. *Pacific Philosophical Quarterly* 81:49–66.

Horsten, Leon. 2005. Canonical naming systems. *Minds and Machines* 15(2):229–257.

Horsten, Leon. 2008. Descriptions and the unknowable. "Versions of the paper were presented at the *Work in Progress* seminar of the philosophy department of the University of Bristol, and at a Workshop on Philosophical Logic, which was organized by Gabriel Uzquiano (Oxford, 20-21 March 2008).".

Kremer, Michael. 1997. Marti on descriptions in Carnap's S2. *Journal of Philosophical Logic* 26:629–634.

Marti, Genoveva. 1994. Do modal distinctions collapse in carnap's system? *Journal of Philosophical Logic* 23.

Shapiro, Stewart. Fall 2007. Classical logic. In E. N. Zalta, ed., *The Stanford Encyclopedia of Philosophy*.

6

Moore, the Sceptic, and the Mysterious Case of the Disappearing Defeasible Justification[1]

DANIELE SGARAVATTI

6.1 Introduction

While defending a version of his anti-sceptical position, Moore claimed that at the root of sceptical arguments there was the unjustified assumption that only infallible justification can turn one's belief into knowledge, so that for instance inductive reasoning, being in principle open to error, can never sustain knowledge. Michael Huemer (2001) also claims that such an assumption is at the root of the most well-known forms of scepticism; however, he notes that there is a powerful argument the sceptic can use to defend it. In fact, according to Huemer the sceptic might argue that the very idea of a defeasible, or non-conclusive, justification, which we are here understanding as a justification that does not entail the truth of the allegedly justified belief, is a non sense, a contradiction in terms.

---

[1] For useful comments and discussion on this work I would like to thank the audiences at the SIFA Graduate Conference in Padua, and at the Philosophy Graduate Research Seminar in St Andrews. Particular thanks, for discussion on these and other occasions, go to Crispin Wright, Martin Smith, Diego Marconi, Gabriele Usberti, and Tim Williamson. Finally I would like to thank the organizers of the SIFA Graduate conference for their effort in publishing this volume.

Language, Knowledge, and Metaphysics.
Massimiliano Carrara and Vittorio Morato (eds.)
College Pubblication, London, 2008.

I consider a detailed version of the argument and some possible attacks on its premises. In the end, however, I claim the solution to the problem is accepting the conclusion. The way I reconcile the conclusion with its apparent unacceptability is by claiming that we actually make a larger than what is usually thought use of deductive reasoning. Very often, what is taken to be an induction or an inference to the best explanation is a sort of deduction, where some of the premises of the reasoning are not made explicit. We tacitly assume, *e.g.*, that sceptic scenarios do not hold (I take this account of the role of assumptions in our epistemic practices to be Wittgensteinean in spirit). A further claim I make is that those assumptions need not always be themselves justified. We have therefore to distinguish (at least) two senses of infallible justification: in the first sense an infallible justification is just a deductive justification. Let's call this "conclusive" justification. In another, stronger sense, an infallible justification is a justification such that the subject having it could not be wrong in the justified belief. My claim is then that most of our justified beliefs are justified by conclusive but not strongly infallible justifications (it might well be that strongly infallible justification is an unattainable ideal).

However, once the disappeared defeasible justification, or something similar enough, is recovered this way, the claim of Moore and Huemer, that the tenability of scepticism depends on an argument to the effect that all knowledge has to be based on infallible justification, turns out to be wrong. The sceptic can safely accept that we have fallible justification in my sense, and still insist that we do not have such a fallible justification to believe the negation of the sceptical hypotheses. We usually just assume they are false.

6.2 Moore and the Sceptic

Consider the prototypical sceptical hypothesis that an evil demon is deceiving us, giving us the appearances of the existence of an external world, while in fact there is none. The cleverness of this kind of hypothesis is supposed to be that they neutralize any putative evidence against them. To see whether this is right, let us consider the "proof" Moore famously claimed to have given for the existence of the external world:

Inference 1 (*Moore's Proof*).

1 Here is a hand
2 Here is another hand
3 ∴ There are at least two external things

The first complaint naturally raised about the proof is that it is question-begging. However, it is not at all easy to give this complaint a clear form, and cogent support. Standardly, we take arguments to be question-begging when one of the premises is identical to the conclusion.[2] But this is not the case for Moore's proof, and he explicitly pointed that out. Of course, if the conclusion of his proof were false, the premises could not be true; but this is not a distinctive feature of question-begging arguments, it is a feature of all deductive arguments! Consider the analogy Moore offers:

> Suppose, for instance, it were a question whether there are as many as three misprints on a certain page in a certain book. *A* says there are, *B* is inclined to doubt it. How could *A* prove that he is right? Surely he could prove it by pointing to three separate places on it, saying "there is one misprint here, another here, and another here".[3]

We can make explicit an argument on these lines and call it "Typo":

Inference 2 (*Typo*).

1 Here is a misprint
2 Here is another misprint
3 ∴ There are at least two misprints

Although the analogy is not explicitly offered against the charge of begging the question, it might have easily been used against it; what is it that is wrong in Moore's proof that is not wrong in the argument considered? There is a great deal to say about that; and indeed much has been said recently.[4] We will also come back to this problem later in this essay; for the moment though we will put it aside, considering another complaint which the sceptic could raise, and which might look less problematic.

The second complaint is that Moore does not know the premises of his proof to be true.

Moore is aware of this kind of possible response as well, and he is ready to admit that he cannot "prove" the premises of his proof to be true; nonetheless, he claims to know them, and to know them "for certain". To understand this answer, which appears to be rather dogmatic, we have to look at "Four Forms of Scepticism", and to come to the problem of defeasible justification. Here Moore is arguing against

---

[2]See Copi (1961, pp. 65-6).
[3]Cf. Moore (1959, p. 147).
[4]See *e.g.* Wright (2000), Wright (2003) and Wright (2004), Davies (2004) and Pryor (2004).

a form of scepticism he attributes to Russell. I think however that the present interest of the following passage should be clear enough:

> That is to say he [Russell] assumes: (1) My belief or knowledge that this is a pencil is, if I do not know it immediately, and if also the proposition does not follow logically from anything that I know immediately, in some sense "based on" an analogical or inductive argument; and (2) What is "based on" an analogical or inductive argument is never certain knowledge, but only more or less probable belief. And with regard to these assumptions, it seems to me that the first one must be true in some sense or other, though it seems to me terribly difficult to say exactly what the sense is. What I am inclined to dispute, therefore, is the second: I am inclined to think that what is "based on" an analogical or inductive argument, in the sense in which my knowledge or belief that this is a pencil is so, may nevertheless be certain knowledge and *not* merely more or less probable belief.[5]

In a more contemporary terminology Moore is saying that the sceptic needs to defend the claim that if perceptual justification is not immediate but inferential, and the inference is not deductive in kind, then there is no real justification for our perceptual beliefs, or at least not enough justification to qualify them as knowledge. But what is the argument for that?

In connection with the proof, the answer the latter passage suggests on behalf of Moore is the following: the only ground for the complaint that he does not know the premises to be true is, in short, the dogma that all knowledge must rest on some kind of infallible justification. Is it perhaps an independently reasonable position that knowledge, and justification, must be infallible? Huemer suggests that there is a very strong case to be made for that.

6.3 The Mysterious Case of the Disappearing Defeasible Justification

6.3.1 The Problem of Defeasible Inferential Justification

In fact, according to Huemer, the sceptic might argue that the very idea of a defeasible justification is a nonsense, a contradiction in terms.

---

[5] See Moore (1959, pp. 225-26), original italics. Let me add an exegetical comment; after this passage, in the essay, there is the much more quoted one in which Moore remarks that propositions such as "I know that p", where p is an everyday obvious fact, are more certain than any of the premises of the sceptical arguments. On the basis of that passage, Moore is often represented as dismissing the sceptic without seriously considering the relevant arguments she can present. This is in a way unfair, since he has just indicated where exactly he thinks there is an unjustified premise in the argument. We will see however that in the end there is some truth in that interpretation too.

Let us look at the argument. We are limiting ourselves, again, to cases in which your evidence is supposed to consist of a set of propositions. We will turn to the import of this limitation later.[6] Let us call justification of this kind inferential justification. We have defeasible, or non-conclusive, inferential justification, when the set of propositions constituting your evidence, call it E, supports the conclusion, call it p, although (E and not p) is consistent. In such cases Huemer notes there will always be an hypothesis H which entails E and is incompatible with p.

Sceptical hypotheses of great imaginative force abound; however, the simplest case is to consider the hypothesis H which is simply (E and not-p).

The support given by our evidence should be at least strong enough for the subject to be justified in believing the conclusion; and strong enough, in the absence of other obstacles, for that belief to qualify as knowledge.

The argument to the effect that this is never going to be the case, in Huemer's version, uses two principles, which I slightly re-formulate, with respect to Huemer's version, as follows:

Principle 1 (P1). *Given any evidence, E, and hypothesis h, in order to justifiably infer h from E, one must have at least some reason independent of h for rejecting each of the alternatives incompatible with h which entails E.*

Principle 2 (P2). *For any set of propositions E and H, if H entails E, then E is not a reason for rejecting H.*[7]

It's easy to see how the argument goes. Take a particular case, *e.g.* my evidence is $E = $ "I have perceptual experience of a hand in front of me", and the desired conclusion is the hypothesis $h = $ "I have a hand". The sceptical hypothesis, although we can suppose there is some story about evil demons or brains in vats to be told to make it vivid, is simply $SH = $ "I have perceptual experience of a hand in front of me, but it's not the case that I have a hand". Since SH implies E, by **P2** it is not the case that E gives reason for rejecting SH; since SH is incompatible with h, by **P1** we cannot justifiably infer h from E, unless we can rule out SH in some other way. Do we have other

---

[6] You might think, as Williamson (2000) does, that all evidence is just propositional; in this case the problem will be more general. I don't agree with that view, but I am not arguing against it.

[7] Huemer (2001) had, at the the end of Principle 1 "in which e would be true". I think what it was meant was just "which entail e", and I use this clearer, to my mind, formulation.

reasons, independent of h, for rejecting SH? We want our justification to be inferential, so the reasons must consist of more statements. So we can add those statements to our initial set E, and get a new set E^*. If E^* rules out every possibility incompatible with h, then we have a conclusive justification after all. Suppose however E^* still does not entail h. We can then consider the new sceptical hypothesis $SH^* =$ "E^* but it is not the case that I have a hand"; and of course we can apply the same reasoning. There seems to be no end to this regress. We will never get to an inferential justification unless the conclusion is entailed by the premises, or we reject either **P1** or **P2**.

In a more general form:

Suppose E is your total propositional evidence. We say that one has an inferential justification for a conclusion when one's propositional evidence suffices for justifiably inferring the conclusion.

(1)	Your total evidence E does not entail h.	Assumption
(2)	There is an hypothesis h^* (E and not-h) which is incompatible with h and entails E.	From (1)
(3)	You do not have reasons independent of h to reject h^*.	From (1), (2) and **P2**
(4)	You cannot justifiably infer h from E.	From (2), (3) and **P1**

However, I have doubts the argument, as it stands, is valid. The problematic passage is from (2) to (3). By **P2**, since h^* entails E, E is no reason to reject it. But E is our total evidence; still, one might think, there might be reasons to reject h^* that are not part of the subject's total evidence, and cannot be added to it (as the informal presentation of the argument presupposed instead), perhaps because they are not of propositional nature. In other words, the argument goes through only if the following presupposition, which I think is therefore worth considering a third principle, is in place:

Principle 3 (P3). *If your total evidence E is not a reason to reject an hypothesis h, then you do not have a reason to reject h.*

There is much to say about **P1**–**P3**. Before discussing them, however, let us have a first look at the conclusion they entail.

6.3.2 The Unacceptable Conclusion

There are different ways one might argue that the conclusion of the argument above is not so worrying after all. Some of these ways I will not have space to discuss adequately here. However, I wish to give some hint as to how and why I think those lines of thinking would not be successful in the end, and in so doing to make a case for the claim that the conclusion that there is no such thing as defeasible inferential justification threatens to have devastating consequences.

The first thing to notice is that the class of beliefs we usually take to have that sort of justification is extremely widespread. Scientific beliefs, in the first place, are based on defeasible inferences. There was perhaps a time someone thought you can deduce all science from the sense-data, but that is surely not the case now. Social and natural sciences do not seem to differ, in this respect; although the methodologies show great diversity, Physics and History, Biology and Psychology, and so on, share the use of inferential defeasible justification. If this is not justification, at least not in a fairly strong sense, it seems that there is no scientific knowledge, except in mathematics and related areas. Highly theoretical matters however do not exhaust the area under attack. Common-sense beliefs are threatened as well; just a few examples of beliefs *prima facie* based on inferential justification: my belief that my house has not moved from where it was this morning; my belief that the building I am in now will not collapse in the next five minutes; my belief that there are people living in Russia (and that there is a place called Russia).

The reason I list these trivialities is to prevent the following reaction: we do not need inferential justification, after all, because we have immediate, non-inferential, perceptual justification. Let us call the latter view "Dogmatism"[8] about perception. I think Dogmatism has problems of its own. However, we do not need to discuss them, since Dogmatism does not guarantee any of the beliefs I mentioned to be justified. Science and common sense both radically exceed the sphere of immediate perceptual warrant. One might think that the problem might be solved adding more sources of immediate justification, such as testimony and memory. Dogmatism about those of course should also be defended on independent grounds; again though, we do not need to discuss this, because even granting that memory and testimony give us immediate justification for our beliefs, without any inferential work on our part going on, and that really is granting a lot, we will not get the desired results; science will not be in any better shape. And among commonsensical beliefs, only a few will be rescued. I would not have a justification to believe that my house is still where it was this morning (memory can only tell that it was there at that time), nor that the building I am in is not just going to collapse.

Another way of making the conclusion less threatening which I will not discuss is one kind of probabilistic, or Bayesian, approach. One

---

[8]See Pryor (2004).

might think that even if we can never use fallible inferences to gain knowledge of a proposition p, we can substitute for those deductive inferences to the effect that p has probability n.

There are at least three problems with this, which I can only name:

(i) The approach requires some kind of knowledge of the priors. It does not matter whether you start with propositions of probability 1 or less than that. You must start knowing that some propositions have probability n, for some n; and those propositions must be about the world, if anything about the world has to be deduced from them. Therefore, you still have to explain in some way how you acquire this knowledge of the world. Since it is conceded that no defeasible warrants obtain, you must have acquired this knowledge through deductive reasoning; it is not clear however how this could happen.

(ii) Psychologically, the Bayesian strategy seems inapplicable. We just do not have the necessary computational capacities.

(iii) Thirdly, the answer seems to concede the sceptic too much. There is no unconditional knowledge to be gained of science or of common-sensical truths about the world. We can only go so far as knowing that *probably* the earth is not flat, and *probably* there are people living in Russia and so on. If one could do better than that, then one surely should.

In the end, I must submit, accepting the conclusion of the supposed paradox is the solution I am going to embrace. Therefore, in some respect, I will have to deal with the objections I roughly sketched above. I will not explore, however, whether the answers I will give are open to a Dogmatist or a Bayesian strategy as well. Quite clearly, those options are not my target here. What the present paragraph was intended to show is just that there are prima facie very good reasons to find unacceptable the conclusion that no defeasible inferential justification is possible.

6.3.3 Principles P1–P3

Principles **P1**, **P2** and **P3** will require some attention. I do not intend to provide a complete defence of them here. I think that the strongest objection they face is just that, together, they lead to the conclusion that there is no defeasible justification. However, as I said, I will argue that this conclusion, once understood properly, is not unacceptable. Putting that aside, **P1**–**P3** have at least, I think, a strong initial plausibility. However, there are a number of possible objections I will briefly consider, to show that the initial plausibility is not easily lost. It will turn out that most, if not all, these objections, actually beg the question against the argument; that is they assume the falsity of the conclusion, and, with other assumptions, conclude that one of the principles is false. This seems to suggest that there is some kind of clash of intuitions going on. If one is unconvinced by my defence, the subsequent sections are going to be interesting, I think, as a conditional argument. Suppose you share those intuitions, and see what follows.

Let us start with **P1**. As Huemer points out, **P1** obviously has some connections with various principles of epistemic closure, which have been widely discussed. Huemer ends up reformulating **P1** in a way remindful of what Brueckner (1994) formulates under the name of the "Underdetermination Principle":

Principle 4 (UP). *For all S, Φ, Ψ, if S's evidence for believing that Φ does not favour Φ over some incompatible hypothesis Ψ, then S lacks justification for believing that Φ.*[9]

To get this from **P1**, we have to equate one's having some reason for rejecting all hypotheses alternative to h, with one's evidence favouring h over all the alternative hypotheses. It's clear that the latter imply the former; if my evidence favours h over all alternative hypothesis, that is surely "some reason" to reject them. The other direction of implication however does not hold, at least in a strong reading of "having reasons to reject"; if having reasons to reject p is read as having justification to believe its negation, it seems I might have reasons to prefer an hypothesis over others without having reasons sufficient to reject the others. If we were thus to weaken **P1**, as Huemer does, we would get:

Principle 5 (P1.1). *Given any evidence, E, and hypothesis h, in order to justifiably infer h from E, one must have at least some reason independent of h for preferring h over each of the alternatives incompatible with h which entails E.*

We would then have to accordingly reformulate **P2** and **P3**:

Principle 6 (P2.1). *For any triple of sets of propositions, H_1, H_2 and E, if H_2 entails E, then E is not a reason for preferring H_1 over H_2.*

Principle 7 (P3.1). *If your total evidence E is not a reason to prefer an hypothesis h_1 over another hypothesis h_2, then you do not have a reason to prefer h_1 over h_2.*

However, we will see that **P2.1** is subject to counterexamples of a sort that do not affect **P2**. I will have accordingly to stick to **P1**.

P1, as I am reading it, is equivalent to a closure principle for justifi-

---
[9]See Brueckner (1994, p. 830).

cation, which could be expressed, following again Brueckner (1994), as follows:

Principle 8 (Closure). *For all S, Φ, Ψ, if S has justification for believing that Φ, and $(\Phi \rightarrow \Psi)$, then S has justification for believing that Φ.*[10]

Despite its intuitive force, putative counterexamples to such a principle are well known. Of course I cannot here provide an exhaustive treatment of the matter. I will however consider two kinds of counterexamples, single premise cases and multiple premises cases, and explain why we can take, for the time being, that they do not work. As an example of the first kind we can think of the zebra case: I am at a zoo, looking to (what apparently is) a zebra. Let us suppose, to adapt the case to the discussion of inferential justification, that I use a (subjective) description of my visual experience as evidence. I am justified, it seems, on these grounds, in believing there is a zebra. However, I am supposed not to be justified in believing something incompatible with it, that what I am seeing is not a cleverly disguised painted mule. I will just deny that this kind of example is convincing. We noted, in presenting the argument, that the sort of justification we were looking for was a justification in itself sufficient for rational belief. It seems in this sense if I am not justified in believing the negation of the alternative hypothesis, then I am not justified in believing there is a zebra.

The other kind of putative counterexample is more problematic. We can think of the lottery case; it seems I have justification in believing one random ticket in a very large lottery will not be the winner. On the same grounds, I could then be justified in believing that of each ticket. Yet I am not justified in believing the negation of something incompatible with the totality of these beliefs, *i.e.* that one of the tickets will win. In fact, I know this to be the case, let alone being justified in believing its negation. Many theorists however will deny the initial point, that I can be justified in believing of some ticket that it will not win. What I am justified to believe it is that it is very likely that it will not win. The main point, however, in this context, is that the counterexample presupposes that I can have inferential defeasible justification, and in particular for believing that the ticket will not win. But this is question begging in this context. Of course that does not

---

[10] See Brueckner (1994, p. 831). There is no need to add to the antecedent a specification to the effect that S believes that Φ implies Ψ, and forms the belief on that basis, because the notion of justification in play is "propositional justification"; you have a propositional justification for p when your evidence is such that if you were to appropriately base the belief that p on it you would be justified in believing that p.

settle the question, but I think it suggests that rejecting closure is an ad hoc move, and alternatives should be explored.

Is the second principle an easier target of criticism? Before answering the question we need to accommodate what I see as an inessential problem with **P2**. As it stands, **P2** has crazy consequences, on a classical understanding of the notion of entailment, both for self-contradictory hypotheses and for evidence consisting of logical truth only. Since contradictions entail everything, they will always entail any evidence, and hence they can never be rejected. Since logical truths are entailed by everything, they can never be a reason for rejecting any hypotheses. We might blame the classical notion of entailment for these unwelcome results, but I don't think we need to discuss this here. The vast majority of the evidence we have for our empirical beliefs is not made of logical truths. And even without considering self-contradictory hypotheses, the alternatives we have to consider are numerous enough for the problem to arise. So we will limit **P2** as follows:

Principle 9 (P2.2). *For any set of propositions E and H, if H is not self-contradictory, and E is not a logical truth, then if H entails E, then E is not a reason for rejecting H.*

Our modified premise **P2.2** (just like its predecessors) seems to follow from some very basic intuitions about evidence, which are reflected in basic principles of probabilistic reasoning. If an hypothesis entails my evidence, then my evidence supports the hypothesis, it increases its probability; how can I gain reasons to rule out this hypothesis from something which supports it? Here is a way one could try to escape this basic thought. Suppose the prior probability of hypotheses h and not-h is 0.5. However the conditional probability of h on E is 0.99, and, of course, the conditional probability of not-h on E is 0.01. In this situation, the hypothesis (E and not-h), although it implies the evidence E, might seem to be reasonably rejected on the ground of E. At the moment we acquire (perhaps by perceptual or testimonial warrant) the information that E holds, it's reasonable to come to believe h, and therefore to reject (E and not-h).

My reaction is the following. Now E entails that h has probability 0.99; we do not have a defeasible warrant there, and I can grant the conclusion. The defeasible warrant would go from "h has probability 0.99" to "h". Our sceptical hypothesis, call it NSH, is therefore "h has probability 0.99 and not-h". By deductive reasoning, we know that NSH has of course a very low probability; but how can we pass from knowledge that a proposition has a low probability to knowledge (or justified belief) that the proposition does not hold?[11] It might be thought that here we can invoke some analytical or *a priori* principle which links probability to rational belief. However, this would clearly be question begging in this context. Surely we cannot in this context take as common ground something like "For any p, if p has a very high probability, then you are justified in believing p". It would be to assume the point at stake, which is just whether we can rationally believe a conclusion that is not entailed by our evidence.[12]

A similar reasoning would answer a possible attack on **P2.2**, or **P3**, based on the notion of simplicity and inference to the best explanation. So, for example, Goldman (2007) argues, against Pritchard (2005), that the underdetermination principle, by itself, does not imply that our perceptual experience does not favour common-sense beliefs over the brain in a vat hypothesis. Our perceptual experience might be a good basis for an inference to the best explanation of the existence of the external world. Inference to the best explanation is a well established way of justifying beliefs; so if the external world hypothesis is the simplest explanation of our perceptual experience, then the latter does justify this hypothesis, he argues. I agree that this result is compatible with **UP** and with **P1** as well, and also that it is in agreement with our ordinary epistemic practices. But note that here the dialectic is not the same as there is between Goldman and Pritchard. We are not just using **P1**, we are also using **P2.2** and **P3**, the combination of which is indeed incompatible with inference to the best explanation, which is a paradigmatic case of defeasible inference. Most importantly, we are not assuming that what we are claiming is compatible with our ordinary epistemic practices; indeed, we find those practices are under attack. But the objection is based on the assumption that our epistemic practice of making inferences to the best explanation is in order.

Finally let us turn to **P3**. The objection in this case would draw on the analogy between deductive and non-deductive inferences; surely the fact that there is an entailment between E and some h, when there is one, need not be added as a proposition to the premises, on pain of regress, as Carroll's clever tortoise taught us at the expense of Achilles. But just like the proposition that the premises entail the conclusion

---

[11] Here is where **P2.1** would fail; surely it might be held, on *a priori* grounds, that the fact that h is much more likely than NSH is a reason to prefer the former over the latter.

[12] Note, however, that **P2** by itself does not entail the conclusion of our argument. If we gave up closure, we could claim that we have justification for h without having justification for not-NHS; admittedly, thinking of evidence in probabilist terms, that would require having the threshold for justification shifting in a strange way.

needs not to be part of our premises when we draw a deductive inferences, so the proposition that our premises inductively, abductively, or otherwise non-conclusively, support the conclusion need not be part of our premises in the non-deductive case. But that surely is a reason to reject the alternative hypothesis.

The last bit, again, seems question-begging. There is however a more radical problem with the objection; I think it takes the moral of Carroll's tale exactly backwards. If I infer q from p and p implies q, there is just no additional reason I need. To suppose so would invite a regress, even if the reason is not propositional in nature, whatever that might mean, because it would imply that the facts that p and p implies q, per se, are not sufficient reasons to infer q; but if one can legitimately question that, one could also question they are a reason to infer q together with the additional reason, and we would then need a further reason, perhaps still non-.propositional, to ensure that, and so on ad infinitum. So I think **P3** stands safely free of counterexamples.

Overall, I think enough has been said to motivate exploring a different way out of the problem.

6.4 Deduction and Fallibility

We were concerned, at the beginning, with the sort of strong justification thought to be necessary for knowledge, our preoccupation being prompted by Moore's contention that the sceptic was relying on the principle that no defeasible justification could produce knowledge. However, the worry we have generated with Huemer's argument is more general, and it relates to the concept of defeasible justification itself. My way out of the problem, as I anticipated, is accepting the conclusion: no defeasible inferential justification is possible. To make this solution acceptable, however, quite a lot of work has to be done. We said, in section 6.3.2, that it seems a vast class of our beliefs, including common-sensical and scientific beliefs, turns out to be unjustified, if the conclusion is accepted. The most difficult part of the work is showing this undeniably intuitive assumption to be wrong, and I will try to do that claiming that we have a deductive justification for most of those beliefs; our apparently defeasible inferences are often, to use the traditional term, enthymemes[13] standing for deductive inferences.

Let me give a couple of examples to show what is meant by our justification being deductive, in cases in which you would think it is not. Consider my belief that there is a desk in front of me. Suppose, for

---

[13] Of course the complete argument is not always a syllogism; I take "enthymeme" in this wider sense.

the sake of argument, that my justification for this belief is inferential. We could suppose that it has the following form:

Inference 3.

1 It looks to me as if there is a desk in front of me.
2 ∴ There is a desk in front of me.

What I would suggest is that the justification is instead:

Inference 4.

1 It looks to me as if there is a desk in front of me.
2 If my perceptual system is working properly, and the environment is favourable, then if it looks to me as if p, then p.
3 My perceptual system is working properly, and the environment is favourable.
4 ∴ There is a desk in front of me.

Secondly, consider my belief that there are people living in France now. We might suppose that my justification is something like this:

Inference 5.

1 There have been people living in France.
2 I don't know of any change in that respect.
3 ∴ There are people living in France now.

Instead, I think the justification for my belief is:

Inference 6.

1 There have been people living in France.
2 I don't know of any change in that respect.
3 It's not possible that there are not people living in France any more and I don't know of any change in that respect.
4 ∴ There are people living in France now.

The pattern should now be clear. What we assume often, but not always, amounts to what I would like to call our "local reliability"; we assume that the circumstances are such that in this case we cannot be wrong (even if we might, very rarely, have been in some other not much dissimilar occasion). The immediate worry one will probably want to raise is asking what justification we have for this assumption, represented by the second and the third premises in the deductive argument 4 and by the third premise in the deductive argument 6.

Before turning to that, let me make two clarifications. Firstly I am not claiming that a similar pattern has to be found all the times we suppose we have knowledge based on defeasible justification. Consider my belief that my car is parked where I left it a few hours ago. It might well be that I do not have a justification for that unqualified claim, and I realize that, when challenged on the possibility of another car having crashed into it, and ended its existence. What I have justification for is perhaps only the belief that it's very likely that my car is still where I parked it. In such a case, I back up on some of the strategies I rejected above. I don't think I need to draw exactly a line between the cases. The second clarification is that I am not claiming that my justification depends on my actually going through some reasoning, be it deductive or not. Just like having a belief, having a justification is here considered as a dispositional state. Having a justification, in this sense, does not require being justified in believing. It does not even require believing. What I am claiming, and this is a claim subject to empirical confirmation or disconfirmation, is that we often have beliefs, either explicit or tacit, of the kind illustrated,[14] which constitute a deductive basis for the beliefs we infer, apparently, through non-deductive reasoning.

Let us turn to the worry I anticipated. What is the justification for these tacit beliefs? Well, there are going to be different kinds of justification; sometimes they are going to be *a priori* justified, and sometimes they are going to be empirically justified themselves. But I also wish to consider the possibility that they are not at all justified. Consider the following principle, which I will call **JE** (for Justified Evidence):

Principle 10 (JE). *For any propositions E and H, H can furnish a reason for accepting or rejecting H only if E itself is justified.*

I will try to convince you that **JE** is to be rejected. Note, however, that this an additional claim with respect to the overall strategy of finding ways in which apparently defeasible inferences are actually enthymematic. The same strategy could be developed holding **JE** and trying to show the relevant tacit beliefs are usually justified.

Sometimes, we may seem to make use of something like JE in rejecting as unjustified the conclusion of an argument whose premises are unjustified. If someone argues that $2 + 2 = 5$, on the ground that $5 - 2 = 2$, we won't regard the conclusion as justified. However, the example is useful only if the reason we would deny justification for the belief is that the first proposition is not justified. Even if it were so,

---

[14]One might worry that the second premise in the first argument (Inference 4) is too "philosophical" for most people; in fact, it is, but I think most people hold some less technical equivalent, such as "if my eyes are fine, and everything is normal, then things are as they look to me".

the general conclusion would not be proved; we could still think that in other cases unjustified propositions can justify derived beliefs. My impression is that the reason we find the initial example convincing is that the proposition supposed to do the justifying work is not only unjustified, but unreasonable and outlandish as well. So I don't see a general argument for **JE**; I see instead a general reason to worry about it, and that is that it puts unreasonable pressure on us.[15] One way to introduce this way of looking at the matter is with Wittegenstein's *On Certainty* § 253,[16] which could be read as the exact negation of **JE**:

At the foundation of well-founded belief lies belief that is not founded.

The thought is that we have to acknowledge our limits. It is often noticed that, when it comes to justification and knowledge, just as well as in other fields, we have to start where we are. We cannot check all our beliefs at a time. Therefore we cannot regard ourselves as irresponsible for not doing so. When we draw an inference, clearly we are responsible for the validity, or the reasonableness, of the inference. If the inference is properly drawn, we therefore meet our primary epistemic responsibility in that respect. Are we also responsible for the premises of our inference? There is a well known risk of regress here. In a sense, we are, but I think we can capture that sense without endorsing **JE**. I propose a weakened version of **JE**, which we may call **RE** (for Reasonable Evidence), which I submit is much closer to our epistemic practice:

Principle 11 (RE). *For any proposition E and H, a subject s can be justified in believing H inferring it from E only if s believes E and it is not unreasonable for s to believe E.*

There are just two necessary and sufficient conditions for someone to have a reasonable belief that p. First, she must have the belief that p; second, she must not be epistemically blameworthy in her belief that p. What does it mean for a belief to be, or not be, epistemically blameworthy? I think the notion can be made intuitive enough to make the work we need it to do here through a couple of examples: suppose I am tossing a fair coin, and for whatever reason I find myself believing that the coin will land head; that's clearly not a situation in which the second condition is satisfied. We have a clear sense that my belief is irresponsible; it is blameworthy, from the epistemic point of view.

---

[15] Other people, such as Williamson (2000), might worry for the opposite reason; justification is not enough, we have to know the propositions constituting our evidence. However, we have to remember that **JE** states necessary, and not sufficient conditions. I do not exclude the necessity of other conditions for a proposition to constitute evidence, or evidence good enough to support knowledge.

[16] See Wittgenstein (1969).

Consider now a different case; I believe that broccoli is healthy, but I just cannot remember where I took this (supposed) information from.[17] Presumably, I have heard it or read it somewhere. In looking at the case, I am not interested here in the question of whether the way the belief was formed was reliable or not, whether it was a good source or not the subject had the information from, and we are not even interested in whether the belief is true. The property we are interested in is one that supervenes on the subject's present mental states; relative to the present mental states of the subject, the belief that broccoli is healthy does not seem blameworthy. Externalists usually do not deny that this property exists, they only deny that it is co-extensive with justification. I need not disagree on that; on the contrary, I am assuming not all blameless beliefs are justified, although probably all justified beliefs are blameless. It might well be, moreover, that some further requirement on the premises of the inference has to obtain in order for the resulting belief to count as knowledge; the most obvious that comes to mind is the truth of the premises. What **RE** is intended to capture is something required from the subject in terms of rational beliefs, from the internal point of view.[18]

It is important to understand where the intuitive difference between the two examples comes from. In the coin case, the available evidence bears on the content of the belief, and it gives a fifty per cent probability to the belief of being false; in the latter case, where the belief is intuitively blameless, there is no evidence, *ex* hypothesis, for or against the content of the belief, except the belief itself. This seems to indicate an intuitive difference between having no evidence for or against something, and having balanced evidence for and against it. I don't think this is the complete explanation, however; if I did not believe that broccoli is healthy, then I surely would be blameworthy if I started believing it just on the basis that there is no evidence for or against it. So the intuition is rather that already believing something gives some kind of default entitlement to believe it; the entitlement is cancelled when there is balanced evidence for and against, but it is not cancelled by the fact that there is no evidence for or against the belief (this could be explained, in turn, by considering the fact that I have the belief as a form of evidence).

---

[17] The example is taken from Goldman (1999); Conee and Feldman (2004, ch. 3), argue that my belief is in fact justified; however they also admit that the class of epistemically blameless beliefs is wider than the class of justified ones.

[18] The resulting notion of justification bears much similarity to the notion of "synchronic justification", justification relative to the subject's beliefs at a given time, described in Swinburne (2001).

Rejecting **JE** in favour of **RE** renders the apparently unacceptable conclusion of our argument acceptable. We often have reasons to reject all the alternatives incompatible with our everyday beliefs; we often not unreasonably believe something that entails those alternatives do not hold, or we simply not unreasonably believe they do not hold. Note all I am claiming is that an inferential justification *can* make use of reasonable unjustified premises. I am not claiming that being in a position to deduce a proposition from reasonable premises is a sufficient condition for having a justification, while I would claim that for deducing from fully justified premises. I might realize, in drawing the inference, that there are reasons against a consequence of my, so far, reasonable belief. Reasonableness is not closed under logical entailment.

Does this mean fallible justification is not possible? In a certain sense of "fallible", yes; to have sufficient reasons for belief, we have to assume (even implicitly) enough to entail the conclusion. If our assumptions are true, the conclusion will also be true. However, our assumptions need not be justified, and this makes room for the fallibility of human beings. Sometimes we assume something wrong, and it turns out that our belief, even if justified, was not true.

We can make more precise the different senses of fallibility of evidence. We can define fallibility for evidence, in the most general form, at least in the three ways sticking to the case of a belief b (allegedly) supported by propositional evidence E, let's first consider the following two:

Definition 1 (FT). *Evidence E for belief b is fallible $=_{def}$ It is possible for a subject s to believe E without b being true.*

Or

Definition 2 (FJ). *Evidence E for belief b is fallible $=_{def}$ It is possible for a subject s to rationally believe E without s being rationally justified in believing b.*

FT (and not **FJ**) encounters well-known problems with the case of necessary truths. Since a necessary truth is entailed (at least on a standard understanding of entailment) by everything, any evidence for a necessary truth is infallible evidence in the first sense (and indeed, any proposition is evidence for a necessary truth). I will not try to accommodate the definition here.[19]

We haven't said anything here about **FJ**, because we did not talk about what is required for being justified in believing something, as opposed to what constitutes a justification for a belief. I have no reason,

---

[19] Haack (1979) and Reed (2002) provide interesting related discussion.

however, to deny that a belief based on deductive inference can be **FJ** fallible; the most obvious case is one in which the deduction is very complicated, and there are circumstances in which you believe the conclusion on the basis of the premises without having properly worked out the entailment. And I am surely granting that we can have evidence which is **FT** fallible: It is possible for us to be wrong in the beliefs that constitute E. The kind of fallibility I am denying is the following modified version of **FT**

Definition 3 (FTT). *Evidence E for belief b is fallible $=_{def}$ It is possible for a subject s to correctly believe E without b being true.*

To correctly believe p here simply means to believe p when p is true, so **FTT** just says that the evidence is fallible when it does not entail the belief. Our conclusion was that if our evidence is fallible in this sense, then it can give no sufficient justification for belief. This is not worrying, I argued, because most of our everyday beliefs enjoy a justification which is not fallible in the **FTT** sense, although it is fallible in the **FT** sense. And it could also be fallible in the **FJ** sense; even if you have beliefs that entail a certain conclusion, you might fail to appreciate the relation there is between the evidence and your belief.

6.5 Scepticism Strikes Back?

What are the consequences of this conception of fallible inferential justification for the problem of scepticism we started with? Let us consider Moore's proof again (see Inference 1 on 124)

Here there are two beliefs which are surely not unreasonable, and they entail the conclusion. Therefore this is, in my sense, a perfectly good inferential justification. So Moore is right, in this sense, to claim that his proof could provide knowledge of the conclusion, even if the premises are not proved. However, the sceptic, we saw, can challenge the premises. This is legitimate. The proof is **FT** fallible, that is, it is possible that Moore is wrong in holding the premises to be true. Nothing in what I have said of course entailed that you do not have to defend the premises of your inferences when they are challenged. I am granting that proofs of the form of Moore's proof can give sufficient justification for belief, and, in appropriate circumstances, knowledge of the conclusion. What happens to this justification, and to the possible knowledge, when the premises are challenged? That will depend on the nature of the challenge. If reasons are given to doubt the premises, and no defence is provided for them, they become unreasonable, and therefore the justification is lost. The sceptic is in effect arguing that the premises of the proof are akin to the belief that the coin will land tail; we should rationally assign them not more than a fifty per cent probability. Moore's reply to the challenge on his premise was, in our reconstruction, that they are justified by defeasible, but perfectly good evidence. What is this evidence however? Let us suppose it consists of a defeasible inferential justification. In my view, it would then need, to be a proper justification, to be something like this

Inference 7.

1 It looks to me as if there is a hand in front of me.
2 If my perceptual system is working properly, and the environment is favourable, then if it looks to me as if p, then p.
3 My perceptual system is working properly, and the environment is favourable.
4 ∴ There is a hand in front of me.

However, it is clear that premise 2, and in particular the part of it that states "the environment is favourable", is somehow assuming the conclusion of Moore's proof. Making explicit what it says would probably require stating the existence of the external world; if you think it wouldn't, then consider that the sceptic is going to challenge it, and its defence will at some point require the assumption that there is an external world. So, overall, Moore's argument would beg the question, after all. I take it, for the time being at least, that it makes no difference how large the circle is. The defence of his premises does beg the question, in something close to the traditional sense, and therefore the original argument does so too, in an indirect way, which is akin to what is known as failure of warrant transmission.[20] The epistemic shortcoming of the proof is that in order to have a warrant for the premises you need to have a belief in the conclusion, and you need that belief not to be blameworthy.

Note that I never claimed that deducing a belief from reasonably believed premises is sufficient for having a justification; if it were so, for any p that we reasonably believed, we would have a justification for believing it, because we could infer p from something that surely implies its truth, that is p itself. So the distinction would collapse; therefore, I have additional good reasons to say that circular arguments cannot help us to move from reasonable belief to justified belief.[21]

---

[20]See note 4 at p. 125 for references.

[21]One might worry that there is tension between this view and a closure principle for justification. Suppose I have a reasonable, but not justified, belief b, and I infer from it a second belief b^*; suppose also b^* entails b. Now it seems that if I realize this, I have a justified belief b^*, I know that b^* entails b, but I am not justified in

To avoid circularity, the premises of Moore's proof should be defended in a non-inferential way. There surely is the possibility of interpreting Moore as claiming a non-inferential warrant, a perceptual one, for his premises. Note that it is possible that, even interpreted that way, Moore's argument would still, overall, be a failure of warrant transmission. The non-inferential justification for my belief that there is a hand in front of me, might still need a background assumption similar to (2). The issue is open.[22] We have seen that Moore's defence of the premises of his proof, going back to his assumption that it is an inferential justification, begs the question against the sceptic. Even if Moore is justified in holding the belief that he has hands, he is unable to use that belief in building an argument against the sceptic.

He cannot even claim that the sceptic is assuming with no motivation that defeasible justification is not enough for knowledge. The sceptic has a strong argument for that assumption. That argument still leaves us a feasible notion of fallible evidence (**FT** fallible evidence) such that many of our beliefs could turn out to be justified, if it could be shown they rest on reasonable assumptions. My belief that I have hands might well be one of those. But this requires that we assume it is reasonable to believe in the existence of the external world. If, however, we could show directly that it is reasonable to assume the existence of the external world, Moore's proof would still not be useful. It would not do the heavy work of giving a first rationale for the existence of the external world, which must be given by some kind of non-inferential warrant, and plausibly it will not even reinforce our position, because of its circularity.

Our conclusion so far is that Moore's proof is utterly useless. Many people, however, will still find something appealing in it. I wish briefly to consider a possible different use of Moore's proof, which I take to be Wittgensteinean in spirit. As a matter of fact, one might suggest, Moore was aware of the circularity in his proof. This is hinted at by the following passage, at the end of "Proof of an External World":

> He [Kant] means to say, I think, that if I cannot prove that there is a hand here, I must accept it merely as a matter of faith – I cannot know it. Such a view, though it has been very common among philosophers, can, I think, be shown to be wrong – *though shown only by the use of*

---

believing *b*. I have two quick replies to this problem; first it's not trivial that all these conditions could hold together; secondly, to make explicit a belief that was tacit, might put new pressure both on itself and on the beliefs I derived from it.

[22] See again Wright (2000), Wright (2003) and Wright (2004), for the view that it would constitute a case of transmission failure, and Pryor (2004) for the opposite view.

premisses which are not known to be true, unless we do know of the existence of external things.[23]

In my reconstruction, Moore was claiming that the sceptic needs to deny the possibility of defeasible justification. However, the possibility of defeasible justification can be shown, it seems, only assuming the sceptic to be wrong. So, after all, Moore is begging the question against the sceptic, in assuming the possibility of defeasible justification for his belief that he has hands, and he is aware of that. Assuming this is correct, what then is he trying to accomplish?

Let us abandon the fiction that the belief in the existence of an external world is just like all other beliefs. It is in fact a very special one, in that a huge deal of our epistemic practice presupposes it. If we cannot reasonably stick to that belief, a lot of what we count as paradigmatic cases of justified beliefs would turn out to be unjustified. If we do not accept the existence of an external world, we are not justified in believing we have hands, and in believing a huge amount of similar things. The very method by which we justify that kind of belief would be less than rational. But isn't that absurd? The proof shows, by its own failure, the absurdity of trying to argue without presupposing the existence of the external world.

Of course, a real sceptic would be unimpressed by the foregoing. I am granting, on behalf of Moore, that his proof is in a way epistemically defective. What I am claiming is that, at the exact opposite of what Pryor (2004) suggests, despite its being epistemically defective Moore's proof is still in a certain sense dialectically effective. By provoking us to think about the pervasive and dramatic consequences that it would have to seriously consider the sceptical hypothesis, Moore's proof invites us not to take it seriously. What the proof provides is not an argument against the sceptic, but rather an illustration of the fact that we are probably psychologically incapable of believing it anyway, and we are probably psychologically incapable not to believe its negation, because we just cannot help believing a huge amount of things, such as our having hands, which entail its negation. I will conclude explaining why I think this is a Wittgensteinean reading of the proof, by glossing on the following quote (*On Certainty*, §495):

> One might simply say "O, rubbish!" to someone who wanted to make objections to the propositions that are beyond doubt. That is, not reply to him but admonish him.

This passage is probably intended by Wittgenstein to be in contrast with Moore's attitude. However, on the reading I am suggesting, what

---

[23]Cf. Moore (1959, p. 150), my italics.

Moore is doing is precisely admonishing the sceptic. Throughout his many papers on the subject, what Moore is saying, in essence, is just "O, rubbish!"; although, admittedly, he is saying that in an extremely complicated and, I would add, gentlemanly manner.

References

Brueckner, Anthony. 1994. The structure of the sceptical argument. *Philosophy and Phenomenological Research* 54(4):827–835.

Conee, Earl and Richard Feldman. 2004. *Evidentialism*. Oxford: Oxford University Press.

Copi, Irwing M. 1961. *Introduction to Logic*. New York: McMillian Company.

Davies, Martin. 2004. Epistemic entitlement, warrant transmission and easy knowledge. *The Aristotelian Society Supplementary Volume* 78:213–245.

Goldman, Alvin I. 1999. Internalism exposed. *The Journal of Philosophy* 96(6):271–293.

Goldman, Alvin I. 2007. The underdetermination argument for brain-in-the-vat scepticism. *Analysis* 67(1):32–36.

Haack, Susan. 1979. Fallibilism and necessity. *Synthese* 41(1):37–63.

Huemer, Michael. 2001. The problem of defeasible justification. *Erkenntnis* 54(3):375–397.

Moore, George E. 1959. *Philosophical Papers*. London: Allen and Unwin.

Pritchard, Duncan. 2005. *Epistemic Luck*. Oxford: Oxford University Press.

Pryor, Jim. 2004. What's wrong with moore's argument? *Philosophical Issues* 14.

Reed, Baron. 2002. How to think about fallibilism. *Philosophical Studies* 107(2):143–157.

Swinburne, Richard. 2001. *Epistemic Justification*. Oxford: Oxford University Press.

Williamson, Timothy. 2000. *Knowledge and Its Limits*. Oxford: Oxford University Press.

Wittgenstein, Ludwig. 1969. *On Certainty*. Oxford: Blackwell.

Wright, Crispin. 2000. Cogency and question-begging: Some reflections on McKinsey's paradox and Putnam's proof. *Philosophical Issues* 10:140–163.

Wright, Crispin. 2003. Wittgensteinian certainties. In D. McManus, ed., *Wittgenstein and Scepticism*, chap. 1, pages 22–55. London: Routledge.

Wright, Crispin. 2004. Warrant for nothing (and foundations for free)? *The Aristotelian Society Supplementary Volume* 78.

7
Taking Externalism Seriously: Externalism, Analyticity, and *A Priori* Knowledge

ASSAF SHARON AND JONATHAN YAARI

7.1

The following sentence has by now become a paradigmatic example of (at least one type of) analytic sentences:

(1)   Bachelors are unmarried men.

Since "unmarried man" is just the meaning of "bachelor," it seems that we can know this sentence without appeal to experience, and thus it is *a priori* knowable. This traditional conception, prominent among philosophers, is exemplified by the following quote from Kripke:

> [A]n analytic statement is, in some sense, true by virtue of its meaning and true in all possible worlds by virtue of its meaning. Then something which is analytically true will be both necessary and *a priori*.[1]

But consider the following scenario. Oscar, who is a competent user of English, has unknowingly been moved to Twin-Earth. On this twin planet, although water is composed of H_2O, the term "bachelor" is used only in reference to unmarried men under the age of 100. An unmarried man over 100 years of age is no longer called a "bachelor," but rather, say, a "sage." Oscar, who has not encountered any elderly bachelors on Twin-Earth, is oblivious to this minor semantic discrepancy and leads

---
[1] Kripke (1980, p. 39).

a happy linguistic life in his new twin-home. What Oscar doesn't know is that on Twin-Earth, not only is the sentence "all unmarried men are bachelors" not analytic, it is downright false.

Since Oscar is not a philosopher, he can go on as if nothing has happened. But for philosophers here on Earth, the mere possibility of Oscar's situation is enough to cast doubt on the status of (1), since it shows that an empirical enquiry is required to establish the sentence's truth. So, although analytic, it is *a posteriori*.

Note that our new predicate, twin-"bachelor," is not simply a grue-like predicate that does not exist in natural languages and may therefore not be taken seriously (as some have responded to Goodman's well-known "grue" argument). Indeed, a very similar predicate exists in English, where the word "spinster" is used to describe an *old* unmarried woman, so an eighteen-year-old unmarried woman is not a spinster.[2] The demarcation between "normal" unmarried women and spinsters is vague, but it just so happens that on Twin-Earth the concepts in question are clearly demarcated. An unmarried man is called a "bachelor" until he becomes 100, and from that day he is exclusively called a "sage." In other words, the classes of things twin-Earthlings call "bachelors" and "sages" are mutually exclusive.[3]

Making the point more apparent, compare the case of our Earthly Oscar and his doppelgänger twin-Oscar. Suppose neither knows about the peculiarity of twin-bachelorness. Much like many people on Earth are not aware of the bachelorette/spinster distinction, twin-Oscar, although growing up in the twin-English linguistic community, does not know that after the age of 100, one is not considered a bachelor but rather a sage. We can now think of Moses, a famous bachelor who has recently turned 100. Both Oscar and twin-Oscar think to themselves the words "Moses is an old bachelor", but only one of them thereby believes a truth. Oscar is of course right in thinking that Moses is an old bachelor, since on Earth "bachelor" doesn't have an age limit.

---

[2] In fact, the OED provides an illuminating discussion of the use of "spinster":
The development of the word *spinster* is a good example of the way in which a word acquires strong connotations to the extent that it can no longer be used in a neutral sense. From the 17th century, the word was appended to names as the official legal description of an unmarried woman: Elizabeth Harris of Boston, *Spinster*. This type of use survives today in some legal and religious contexts. In modern everyday English, however, *spinster* cannot be used to mean simply "unmarried woman"; it is now always a derogatory term, referring or alluding to a stereotype of an older woman who is unmarried, childless, prissy, and repressed.

[3] This is quite similar to the relationship between the English words "Bachelorette" and "Spinster", except there is a clear cut-off point. As a matter of fact, the concept bachelorette is unlike bachelor and similar to twin-bachelor since it applies only to young unmarried women.

But twin-Oscar is mistaken in the same way as someone on Earth who thinks that a fifteen-year-old girl is a spinster.[4] So, it turns out that the word "bachelor" behaves similarly to "water" in Putnam's famous Twin-Earth scenario. Only through empirical inquiry can one know the truth of sentences specifying the meaning of the word "bachelor"; "bachelors are unmarried men" and "water is H_2O" are both *a posteriori*.[5]

Thus, in more general terms, if semantic externalism is accepted, *i.e.*, that external factors, physical or social, count in determining the meanings of one's terms, it follows that some analytic truths are *a posteriori*.

The discussion above shows that at least some analytic sentences are not strictly *a priori*. In order to lend further support to a comprehensive claim regarding the relationship of analyticity and apriority, we must now specify how we understand some of the key notions being invoked.

What exactly counts as an analytic sentence is of course debatable, and we shall discuss this in due course. For now, let us use the following simple definition: a sentence is analytic if and only if it is true solely by virtue of the meaning of the terms appearing in it and its logical structure. The truth of the sentence "bachelors are unmarried men" is determined strictly by the meanings of the words comprising it and the logical form in which they are cast.

Externalism is taken here to be the family of semantic theses that state that there are factors external to one's mind that play a part in determining the meanings of one's utterances. These factors are usually thought to be either physical or social or both. The examples often put forward in support of externalism are utterances of *natural kind terms*

---

[4] As was established in debates on "slow-switching" in recent years, it should be noted that after a while (maybe a couple of years) on Twin-Earth, Oscar, too, will be mistaken when thinking the words "Moses is a bachelor" (because in so thinking he will no longer be thinking that Moses is a bachelor, but rather he's a twin-bachelor). But this does not bear on the current case.

[5] Those who think the externalist analysis of meaning applies only to natural kind terms and names may find the attribution of the concept "bachelor" to twin-Oscar objectionable. However, it seems to us that the case we have articulated establishes the requisite similarity between terms such as "bachelor" and natural kind terms like "water." Acknowledging that the meanings of terms of both sorts are determined externally, the specific mechanism being what it may, is just what it is to take externalism seriously. For further argumentation, see Burge (1986) and Brown (2001), who convincingly argue that the meaning of the term "sofa" – clearly not a natural kind term – is determined externally. As a side note, let us mention that Brown does think that "it is vital to consider whether anti-individualism rules out that the subject can ever have *a priori* knowledge of an analytic truth" (p. 220). But she does not pursue this suggestion.

and *names*.[6] According to the standard view, sentences such as "water is H_2O" are *a posteriori* even though they are necessary, but sentences such as "bachelors are unmarried men" are *a priori* and analytic. Our contention is that by accepting externalism one must also accept the *a posteriori* nature of at least some analytic sentences. The main idea is the following: the truth-value of a given sentence is determined by two factors: its meaning and the relevant facts in the world. The traditional classification of sentences into those that can be known *a priori* and those that are *a posteriori* turned on the latter component (the facts) while neglecting the role of the former in the determination of the epistemic status of sentences. In other words, it is usually thought that the categorization of sentences into those that can be known *a priori* and those knowable *a posteriori* is done, as it were, after the meaning of the sentence is known, so that if one knows the meaning of "bachelor," one can then know *a priori* that the sentence "bachelors are unmarried men" is true. We do not object to this position, but our claim is that semantic externalism requires, when determining whether a given sentence is knowable *a priori*, that the ways in which the meaning of the sentence (and, in particular, of the terms comprising it) are fixed be taken into account. Taking externalism seriously is not taking knowledge of meaning for granted. So while a category of *a priori* can be fixed as what is knowable without recourse to experience *given that the meanings are known*, such a demarcation of the epistemic categories would be – from the point of view of externalism – unprincipled and theoretically uninteresting.

By drawing a distinction between sentences whose truth is knowable once their meaning is (fully) grasped and sentences whose truth cannot be known without taking further account of facts in the world, one can continue to maintain a sense in which analytic truths are *a priori*. However, this is hardly what the apriority of analytic truths was meant to be. Under this conception, the clear-cut distinction between sentences requiring empirical inquiry for their truth-evaluation and those that can be evaluated "from the armchair" collapses. When considering whether a sentence is *a priori* in the substantive sense, we argue, one must take into account both stages of determining its truth-value. And once it is conceded that external factors play a part in the determination of

---

[6]The argument for names is usually not presented as an argument for externalism but for a "causal theory of reference." For our purpose, there is no real difference between the two, since our argument would work for tracking the meaning of a term that got its reference (and meaning) causally. If a name's reference is determined causally, then in order to know to which object a name refers, one has to track the causal chain, which is clearly an empirical undertaking.

meanings (and that in order to account for these external factors one must appeal to some empirical, non-*a priori* investigation), then even analytic sentences containing terms of this sort would ultimately have to be regarded as *a posteriori*.

Let us consider the notion of *a priori* knowledge more explicitly. Considerations similar to those being discussed here have led some epistemologists to understand *a priori* knowledge as truths knowable without recourse to experience beyond the extent needed for understanding them. A characteristic example of this is BonJour's conception of *a priori* justification:

> The key point is that while not only the allegedly *a priori* justification in these cases, but indeed *any* sort of justification *of course* presupposes an understanding of the proposition (or propositions) in question, that understanding does not thereby constitute a part of the justification itself, that is, a part of the reason for thinking that the proposition in question is true.[7]

Thus, according to BonJour, the classification of what is knowable *a priori* and what is knowable *a posteriori* comes, so to speak, after the meanings of the stated terms have been understood.[8] But what exactly is meant by "understanding"? There are two possible answers to this question. One option is that by "understanding" BonJour means complete comprehension, *i.e.*, a full understanding of the meanings of the terms in question. A second option is that by "understanding" he means knowing all that is needed in order to qualify as a competent user of the terms, *i.e.* a person who knows enough about the meaning of the terms to be able to use them correctly in all practical circumstances.

The first notion of understanding may indeed support BonJour's conclusions, but it has some very unwelcome consequences. Consider the case of sentences that are knowable *a posteriori* such as "water is H_2O." Surely, part of the "full meaning" of "water" is the fact that it is H_2O.[9] So if the epistemic status of this sentence is determined post-understanding, and "understanding" means knowing all there is to know about the meaning of the terms (including "water"), then the sentence is knowable *a priori*. Once it is known that the meaning of "water" includes the fact that it is H_2O, the sentence stating their identity is *a priori*. Notice that this applies not only to identity sentences.

---

[7] BonJour (2000, p. 80).

[8] BonJour talks here of propositions, whereas our argument is phrased in terms of sentences. There is, of course, a deep and important difference between the two. This issue is discussed at length below in the third section.

[9] We take "full meaning" to include all that goes into the determination of the truth values of sentences in which a term figures.

Consider, for instance, the sentence "whales are mammals." Again, it seems very plausible that part of the full meaning of the term "whale" is that it is a mammal, *i.e.*, one could not be considered to possess a full understanding of the meaning of "whale" if one thinks that "whales are fish." So, again, if apriority pertains to the epistemic status of the sentence after all is known, then this sentence, too, comes out *a priori*. In sum, endorsing this notion of understanding, requiring complete knowledge of meaning before assessing whether a given sentence is *a priori*, leads to unpalatable results, namely that many sentences that seem *a posteriori* turn out to be knowable *a priori*.

The second conception of understanding is therefore more appealing. Indeed, why require a speaker to have *complete* understanding of the meanings of terms in order to be considered a competent user of them? Children are competent users of "water" even though they know nothing about chemical composition. And here is another example, more closely related to the earlier case, discussed above. Others have noted that the question of whether or not the predicate "bachelor" may properly be applied to the Pope might not be answerable unequivocally. Yet it seems unreasonable to claim that our failure to possess this semantic knowledge renders us incompetent in the use of the term "bachelor."[10] Surely, twin-Oscar is a competent speaker of twin-English, and specifically a competent user of the term "bachelor," even though he is unaware that its application is limited to men under a certain age. But under this conception, sentences such as "all unmarried men are bachelors" fall once again into the category of *a posteriori* knowable. Although he understands – in this second sense of understanding – the sentence "all unmarried men are bachelors," twin-Oscar doesn't know that it is false. The truth-value, and more importantly, the justification of this sentence, in Oscar's case, involves recourse to some empirical investigation, since in order to determine truth-value Oscar must first determine whether he is a speaker of English or of twin-English.

The upshot of the foregoing argument is that all sentences containing terms that require some empirical tracking in order to determine their meanings are *a posteriori*. The question now remains of specifying which are these terms. Generally speaking, the same sort of argument that we have offered in the example of "bachelor" is also applicable to other terms in a *natural language*. Without committing ourselves to a specific metaphysical doctrine, it is reasonable to say that (accord-

---

[10] Assuming this is not a case of vagueness or semantic indeterminacy but of epistemic unclarity.

ing to externalism) the meanings of most terms in natural language are determined either by objects in the physical world to which they refer or by the social circumstances of their use. Since these physical and social features are factual, hence empirically cognized, it follows, we contend, that the meanings of the corresponding terms in natural language cannot be known strictly *a priori*.

The status of natural language can be contrasted with terms that are introduced *via stipulation*. Kripke's, complete paragraph from which the quote at the beginning of this paper is taken, illustrates what is meant by stipulation:

> Another term used in philosophy is "analytic". Here it won't be too important to get any clearer about this in this talk. [...] At any rate, *let's just make it a matter of stipulation* that an analytic statement is, in some sense, true by virtue of its meaning and true in all possible worlds by virtue of its meaning. Then something which is analytically true will be both necessary and *a priori*. (That's sort of stipulative.)[11]

In addition to articulating the traditional view of analyticity, this passage exemplifies the notion of definition by stipulation. By Kripke's stipulation, it becomes *a priori* knowable that, *e.g.*, an analytic statement is necessary. However, it is quite clear that although Kripke has articulated some features of the term "analytic" in natural language, he has not provided, nor did he intend to provide, the exact meaning of "analytic." The specific notion as it appears in statements of natural language was not fully accounted for.[12] Indeed, even after accepting Kripke's stipulation it is completely reasonable to claim that Kripke's "analytic" has not captured the extension of that which is actually analytic. Such a reaction to stipulative definitions is quite common, notably in the field of mathematics. Mathematicians frequently use stipulative definitions in order to introduce new terms. Even those mathematical terms that were first introduced intuitively, as an extension of natural language terms, are later given a formal definition that gives their

---

[11] Kripke (1980, p. 39), emphasis added.

[12] As a side note, it should be mentioned that Kripke's view on the matter in *Naming and Necessity* is not entirely clear. He writes: "I am presupposing that an analytic truth is one which depends on meanings in the strict sense and therefore is necessary as well as *a priori*" (Kripke, 1980, p. 122). What is "the strict sense" of meaning? Kripke goes on to say: "If statements whose *a priori* truth is known via the fixing of a reference are counted as analytic, then some analytic truths are contingent." In a footnote earlier in the book, Kripke says that he chooses not to call statements of the latter type analytic, "stipulatively requiring analytic truths to be both necessary and *a priori*" (p. 56). As far as stipulation goes, this choice is surely legitimate. However, in the context of the present discussion (of the possibility of analytic *a posteriori* statements, which, admittedly did not concern Kripke), assuming this Kripkian notion of analyticity is begging the question.

exact meaning by stipulation. A good example of this practice is the concept of limit in modern mathematics. Today, any mathematical consequences that are arrived at from premises that use the definition of "limit" are *a priori*, precisely because they are derived from the stipulated meaning of "limit." Moreover, mathematicians would agree that "their" "limit" is not coextensive with the natural language term "limit", since what determines the meaning of the mathematical "limit" is the stipulation, and not its origin in natural language.[13] But how does one determine the connection between natural language terms and their references and meanings? It could be argued that all one needs is a good dictionary, listing the definition of every given term. This route, however, is not open to the proponents of *a priori* knowledge of meaning, as shown by Quine in his famous "Two Dogmas":

> There are those who find it soothing to say that the analytic statements of the second class reduce to those of the first class, the logical truths, by definition; "bachelor," for example, is defined as "unmarried man." But how do we find that "bachelor" is defined as "unmarried man"? Who defined it thus, and when? Are we to appeal to the nearest dictionary, and accept the lexicographer's formulation as law? Clearly this would be to put the cart before the horse. *The lexicographer is an empirical scientist*, whose business is the recording of antecedent facts; and if he glosses "bachelor" as "unmarried man" it is because of his belief that there is a relation of synonymy between these forms, implicit in general or preferred usage prior to his own work.[14]

Unlike the case of stipulation, where the definition determines the meaning of a term *a priori*, in the case of natural languages, a dictionary definition is the product of empirical observation, and therefore cannot be considered a basis for *a priori* knowledge of meaning.

Finally, we note that the meanings of terms appearing in natural languages, such as English or twin-English, are determined *naturally*. A consequence of taking externalism seriously is understanding it as alluding to the involvement of environmental factors that play a part in the determination of meanings, which may be epistemically independent of the speaker. Therefore, in order to determine the precise meanings of the terms one uses, one may have to track some environmental features of the language community. This activity is clearly an

---

[13]This point is articulated eloquently in the classical "Introduction to Knot Theory" by Crowell and Fox (1963): "Mathematics never proves anything about anything except mathematics, and a piece of rope is a physical object and not a mathematical one. So before worrying about proofs, we must have a mathematical definition of what a knot is." This conception is emphasized by Shapiro (1981, p. 360), from whom the quote is taken.

[14]Quine (1951, p. 24), emphasis added.

empirical undertaking, since it involves an investigation into the nature of the physical and social environment. The result is that the first step in determining the truth-value of a sentence in natural language, particularly in discovering the meanings of the terms comprising it, is (often) empirical. Thus, there is an unavoidable empirical element in determining the truth-value of most natural language sentences, even of some analytic sentences.

7.2

In order to gain further insight into the significance of the argument of the preceding section, we shall now consider some features of semantic externalism. We examine a particular argument that was proposed against semantic externalism and show how the claim that some analytic sentences are *a posteriori* helps to diffuse it.

Considering the case of Peter, the opera buff, Paul Boghossian raised the following argument against externalism:[15]

> While still on earth, [Peter] goes hiking in the mountains of northern New Zealand. Here he comes across Lake Taupo and is startled to see the famous tenor Luciano Pavarotti floating in its pristine waters.
>
> ...
>
> Well, some years go by and Peter moves to Twin-Earth and becomes happily ensconced there. Of course, he maintains his interest in opera and so continues to read and hear about his favourite performers. Eventually, some of the tokens of his mental names come to refer to the twin counterparts of the familiar earthly performers: tokens of "Domingo" come to refer to twin Domingo, tokens of "Pavarotti" to twin Pavarotti, and so on.

Now suppose Peter went to a Pavarotti concert yesterday. Boghossian then considers the following inference made by Peter on Twin-Earth:

(2) Pavarotti once swam in Lake Taupo.
(3) The singer I heard yesterday is Pavarotti.

Therefore:

(4) The singer I heard yesterday once swam in Lake Taupo.

The problem is straightforward: Both premises of the argument are true, the inference appears to be valid, and yet the conclusion is false. Thus, in Boghossian's words:

---

[15] The following and all other quotes by Boghossian in this section are taken from Boghossian (1992).

In travelers like Peter, both the relationship between derivability and validity and the transparency of thought content break down, with the result that inferences that look to be, "from the inside", valid, aren't. And *the thesis of the apriority of logical abilities is shown, thereby, to be inconsistent with externalist assumptions.*[16]

Although Boghossian does not state this explicitly, it is quite clear that he views this result as fatal for externalism: if externalism is inconsistent with "the apriority of our logical abilities," then one must uphold the latter and abandon externalism.

Boghossian's point is that Peter's argument appears valid, when in fact it is not. The name "Pavarotti" when appearing in the first premise refers to Earth-Pavarotti, whereas in the second premise the name "Pavarotti" refers to twin-Pavarotti. The conclusion, therefore, simply doesn't follow from the premises.

Some of the attempts to resolve Boghossian's puzzle rest on the claim that one of the premises is false to begin with, *i.e.*, that in slow-switching scenarios either the reference of the terms changes over completely to the twin-objects, or else that none of the terms change their reference to twin-objects. In the former case, the first premise is simply false, and in the latter case, the second premise is false, so logic remains *a priori*. But this answer is too cozy and apparently unavailable to those who take externalism seriously. We agree, therefore, with Boghossian that the plausible analysis is that both premises are true while the conclusion is false.

A more modest response to Boghossian's argument runs as follows. Suppose it is agreed that in slow-switching scenarios, like Peter's, terms involved in memory descriptions generally retain their original reference while others switch reference. Then the claim is that, nevertheless, when one is in the process of making inferences the references of terms used in the inferences remain fixed throughout the inference. In other words, even if we agree that when Peter thinks of Pavarotti *vis-à-vis* swimming in Lake Taupo he is thinking of Earth-Pavarotti and when Peter thinks of Pavarotti *vis-à-vis* the concert last night he is thinking of twin-Pavarotti, when making an inference using the term "Pavarotti" in both premises, its reference must be the same in both. Therefore, the reply goes, there is no equivocation in Peter's reasoning, and the inference is indeed valid (with one of the premises being false).[17]

To us, this reply does not appear very convincing. The main problem with the proposed solution is that it looks rather *ad hoc*-ish. If one

---

[16] Emphasis added.
[17] For this suggestion, see Schiffer (1992).

accepts that when on Twin-Earth Peter evokes memories of Pavarotti from his days on Earth he normally refers to Earth-Pavarotti, and when speaking of a recent encounter with him (say at a concert last night) he refers to twin-Pavarotti, it doesn't seem plausible that when used as premises of an inference, the reference in one of the sentences somehow changes. One would have to provide a detailed account of how the reference of names is shifted when names are used in the context of inferences, and such an account does not seem forthcoming. Moreover, even if such an account exists, there still remains the problem of identifying the wrong premise *a priori*.[18]

We believe that a more straightforward response to Boghossian's argument is called for. But first let us examine exactly what the problem is. Here is how Boghossian puts it:

> Peter will not be able to judge *a priori* the logical properties of his inferences. (p. 21)

This does indeed sound like trouble. However, consider Boghossian's later footnote:

> I am not saying that externalism undermines our ability to tell *a priori* what form an argument would have to have in order to be logically valid; I am arguing that externalism undermines our ability to tell *a priori* whether any particular inference of ours satisfies one of those forms.

But what's the problem with that? Indeed, Peter's inference seems valid when actually it is not – allowing him to derive a false conclusion from true premises. Moreover, we agree that Peter is unable *a priori* to detect whether his inference (or any other inference laid out in natural language) is a token of a valid inferential form. However, Peter is capable of detecting, *a priori*, the validity of forms. *A priori* knowledge of logical relationships is not undermined by a possible failure to *a priori* recognize a particular token of some logical form. Logical relationships of the type that is relevant to the discussion of *a priori* knowledge are relationships between forms. We may know *a priori* that the form codified by *modus ponens*, for instance, is the form of a valid inference, yet at the same time we may fail to recognize some particular inference as a token of *modus ponens*. Nowhere does Boghossian spell out why he thinks anyone should expect us to have knowledge of the latter sort *a priori*. So it seems that the appropriate response to Boghossian's argu-

---

[18] For a comprehensive analysis and criticism of Schiffer's and similar responses to Boghossian's argument, see Goldberg (2007). Goldberg convincingly shows that, even if accepted, this line of argument does not overcome other versions of the problem raised by Boghossian's example.

ment is just to accept its conclusion and reject its ominous tone. The possibility does exists of failure to recognize tokens of valid inferences *a priori*, but this does not threaten "the apriority of logical abilities."

But this is not the whole story. Interestingly, given the point of the first part of this paper, externalism emerges in a better position than competing theories to deal with the possibility of mistaken identification of a logical form. Since semantic externalism admits the aposteriority of some analytic sentences, it also allows for the aposteriority of inference-recognition to be accounted for. The epistemological gist of externalism consists of the idea that in most instances the relation between words (and sentences) and their meanings is not trivial. Linguistic entities are connected to their meanings in empirically complex ways, so quite often, knowledge of meaning rests unavoidably on empirical knowledge. One must therefore reject the hypothesis that if the truth of a sentence depends only on its meaning then it is *a priori*, and can be known (justified) without recourse to experience. Since knowledge of meaning is itself, more often than not, an empirical matter, determining truth-values, even when they depend only on meaning and logical form, will also be an empirical matter. This explains why a subject may not always be able to tell by reflection (*a priori*) whether an inference she makes is valid or not.

Now we can see how Boghossian's argument sidesteps a crucial point concerning the nature of the semantic commitments of externalism, namely its implications for the relationship between analyticity and apriority. To see this, let us recast the argument in a form that brings out its relationship to the issue of analyticity. Since any valid inference can be made into an analytic sentence by constructing an implication leading from the conjunction of the premises to the conclusion, we can restate Boghossian's argument as the following analytic sentence:

(5) *If* Pavarotti once swam in Lake Taupo *and* the singer I heard yesterday is Pavarotti, *then* the singer I heard yesterday once swam in Lake Taupo.

Sentence (5) appears analytic, but it turns out that in Peter's case it is not even true. Even when the sentence is true, one cannot know this *a priori*. So we obtain a strengthened version of Boghossian's thesis and arrive at our own claim – externalism implies that for some analytic sentences, *a priori* recognition of the truth-value is impossible. The point is this: The novel consequences of externalism for the seam connecting language and epistemology do not pertain to knowledge of logical abilities, but rather to the relationship between the semantic category of analytic and the epistemological category of *a priori*. We have argued that not only does externalism render the meanings of names and natural kind terms *a posteriori*, but it does so also for many other terms of natural language. It follows that many sentences that are traditionally considered analytic, even paradigmatically analytic, are – given externalism – nevertheless *a posteriori*.

7.3

In this final section, we address possible objections and clear up a few issues related to the position advanced above. The first of these has to do with the issue of *propositions*. In the foregoing discussion, propositions were deliberately suppressed, in order to avoid committing ourselves to any specific doctrine regarding the existence of such entities. However, since realism about propositions, loosely defined as language- and thought-independent abstract entities that convey meanings (in the sense of being either true or false), is quite common, let us briefly address it. Once the existence of entities of this sort is accepted, it is easy to restate the position advanced here claiming that while the truth of some propositions can be known *a priori*, determining exactly *which* proposition a given sentence expresses is often a matter of *a posteriori* investigation. Thus, to recap our reply to Boghossian's argument concerning Peter's inference, we can now say that the validity of inferences can be decided *a priori only* at the level of propositions. Peter's mistake in thinking that his inference is valid is the result of his ignorance about which propositions are expressed by sentences (2) and (3). The crucial point is, of course, that the name "Pavarotti" appearing in both sentences denotes two different objects, so the conclusion simply does not follow. This is very clear at the level of propositions. If Peter knows the propositions, he can surely know *a priori* whether the inference that they comprise is valid or not. The case of Oscar (in section 7.1 above) can be clarified in the same way. Oscar's inability to know *a priori* that "all unmarried men are bachelors" is due to his being incapable of telling *a priori* whether that sentence expresses a proposition about Earth-bachelorness or about Twin-Earth-bachelorness. If our argument is cogent, semantic externalism implies that discovering which proposition is expressed by a sentence is often an empirical matter, but once this is settled, the truth of the proposition can be known, so to speak, *a priori*.

Another matter that needs to be explicitly addressed has to do with the notion of *a priori* knowledge. In the discussion thus far, no mention has been made of the difference between *a priori* knowledge and *a priori* warrant or justification. However, it is common in this context to distinguish between how truths get to be known and the epistemological warrant or justification of these truths.[19] To take an example discussed by Boghossian and Peacocke, one can come to know the logical truth $(p \to q) \lor (q \to p)$ by reading a proof of it. Seeing the proof written down is what causes the belief that $(p \to q) \lor (q \to p)$ is true, yet the warrant for this belief has nothing to do with the *a posteriori* process of reading pencil marks on paper. The belief is warranted by different, *a priori*, considerations, namely that it is a logical truth. Important as this distinction is, it has no implications for our account of *a posteriori* analytic sentences and the validity of inferences, because here *a priori* knowledge is understood in the justificatory sense. In other words, when noting the *a posteriori* nature of the process of discovering the meanings of terms in natural language sentences, we refer to the impossibility of a non-empirical, *a priori*, warrant for knowledge of these meanings. The point is not that one must use one's senses to discover some meaning-facts that are in fact *a priori* warranted, but rather that there is no *a priori* warrant for believing these meaning-facts.

As a further objection, it may be proposed that externalism, in our interpretation, leads to unsettling skepticism.[20] Since the meanings of Oscar's words depend on his terrestrial location, it would seem that he cannot know the meaning of the word "bachelor" before conducting an empirical investigation as to which planet he resides on. Thus, in order to be considered as knowing the meaning of the word "bachelor," or any other word for that matter, Oscar would have to embark on an empirical investigation eliminating the possibility of the word having a deviant meaning. Since for every word in natural language there are infinite possible deviant meanings, Oscar would never be able to know the meanings of the words he uses. The reply to this worry – which is a variant of the general concern about the compatibility of externalism with knowledge of meaning – is related to the previous issue. The imaginary Twin-Earth scenario is not an illustration of how Oscar – or any of us – actually go about using terms in English and figuring out their meanings. Rather, the purpose of the scenario is to highlight the source of Oscar's epistemological warrant for knowing the meanings of the words he uses. In other words, it is assumed that in real-world scenarios Oscar, and other competent users of natural language, does not empirically investigate his environmental surroundings to determine the meanings of his words before using them. Speakers are entitled to the presumption that the meanings of their words are

---

[19] Boghossian and Peacocke (2000).
[20] This objection was raised by Timothy Williamson in discussion.

what they take them to be and their beliefs regarding meanings are normally warranted. The point is, however, that according to externalism their knowledge of meanings is warranted by the empirical facts of their surroundings. This, of course, is no surprise for the proponents of semantic externalism and does not entail a radical skeptical thesis according to which every time a speaker uses words that the speaker needs first to empirically rule out the possibility that these words have deviant meanings in the environment in which the speaker resides.

We turn now to a possible objection that bears on the scope of analyticity as it emerges from the present proposal. It may seem that the argument unavoidably extends to the field of mathematics, and this will carry unfortunate consequences. Mimicking our treatment of "bachelor," a Twin-Earth scenario can also be constructed around the concept of "prime number." Suppose that on Twin-Earth "prime" is not defined as a number evenly divisible only by itself and one, but rather as a number smaller than $1,000,000$ divisible only by itself and one. By this new definition, the number $1,000,003$, which is a prime number, cannot properly be called "prime" on Twin-Earth. Next we consider Oscar and his doppelgänger twin-Oscar both thinking the words "$1,000,003$ is a prime." It seems that much like the sentence "Moses is a bachelor," the truth-value of this sentence differs between Earth and Twin-Earth. When uttered on Earth, this sentence expresses a truth (and indeed a necessary one), and when uttered on Twin-Earth a falsehood. Therefore, the objection would proceed, the present account would render sentences containing the term "prime number' *a posteriori* (just like "bachelor"), since knowledge of the truth of the sentence "$1,000,003$ is prime" depends, among other things, on external conditions that must be ascertained empirically. Therefore, our argument would seem to imply that at least some parts of mathematics (arithmetic, in this case) are *a posteriori*.

A possible reply to this objection is to accept that mathematics is *a posteriori*. However, this is, if nothing else, a controversial position, and it is one we do not wish to endorse. Luckily, we don't have to. The objection relies on the assumption that mathematical terms can, and should, be given an externalist account. But this assumption is widely contested even by those who advocate semantic externalism for other terms. Recall that externalism is a theory about the semantics of natural languages and in this sense mathematics is not a natural language. In order to be considered as having knowledge of specific mathematical statements, one must be fully knowledgeable of the definitions of the relevant mathematical terms. So in this case, to know that "$1,000,003$ is prime" is true, one must fully understand the meanings of the terms appearing in that sentence. Given such complete understanding, the sentence is either *a priori* (as in Earthly Oscar's case), or else it is knowably false (as in the case of twin-Oscar). It is of course possible that both Oscars were told by expert mathematicians that certain specific numbers are primes. Thus, it is possible that our Oscars know specific mathematical truths, just like children might know the truth of a specific mathematical statement through testimony. However, if neither Oscar was ever specifically told by an expert that "$1,000,003$ is prime" is true, then although they might think this sentence is true, they should not be considered as knowing it (even when it is true – as in Earthly-Oscar's case), since they lack proper justification (*a priori* or *a posteriori*). In other words, Oscar's belief in the truth of this sentence is, in a way, accidental. It is at best an educated guess, and accidental beliefs and guesses do not constitute knowledge. The conclusion is that neither Oscar nor twin-Oscar can be said to know any truth about primes other than what they know by expert testimony. Thus, we see that this scenario cannot be alleged to lead to the possibility of *a posteriori* mathematical knowledge, since it does not lead to knowledge of mathematics at all.

Placing this conclusion within the context of the general position advanced in this paper, it can be stated that terms of mathematics are not the kind of terms whose meaning are determined externally. Unlike the case of the term "bachelor," in the case of mathematical terms, one is not considered competent in their use if one does not already possess a complete understanding of them. In this sense, the meanings of the terms used in mathematical discourse are not determined externally, and mathematical sentences do not belong to the identified class of *a posteriori* analytic sentences.

To sum up, we identify three main classes of *a priori* statements to which our argument concerning the scope of analytic *a posteriori* sentences does not apply. First, there are logical truths in an explicitly defined formal language. A good example of this case is Boghossian's and Peacocke's $(p \to q) \vee (q \to p)$ cited above. A second class includes all truths brought about by stipulation, as was discussed in Section 7.1. Thus, the following is an example of an *a priori* knowable sentence: "if 'Bachelor' is stipulated to mean 'unmarried man' and Moses is unmarried, then Moses is a bachelor." Lastly, the truths of mathematics are also *a priori*, for reasons mentioned above.[21] The common feature of

---

[21] We do not contend that this list of types of *a priori* sentences is exhaustive. Examples of other possibly *a priori* sentences may include "I am here now" or "x is identical to itself." The apriority of sentences of this type may perhaps be explained similarly to the way the apriority of mathematics is explained – they are comprised

these three classes is that they have to do with sentences whose truth-conditions are based on logical structure, independently of referential and other links to the external world. Our contention that many of the sentences traditionally considered analytic (specifically those called conceptual truths) are *a posteriori* is entirely consistent with maintaining, as indeed we do, that logic is *a priori*.[22]

To recap: our main purpose in this paper has been to argue that, given semantic externalism, many analytic sentences are *a posteriori*. It must be stressed, however, that this must not be considered as obliterating the epistemological difference between the two types of *a posteriori* sentences, namely, analytic and non-analytic (synthetic) sentences. The truth-value of sentences of the former type is determined once the meaning of the terms comprising them is, which is not the case when it comes to sentences of the latter type. Knowledge of non-analytic sentences requires some empirical input beyond what is needed to know their meaning. So while both types of statements are *a posteriori*, we can speak of two classes of *a posteriori* sentences: those where empirical investigation is required only for the determination of their meanings and those requiring such investigation both for determining precise meaning and for determining truth-value.

It is perhaps appropriate, in conclusion, to place the present argument in the context of the traditional debate about the *a priori* and conclude with a suggestion of a more promissory nature, the development of which goes beyond the reach of this paper. Inasmuch as the Quinean argument targeted not only the idea of analytic sentences, but also specifically the possibility of *a priori* analytic sentences, the argument proposed herewith can be viewed as a vindication of analyticity. Our argument relies on semantic externalism to suggest the divorce of the purely semantic category of analyticity from the epistemic category of *a priori* knowledge. This divorce, in our opinion, allows statements of the type "all unmarried men are bachelors," traditionally regarded as analytic, to maintain this semantic status even though they may not be knowable *a priori*. Thus, to the extent that arguments against analyticity hinge on a rejection of *a priori* knowledge of their truth,

---

of terms the meanings of which are not determined externally, at least not in way that is epistemically independent of their user. However, a complete survey and discussion of all possible categories of sentences and their epistemological status is beyond the scope of this paper. Here we limit ourselves only to the identification of some such categories.

[22] In a recent paper, Ludlow (2003) has suggested an even more radical approach, according to which the consequence of externalism is that even logic is *a posteriori*. Ludlow himself does not consider his suggestion to be complete, so we shall refrain from discussing it here.

the present argument can be considered a vindication of analyticity.[23]

References

Boghossian, Paul A. 1992. Externalism and inference. *Philosophical Issues* 2:11–28.

Boghossian, Paul A. and Christopher Peacocke. 2000. Introduction. In P. A. Boghossian and C. Peacocke, eds., *New Essays on the A Priori*, pages 1–10. Oxford: Oxford University Press.

BonJour, Laurence. 2000. *Epistemology: Classic Problems and Contemporary Responses*. Lanham UK: Rowman and Littlefield.

Brown, Jessica. 2001. Anti-individualism and agnosticism. *Analysis* 61(271):213–224.

Burge, Tayler. 1986. Intellectual norms and the foundation of mind. *Journal of Philosophy* 83(12):697–720.

Crowell, Richard H. and Ralph H. Fox. 1963. *Introduction to Knot Theory*. Boston: Ginn.

Goldberg, Sanford. 2007. Semantic externalism and illusions of epistemic relevance. In S. Goldberg, ed., *Internalism and Externalism in Semantics and Epistemology*. Oxford: Oxford University Press.

Kripke, Saul A. 1980. *Naming and Necessity*. Cambridge MA: Harvard University Press.

Ludlow, Peter. 2003. Externalism, logical form and linguistic intentions. In A. Barber, ed., *The Epistemology of Language*, chap. 12, pages 399–415. Oxford: Oxford University Press.

Quine, Willard van Orman. 1951. Two dogmas of empiricism. *Philosophical Review* 60(1):20–43. Reprinted in (Quine, 1961, pp. 20–46).

Quine, Willard van Orman. 1961. *From a Logical Point of View*. Cambridge MA: Harvard University Press, II edn.

Schiffer, Stephen. 1992. Boghossian on externalism and inference. *Philosophical Issues* 2:29–37.

Shapiro, Stewart. 1981. Understanding church's thesis. *Journal of Philosophical Logic* 10(3):353–365.

---

[23] We thank Hagit Benbaji, David Enoch, Sanford Goldberg, Arnon Levy, Ofra Magidor, Alik Pelman, Oron Shagrir, and Levi Spectre for many very helpful comments on earlier versions of this paper. We would also like to thank the participants of the SIFA graduate conference 2007 for insightful discussion. Lastly, we wish to express our thanks to the conference organizers for their generosity and hospitality, which made this conference particularly rewarding.

Section III: Metaphysics

8

Is an "Olsonian" Critique of Hitchcock's View on Causality successful?[1]

BENGT AUTZEN

8.1 Introduction

The philosophical analysis of causality and the philosophical analysis of personal identity are commonly perceived as two distinct projects in contemporary analytic philosophy. The literature on causality rarely mentions the literature on personal identity and *vice versa*. However, the walls between these two fields have not always been so high. As James Humber points out, David Hume's analysis of personal identity parallels his analysis of causality in a several ways.[2] For instance, Humber states that, as is the case in Hume's analysis of causality, Hume fails to find an impression that could serve as the basis for an idea of a self that remains essentially unchanged throughout time. In the case of causality, introspection does not lead Hume to the impression of any necessary connection between the alleged cause and its alleged effect. According to Hume, we only find that cause and effect appear together. Let us, for instance, take the statement "friction causes heat". When we observe a heavy object moving on a surface, we can only observe the movement of the object on the surface and that the surface gets warm

---

[1] I would like to thank Jason Alexander, Nancy Cartwright, Katy Dineen and Matthew Parker for very helpful suggestions on earlier drafts of this paper.
[2] See Humber (1999, p. 314).

on the paths of the moving object. We cannot observe any "bond" between the movement of the object and the rising of the temperature of the surface.

Similarly in the case of personal identity: Here, introspection leads Hume only to the discovery of a stream of successive thoughts or perceptions that are distinct and separable from each other. For instance, at time t_1 we see a car driving fast towards us, at time t_2 we think that we should get out of the way of the car in order not to be hit by it, at time t_3 we jump to the side, and so on. Introspection does not lead Hume to the discovery of an invariable thinking substance that might ground our notion of personal identity.

The details of Humber's as well as Hume's analysis do not concern us here. What can be learned is a more general, methodological point, namely, that the philosophical analyses of causality and personal identity can be very similar from a structural point of view. Further, Humber's discussion suggests that when philosophers analyse personal identity something can be learned from the analysis of causality and vice versa. In this paper I will illustrate this methodological point in a more contemporary debate. That is, I will show that Christopher Hitchcock's discussion of causality parallels Derek Parfit's view on personal identity from a structural point of view. Further, I will argue that in the contemporary discussion about causality something can be learned from Parfit's writing on personal identity.

More specifically, I will examine whether Hitchcock's position put forward in his paper "Of Humean Bondage"[3], can be successfully criticised by an argument similar to one given by Eric Olson in the context of the debate about personal identity.[4] In particular, I will assess if Olson's argument used against the "decision thesis"[5] can be used in a modified version against Hitchcock's position. I will argue that an 'Olsonian' critique leads to a difficulty in Hitchcock's account and suggest how it might be overcome by looking at Parfit's writings on personal identity.

In the next section I will sketch the similarities between Hitchcock's view on causality and Parfit's view on personal identity.

8.2 Hitchcock and Parfit

In his paper "Of Humean Bondage" Christopher Hitchcock argues against, what he calls, the "Thesis of Humean Bondage" (THB). The

---
[3] See Hitchcock (2003).
[4] See Olson (2006).
[5] See Olson (2006, pp. 253–254).

THB reads as follows:

> In any concrete situation, there is an objective fact of the matter as to whether two events are in fact bound by the causal relation. It is the aim of philosophical inquiry to analyze this relation.[6]

In other words, Hitchcock argues that the idea that there is an objective fact of the matter as to whether two events are bound by the causal relation is mistaken. In particular, Hitchcock thinks that the word "the" preceding "causal relation" is misleading since there is no unique causal relation. Rather, he argues in favour of a certain form of pluralism about causality. The "causal pluralism" Hitchcock is advocating suggests that there is a variety of causal relations. He thinks that once one has, for instance, established what probabilistic correlations hold between certain events or what counterfactuals are true, one can identify a number of relations that are all causal in a broad sense of the word.[7]

Hitchcock thinks that in most cases when philosophers dispute whether two events stand in the causal relation there is no dispute about what he calls the "stage-one-facts" of an example. By saying that the 'stage-one-facts' of a case are clear, Hitchcock means that everybody involved in the debate agrees on what (non-backtracking) counterfactuals are true, what probabilistic correlations hold, and what events are connected by the type of processes which Wesley Salmon has called "causal processes"[8]. Further, Hitchcock means that "[t]here is no controversy over whether the cases rely on accidental generalizations, spurious correlations, backtracking counterfactuals or pseudo-processes" (*ibid.*). Rather, the conflicts arise when we ask: what causes what? Although it leads to endless debates Hitchcock does not think that anything of import hinges upon an answer to this causal question. He writes:

> Would our understanding of why the outcome occurred be enhanced? Would we be better placed to make decisions about how we should act if we knew? Would we be better placed to assign praise and blame? The answer to each of the three questions is a resounding "no". (*ibid.*)

One of the examples Hitchcock presents in order to illustrate his point is the example of the "two assassins" which is due to Michael McDermott. The example goes as follows: Two assassins, say a captain and his assistant, intend to kill a victim. Upon spotting the victim, the captain shouts "fire", and the assistant fires. The victim overhears the

---
[6] See Hitchcock (2003, p. 4).
[7] See Hitchcock (2003, p. 8).
[8] See Hitchcock (2003, p. 9).

order, ducks and survives unscathed.

According to Hitchcock, the stage-one-facts of the example are clear. For instance, the non-backtracking counterfactual "If the captain had not yelled 'fire', then the assistant would not have fired, the victim would not have ducked, and the victim would have survived" is true. Analogously, given the relevant background information, we can agree, at least to a large extent, on the probabilistic correlations which hold between yelling "fire" and shooting, yelling "fire" and ducking, ducking and surviving and so on. Further, there is no dispute that the captain's order "fire" was transmitted via sound waves that fall in the category of processes which Salmon labels causal processes. Similarly, the shooting of a bullet represents a process that counts as a causal process for Salmon. Salmon initially introduced the concept of a causal process in his book *Scientific Explanation and the Causal Structure of the World*.[9] For Salmon a "process" is anything that has a consistent structure over time.[10] He then distinguishes between "causal" and "pseudo processes". Causal processes are those processes that are able to transmit a "mark" (*i.e.* a modification in structure).[11] Coming back to the "two assassins" example, both the sound waves transmitting the captain's order and the shooting of a bullet represent processes which are able to transmit a "mark" and therefore count as causal processes for Salmon.

Hitchcock concludes from the "two assassins" example that regarding the stage-one-facts, there is no dispute. Rather, the dispute starts when we ask the question: Did the captain's yelling "fire" cause the victim to survive? However, for Hitchcock we do not need an answer to this question to answer the questions which usually interest us in the context of the "two assassins" example. Hitchcock writes:

> Does Captain deserve praise for saving Victim's life? Clearly he does not. If Captain actually wanted Victim to survive, did he pursue a rational course of action? No more rational than the alternative of withholding of the order. Do we lack anything by way of understanding of why Victim survived this incident? No we do not. What possible grounds could we have, then, for caring whether Captain's order really caused Victim's survival? (Hitchcock, 2003, p. 10)

One point that seems peculiar about Hitchcock's position is that he considers counterfactuals as stage-one-facts. In the "two assassins" example, for instance, Hitchcock takes it for granted that the counterfactual "If the captain had not yelled 'fire', then the assistant would not have fired, the victim would not have ducked, and the victim would

---

[9] See Salmon (1984).
[10] See Salmon (1984, p. 144).
[11] See Salmon (1984, p. 147).

have survived" is true. However, as the name counterfactual suggests, the situation in which the captain did not yell "fire" did not occur. We have made no observation that tells us what happened after the captain had not yelled "fire". It has therefore to be asked how we evaluate the truth values of counterfactuals assuming, of course, that counterfactuals have truth values. Hitchcock does not address this issue in his paper. However, this seems necessary because one might object to Hitchcock's position that he smuggles in causal knowledge, that is, knowledge of the form "x causes y", in the evaluation of counterfactuals. For instance, in order to evaluate the counterfactual in the "two assassins" case one might make use of the some knowledge of the form "hearing the order 'fire' causes pulling the trigger", "pulling the trigger causes a bullet to be shot", "being shot by a bullet causes one's death", and so on. What Hitchcock needs is a semantic for counterfactuals that does not make use of any causal knowledge.

One candidate which comes to mind is David Lewis's "possible worlds" semantics for counterfactuals.[12] For Lewis a possible world is a way the world could be, or – when it comes to past events – could have been. Lewis proceeds to rank possible worlds according to their "comparative similarity". That is, he introduces a two place relation R_w among worlds (*i.e.* actual and possible worlds), regarded as the ordering of worlds with respect to their comparative similarity to world w. For reasons which are not important in this context Lewis introduces the notion of an "accessible" world from w. Lewis calls a world v accessible from world w if and only if it satisfies a restriction depending on the context of the similarity ranking. For instance, one might think that what possible worlds are admitted as accessible depends on what the actual laws of nature are. Hence, the restriction will be different from the standpoint of worlds with different laws of nature.[13] Finally, Lewis calls a world where A is the case an "A-world". Then, the counterfactual "If it were the case that A, then it would be the case that B" is true at world w if and only if, if there is an A-world accessible from w, then B holds at every A-world at least as close to w as a certain accessible A-world.[14]

Given this semantic for counterfactuals, for us the crucial question is whether we can make sense of the similarity ranking of worlds without making recourse to any causal knowledge? Although Lewis makes use of the notion of a "law of nature" to rank worlds with respect to their comparative similarity his notion of a "law of nature" should

---

[12] See Lewis (1973).
[13] See Lewis (1973, p. 5).
[14] See Lewis (1973, p. 49).

not be understood as what Nancy Cartwright calls a "causal law". For Cartwright causal laws "have the word 'cause' – or some causal surrogate – right in them".[15] For instance, "smoking causes lung cancer" or "force causes change in motion" are causal laws for Cartwright. According to Cartwright, the true laws of nature are not exceptionless regularities rather they are descriptions of, what Cartwright calls, "causal powers". Cartwright distinguishes between the possession of a (causal) power and the exercise of it. For instance, the law of gravitation claims, according to Cartwright, that two bodies have the power to produce a force of a certain size. However, two bodies do not always succeed in the exercise of it.[16] In contrast, for Lewis laws of nature are those regularities that are members of a coherent system, in particular, a system that can be represented as a deductive axiomatic system striking good balance between simplicity and strength.[17] More specifically, Lewis proposes that laws are the axioms and theorems common to all deductive systems which are well balanced between simplicity and strength.[18] This suggests that Lewis provides a semantic for counterfactuals that does not need any causal knowledge in the first place. However, I would like to leave the question open whether by adopting Lewis's "possible worlds" semantics Hitchcock can resist the criticism that he is smuggling in causal knowledge by calling counterfactuals stage-one-facts. For the rest of the paper I just assume that some semantics for counterfactuals can be found that enables us to evaluate counterfactuals without making recourse to some sort of causal knowledge and, hence, to make sense of Hitchcock's idea of counterfactuals as stage-one-facts.

Let me stop talking about Hitchcock's view on causality here and take a look at the literature on personal identity, particularly, Derek Parfit's writings on the subject. Parfit thinks that questions about identity are often "empty questions". In his book *Reasons and Persons*[19], Parfit presents the example of a club which exists for several years. After a while the meetings of the club members cease. Some years later, a few of the members of this club form a club with the same name and the same rules. For Parfit the question whether the club is still the same is an "empty question" since we can know everything without answering that question. Parfit writes:

The claim "This is the same club" would be neither true nor false.

---
[15]See Cartwright (1983, p. 21).
[16]See Cartwright (1983, p. 61).
[17]See Psillos (2002, p. 149).
[18]See Lewis (1973, p. 73).
[19]See Parfit (1986).

Though there is no answer to our question, there may be nothing that we do not know. This is because the existence of a club is not separate from the existence of its members, acting together in certain ways. The continued existence of a club just involves its members having meetings, that are conducted according to club's rules. If we know all the facts about how people held meetings, and about the club's rules, we know everything there is to know. This is why we would not be puzzled when we cannot answer the question, "Is this the very same club?" We would not be puzzled because, even without answering this question, we can know everything about what happened. (Parfit, 1986, p. 213).

And further:

When an empty question has no answer, we can decide to give it an answer. We could decide to call the later club the same as the original club. Or we could decide to call it another club, that is exactly similar. This is not a decision between different views about what really happened. Before making our decision, we already knew what happened. We are merely choosing one of the two different descriptions of the very same course of event. (*ibid.*)

Parfit considers the idea that questions of identity might not have a determinate answer as a consequence of his "reductionist" view on identity. By a "reductionist" view on personal identity Parfit means that "the fact of a person's identity over time just consists in the holding of certain more particular facts".[20] More specifically, Parfit claims that "[a] person's existence just consists in the existence of a brain and body, and the occurrence of a series of interrelated physical and mental events". That is, for Parfit identity is constituted by relations of physical and psychological continuity and connectedness. By "physical continuity" Parfit just refers to the ordinary concept of spatio-temporal physical continuity.[21] For instance, a brick yesterday is physically continuous with a brick today if a physically continuous spatio-temporal path leads from the brick yesterday to the brick today. Parfit's notion of psychological continuity is similar to his notion of physical continuity but its formulation requires the notion of psychological connectedness. For Parfit "psychological connectedness" is "the holding of particular direct psychological connections".[22] A direct psychological connection is, for instance, when a belief or desire continues to be had. Then, "psychological continuity" is "the holding of overlapping chains of strong connectedness" (*ibid.*). "Strong connectedness" is given when

---
[20]See Parfit (1986, p. 208).
[21]See Parfit (1986, p. 203).
[22]See Parfit (1986, p. 206).

there are enough direct connections. By "enough direct connections" Parfit means that "the number of direct connections, over any day, is at least half the number that hold, over every day, in the lives of nearly every actual person" (*ibid.*). It follows from the definitions that psychological connectedness is not a transitive relation whereas psychological continuity is.

For Parfit psychological relations are of much greater importance than physical ones. That is, when we raise questions about identity what we really care about, according to Parfit, is psychological continuity and connectedness.[23]

When we compare Parfit's view on personal identity and Hitchcock's view on causality then we can see that there is structural similarity between the two positions. That is, for both Hitchcock and Parfit certain questions – in Hitchcock's case "Does x cause y?" and in Parfit's case "Is x identical with y?" do not require an answer in order to learn something new in the examples Hitchcock and Parfit present. Of course, Hitchcock's and Parfit's formulations are not congruent. While Hitchcock does not think that "anything of import" hinges upon the question whether one event or factor really causes another, Parfit thinks that in the case of an empty question there is "nothing" that we do not know even if we do not know an answer to such a question. However, I do not consider these different terminologies as a substantive difference between the two positions.

Since Hitchcock's and Parfit's positions are very similar from a structural point of view, they may be susceptible to the same sort of criticism. In the next section I will therefore present one objection that has been raised against Parfit's view by Eric Olson. I will then develop an "Olsonian" critique of Hitchcock's view on causality.

8.3 An "Olsonian" critique of Hitchcock's view on causality

In his paper "Imperfect Identity" Eric Olson attacks the idea that (some) questions of identity over time have no unique, determinate answer and disputes over such questions are merely verbal.[24] Olson argues that depending on how the claim that questions of identity over time have no unique, determinate answer and that disputes over such questions are merely verbal, is understood, it is either false or presupposing a highly contentious metaphysical claim. In our context Olson's criticism of Parfit's view on personal identity is of particular interest.

---

[23]See Parfit (1986, p. 215).
[24]See Olson (2006).

Olson takes up Parfit's idea that we can *decide* whether two persons (or objects) are identical. He labels this aspect of Parfit's position the "decision thesis". Olson then uses the following example originally due to Roderick Chisholm[25] to illustrate that the "decision thesis" is misleading:

> Suppose you are worried about a surgical operation that you have to undergo without anaesthetic. Now imagine that the Queen offers to declare officially that when the operation takes place, the one who suffers the pain will not be you, but someone else – perhaps someone newly created who takes your place temporarily and insensibly, perhaps someone who already exists and insensibly swaps places with you. If the Queen's word is effective, your attitude towards the operation ought to be no different for your attitude towards anyone else's painful operation. Would her offer set your mind at ease? I don't think so. (Olson, 2006, p. 256)

Independent of whether or not Olson's modification of Chisholm's example shows that Parfit's position is untenable, one can construct a similar example in order to argue against Hitchcock's view on causality. If, as Hitchcock thinks, there is no objective matter of fact whether two events stand in the causal relation, then one might conclude that it is up to our decision whether two events stand in the causal relation. I will call the idea that we can decide whether two events stand in the causal relation the "causal decision thesis". In order to argue against the causal decision thesis consider the following modification of Olson's example: Suppose you are worried about a surgical operation that you have to undergo. Now imagine that the Queen offers to declare officially that drinking a glass of milk will cause you to feel no pain during the operation. Would you be happy when you get offered a glass of milk by the nurse before the operation instead of a traditional anaesthetic?

I take it that the hypothetical patient in this example would not be happy with this treatment. However, the crucial question is whether this example poses a problem for Hitchcock's position.

Hitchcock's response would presumably play the causal pluralist's card and point out that although there does not exist *the* causal relation there exist a variety of causal *relations*. From this perspective the reason why we feel uncomfortable in saying that drinking a glass of milk causes to have no pain is that the events "drinking a glass of milk" and "being painless during a surgical operation" do not stand in *any* causal relation. There is no counterfactual dependence between these two events, there cannot be found any non-spurious probabilistic

---
[25] See Chisholm (1976, p. 111).

correlations and no causal process is linking the two events. Drinking the glass of milk does not cause, in any sense of the word, to be without pain during an operation.

This objection asserts that we are not entirely free to decide whether or not an event causes another. Hitchcock believes in the distinction between causal and non-causal relations. That is, for him there is an objective fact of the matter whether two events stand in some causal relationship. What he opposes is the idea of the uniqueness of the causal relation. Hitchcock thinks there is no mono-criterial concept of causation which captures all our intuitions behind causal judgements.

This response to the "Chisholmian" example raises one question: on what grounds does Hitchcock label certain relations as causal? Assuming that Hitchcock would presumably call the relation of (non-backtracking) counterfactual dependence or the relation induced by Salmon's causal processes a causal relation, one has to ask what makes these relations "causal relations"? Before I explore Hitchcock's possible answer to this question, let me point out that the issue of clarifying what it means to be a pluralist is not as trivial for the causal pluralist as it is for pluralists about other concepts, such as pluralists about probability. In the case of pluralisms about probability it is easy to say what it means to be a pluralist about this concept. A pluralist about probability, such as Donald Gillies, suggests that there are different probability concepts, that is, in Gillies's case an objective and a subjective concept of probability.[26] When asked what makes these two different concepts, "probability concepts", Gillies can refer to the fact that any interpretation of probability, be it an objective or a subjective interpretation of probability, gives meaning to the same set of axioms of mathematical probability theory. Hence, a concept is a probability concept if and only if it satisfies the axioms of mathematical probability theory. However, when it comes to philosophical theories of causality there is no axiom system which has to be interpreted. Rather, we are only given the use of the word "cause" in our ordinary language.

Let me come back to Hitchcock's causal pluralism. On what grounds does Hitchcock label certain relations as causal? Following Nancy Cartwright[27], Hitchcock believes that "a distinction between causal and non-causal relations grounds the essential distinction between effective and ineffective strategies".[28] For instance, Hitchcock mentions that lung cancer is correlated both with smoking and with stained teeth, but if you wish to avoid getting lung cancer, it will be effective

---

[26] See Gillies (2000).
[27] See Cartwright (1979).
[28] See Hitchcock (2003, p. 4).

to quit smoking but not to whiten your teeth.

Hitchcock does not explore the distinction between effective and ineffective further, although such an exploration seems necessary. We have to know when a certain strategy is effective. For instance, even non-smokers get lung cancer. Does this imply that not smoking is an ineffective strategy against getting lung cancer and therefore there is no causal relation between these two events?

It seems not clear whether Hitchcock fully endorses the characterisation of effectiveness suggested by Cartwright. If he does, then this characterisation of an effective strategy is not helpful in the context of a causal pluralist response to the "Chisholmian" example since Cartwright defines strategy S as effective for obtaining (outcome) G in terms of the causal factors other than S for G.[29] That is, in order to define an effective strategy for G we already need all and only the causal factors for G. As a result of this definition the choice of causal factors for G determines whether a certain strategy is effective for obtaining G. However, on what grounds do we decide whether a certain relation is causal? What is needed in our context would be a characterisation of a causal relation.

It should be noted that in the previous paragraph I have assumed that the statements "A is a causal factor for B" and "A stands in a causal relationship with B" are equivalent. This assumption seems necessary in order to apply Cartwright's definition of an effective strategy which makes use of the notion of a "causal factor" to Hitchcock's position, which is a view about "causal relations".

If Hitchcock intends to base the difference between a causal and a non-causal relation on the difference between effective and ineffective strategies, then certain problems of such a project appear on the horizon: This approach would imply that Hitchcock puts forward the idea of a plurality of causal relations while at the same time offering a mono-criterial account of what makes a causal relation. It seems that this position is a hidden mono-criterial account of causation. If this assessment is correct, then Hitchcock's position will face problems similar to the ones of the mono-criterial accounts of causation he is arguing against.

The worry that Hitchcock's position is inconsistent since, on the one hand, he is calling himself a causal pluralist while, on the other hand, he is advocating a – more or less hidden – mono-criterial account of causation can be further substantiated by looking at one of Hitchcock's more recent publications. In "On the Importance of Causal

---

[29] See Cartwright (1983, p. 35).

Taxonomy"[30] Hitchcock addresses the question of how to distinguish causal and non-causal relationships[31]. In regard to the question of what positive characteristics distinguish causal and non-causal relationships, Hitchcock suggests that Woodward's "interventionist" approach to causation is particularly promising.[32] For Woodward, causal relations, in contrast to non-causal relations, remain stable under interventions.[33] Interventions are manipulations or changes in the value of one variable that have the right sort of "surgical" features. That is, the notion of an intervention attempts to capture the idea of a "surgical" change in a variable X which is such that if any change occurs in a variable Y, it occurs only as a result of its causal connection, if any, to X and not in any other way. For instance, consider the following claim: Changes in the position of the moon with respect to the earth (variable X) cause changes in the motion of the tides (variable Y). According to Woodward's theory, this is a true statement if and only if there is a "possible" intervention by which the distance of the moon with respect to the earth is varied such that the motions of the tides would change.

The details of Woodward's theory of causality are not of interest in our context. However, what is important is that, in contrast to Hitchcock, Woodward does not consider himself as a causal pluralist. Rather, Woodward makes it clear in the introduction of his book *Making Things Happen*[34] that he is developing a mono-criterial account of causation.[35] Of course, Hitchcock is aware of this point. For instance, Hitchcock acknowledges that for Woodward the "invariance of a relationship under interventions is a defining feature of a genuinely causal relationship".[36] It seems therefore problematic to make use of Woodward's theory in order to distinguish causal and non-causal relations from a causal pluralist's perspective.

As it stands the causal pluralist's response to the "Olsonian" critique is not satisfactory. How might Hitchcock then deal with the "Olsonian" critique? Here, the analogy between Hitchcock's view on causality and Parfit's position in regard to personal identity is helpful again. Parfit says that when we raise questions about personal identity what we re-

---

[30] See Hitchcock (2007).
[31] In his 2003 paper "Of Humean Bondage" Hitchcock is talking about "causal relations" whereas in his 2007 paper "On the Importance of Causal Taxonomy" Hitchcock is talking about "causal relationships". For the purpose of this paper I do not distinguish between these two notions.
[32] See Hitchcock (2007, p. 104).
[33] See Woodward (2003).
[34] See Woodward (2003).
[35] See Woodward (2003, p. v).
[36] See Hitchcock (2007, p. 104).

ally care about is psychological continuity and psychological connectedness.³⁷ Parfit does not call his position a "pluralism about identity". He does not label psychological continuity as "identity relation I_1" and psychological connectedness as "identity relation I_2". Parfit does not suggest a distinction between "identity relations" and "non-identity relations". By adopting this position Parfit can easily respond to Olson's original "Queen" example. If psychological continuity and connectedness are what we really care about when we normally talk about identity these relations in the world are not touched if the Queen does stipulate how we use the words "identity" or "same person". Hence, Olson is right that the patient in Chisholm's example has good reasons to be worried about the operation but this is in accordance with Parfit's view on identity.

Olson seems to anticipate this reply to his example by saying that the "decision thesis", if not blatantly false, has to be understood as about linguistic facts, and not as about the "facts of identity" as he puts it.³⁸ Take the example of an old church whose stones have all been replaced over the centuries. When we ask whether the church today is the same as the church 400 years ago, we might have different answers to this question depending on whether we focus on the form (or geometrical structure) of the church or the material of the church. Someone who considers only the form of the church will call it the same church, while someone who takes only the material of the church into consideration will say that it is not the same church. Both answers can be correct, if speakers adopt different criteria in regard to the question whether the church is the same as the church 400 years ago. By reading along these lines you might wonder what the difference is between this position and Parfit's position? The difference between the two positions is that Olson suggests – by referring to the writings of Thomas Reid – that in the example of the church we seem not to be talking about the identity relation but about something else. Olson writes: "[...] we seem to be disagreeing only about whether the expression 'same' when applied to churches existing at different times means having the same form or having the same matter, or the like".³⁹ In other words, in the example of the church we are not talking about genuine identity but about a different relation applied to churches. However, by stating this position Olson does not provide a reason why Parfit's possible reply to Chisholm's example is untenable. Rather, Olson just suggests an alternative reading of the "decision thesis". Hence, Chisholm's example

---

³⁷See Parfit (1986, p. 215).
³⁸See Olson (2006, pp. 256-257).
³⁹See Olson (2006, p. 260).

does not pose a problem for Parfit's view on identity.

Coming back to causality: Similarly to Parfit, Hitchcock might point out that when we talk about whether one event causes another what we really care about are the relations, say, (non-backtracking) counterfactual dependence (A), probabilistic correlations of a certain type (B) and the relation induced by Salmon's causal processes (C). These three relations A, B and C exist in the world and are not affected by the Queen's declaration about the word "cause". By taking this route we do not have to provide a further criterion about what makes certain relations causal and we avoid the difficulties I have diagnosed in Hitchcock's account.

One might object that this "Parfitian" position simply transfers the problems of Hitchcock's position to a different level. That is, one might ask: according to what criterion is a relation put into the set of relations we care about when we talk about causality? However, this problem does not seem to be as severe as Hitchcock's difficulty of explaining the distinction between causal and non-causal relations within his causal pluralist's paradigm. A "Parfitian" can accept that the set containing the relations we care about when we talk about causality is a dynamical entity, that is, an entity which changes over time. Those relations that are currently included in this set depend on our current usage of the word "cause". However, this usage can change; relations can be added or subtracted from the set of relations we care about when we talk about causality. There is no further (or "deeper") criterion according to which a relation is part of the set of those relations under consideration. Hence, a "Parfitian" view on causality seems to improve Hitchcock's argument outlined in "Of Humean Bondage".

8.4 Conclusion

Is an "Olsonian" critique of Hitchcock's view on causality successful? I used the structural similarities between Hitchcock's view on causality and Parfit's view on personal identity as a starting point to assess whether an argument similar to the one given by Olson against Parfit's view on personal identity can be used against Hitchcock's view on causality. The "Olsonian" critique which made use of a modification of Chisholm's example leads us to a difficulty in Hitchcock's account. That is, Hitchcock's distinction between causal and non-causal relations seems to be in conflict with his "causal pluralism". Hitchcock's explanation of the distinction between causal and non-causal relations seems to lead to a mono-criterial account of causation, a position he is initially arguing against in his paper "Of Humean Bondage".[40]

In order to counter the "Olsonian" critique I suggested to look at Parfit's view on personal identity as expressed in *Reasons and Persons*.[41] Parfit's writings suggest how one might reply to the "Olsonian" critique without the need of explaining the distinction between causal and non-causal relations. In effect, the "Parfitian" view on causality says that when we talk about causality what we really care about is a set of distinct relations, such as, (non-backtracking) counterfactual dependence or probabilistic correlations of a certain kind. Hence, by adopting a "Parfitian" view on causality Hitchcock's argument can be improved. If one adopts the "Parfitian" strategy, then the "Olsonian" critique fails.

References

Cartwright, Nancy. 1979. Causal laws and effective strategies. *Nous* 13(4):419–437. Reprinted in Cartwright (1983, pp. 21–43).

Cartwright, Nancy. 1983. *How the Laws of Physics Lie*. Oxford: Clarendon Press.

Chisholm, Roderick. 1976. *Person and Object*. London: Allen and Unwin.

Gillies, Donald. 2000. *Philosophical Theories of Probability*. London: Routledge.

Hitchcock, Christopher. 2003. Of Humean bondage. *British Journal for the Philosophy of Science* 54(1):1–25.

Hitchcock, Christopher. 2007. On the importance of causal taxonomy. In A. Gopnik and L. Schulz, eds., *Causal Learning: Psychology, Philosophy and Computation*, pages 101–114. Oxford: Oxford University Press.

Humber, James. 1999. Hume. In R. Arrington, ed., *A Companion to the Philosophers*, pages 309–317. Oxford: Blackwell.

Lewis, David K. 1973. *Counterfactuals*. London: Routledge.

Olson, Eric. 2006. Imperfect identity. *Proceedings of the Aristotelian Society* 106(2):247–264.

Parfit, Derek. 1986. *Reasons and Persons*. Oxford: Oxford University Press.

Psillos, Stathis. 2002. *Causation and Explanation*. Chesham: Acumen Books.

Salmon, Wesley. 1984. *Scientific Explanation and the Causal Structure of the World*. Princeton: Princeton University Press.

Woodward, James. 2003. *Making Things Happen*. Oxford: Oxford University Press.

---

[40] See Hitchcock (2003).
[41] See Parfit (1986).

9
Actuality in the Garden of Forking Paths
ROBERTO LOSS

9.1 Introduction

Truth-relativism can be described as the thesis that utterance-truth must be relativized to a context of assessment. John MacFarlane (2003) has argued that a truth-relativist semantics is necessary for an adequate treatment of future contingents, since it appears better fit to accommodate our intuitions about the retrospective assessment of future-directed assertions than the standard supervaluationist approach first put forward by R. Thomason (1970).

Recently, however, MacFarlane (forthcoming) has restricted his earlier claim. He now concedes that in most cases the supervaluationist can accommodate the intuitions elicited by an indeterministic setting. This can be done by introducing a monadic truth-predicate for propositions in the object-language to thereby analyse statements like "What you said yesterday *was true*". Nevertheless, he argues, even with this truth-predicate in play the supervaluationist appears unable to give an adequate treatment of "actually".

In section 9.1 I shall be involved in a brief stage-setting, moving from the classical Kaplan/Lewis framework to a supervaluationist semantics for future contingents and then to MacFarlane's relativist proposal; in section 9.2 I will explain the criticism which MacFarlane (forthcoming) brings out to his earlier argument from retrospective assessment; in section 9.3, after having defined two ways in which the actuality oper-

Language, Knowledge, and Metaphysics.
Massimiliano Carrara and Vittorio Morato (eds.)
College Pubblication, London, 2008.

ator may be construed, I will prove that by embracing a *nonindexical* reading of "actually" the supervaluationist is able to deliver the right predictions about retrospective assessments even when the actuality operator is involved.

The conclusion will be that, if the standard supervaluationist can make use of the monadic truth-predicate for propositions which MacFarlane (forthcoming) envisages, then truth-relativism is by no means necessary for an adequate treatment of future contingents.

9.2 Open future and relative truth

9.2.1 The standard framework

According to the classical Kaplan-Lewis framework, sentence-truth must be relativized both to a *context*, to handle indexicals, and an *index*, to handle operators.[1] A context is a possible scenario in which a sentence might be uttered or used (or a representation thereof); an index is a collection of shiftable parameters, the number of which will depend on what operators the language contains. The index stands for the Kaplanian *circumstance of evaluation, i.e.* the circumstance with respect to which the proposition expressed by a sentence in a certain context has to be evaluated. In what follows, I will take an index to be simply a possible world.

Following MacFarlane's (2003) useful taxonomy, let us call "semantics proper" the recursive definition of *truth at a point of evaluation* (where a "point of evaluation" is a <context, index> pair), and "postsemantics" the definition of *truth at a context*. Intuitively, sentence-truth at a point of evaluation can be understood on the basis of the fundamental notion of proposition-truth at a world, along the following lines:

(1)   For every sentence Φ and point of evaluation $\langle c, w \rangle$, Φ is true at $\langle c, w \rangle$ iff the proposition expressed by Φ in the context c is true with respect to the world w.

The job done by postsemantics, on the other hand, is to define the notion of truth at a context on the basis of the notion of truth at a point of evaluation:

(2)   A sentence Φ is true at a context c iff Φ is true at $\langle c, w_c \rangle$, where w_c is the world of the context c.[2]

This, in turn, allows the following definition of utterance-truth:

---

[1] See Kaplan (1989) and Lewis (1996).
[2] See MacFarlane (forthcoming, p. 4).

(3) An utterance u of a sentence Φ is true iff Φ is true at $\langle c_u, w_u \rangle$, where c_u is the context in which u is uttered and w_u the world of the context c_u.

From (2) we can observe that the role of the context of use in postsemantics is to determine the circumstances against which the proposition expressed by the sentence in question has to be evaluated. In our specific case, the context of use determines the world of evaluation, to the effect that sentence-truth at a context is understood in terms of proposition-truth at the world of the context of use.

9.2.2 Determinacy and Indeterminacy

Suppose now that the future is objectively open: in some possible futures there will be a sea battle tomorrow, in others there won't. Suppose that I utter today (at t_1):

(4) There will be a sea battle tomorrow.

Suppose furthermore that, as it turns out, a sea battle takes place the next day (at t_2). MacFarlane (2003) has claimed that this scenario elicits two different intuitions which he calls, respectively, the "determinacy–" and the "indeterminacy–intuition". Letting "U" denote my utterance of (4) at t_1, these intuitions can be cashed out as follows:

INDETERMINACY: At t_1, when it is still objectively unsettled whether a sea battle will occur the next day, U is neither true nor false.

DETERMINACY: At t_2, once a sea battle has in fact taken place, U is true.

The most attractive semantics for future contingents – Thomason's supervaluationism – was first put forward to accommodate INDETERMINACY.[3] The supervaluationist approach embraces a branching picture of time: instead of a single line representing the actual world-history, we have a set of worlds overlapping towards the past and branching towards the future. With this model at hand it is easy to see that the postsemantics given in (2) must be refined: as a matter of fact, the openness of the future entails that there is no such thing as *the* world of the context. Here is where supervaluationism comes in. The main change to the classical framework which needs to be brought about in order to deal supervaluationistically with INDETERMINACY is

---

[3] "This paper will consider the problem of working out a semantic theory for indeterministic model structures. Its principal contribution is in developing a rigorous form of the traditionally popular view that "future contingent" statements can be neither true nor false." (Thomason, 1970, p. 265).

postsemantical; sentence-truth at a context has to be defined in terms of truth at *every* world overlapping at the context:

(5) A sentence Φ is true/false at a context c iff Φ is true/false at every point of evaluation $\langle c, w \rangle$, where w is a world overlapping at c.
Otherwise, Φ is neither true nor false at c.

Utterance-truth has to be redefined accordingly:

(6) An utterance u of a sentence Φ is true/false iff Φ is true/false at every point of evaluation $\langle c_u, w \rangle$, where c_u is the context in which u is uttered and w is a world overlapping at c_u.
Otherwise, u is neither true nor false.

Given this definition of utterance-truth, it is straightforward to see that u is predicted to be neither true nor false by the supervaluationist, since only in some worlds overlapping at the context in which u is uttered is there a sea battle at t_2. Thomason's supervaluationism appears therefore able to vindicate INDETERMINACY.

Nonetheless, as MacFarlane (2003) argues, the supervaluationist appears to have some trouble in coping with DETERMINACY, since (5) predicts U to be neither true nor false even from the advantaged point of view of t_2 (in which a sea battle does take place). The fact that only in some worlds overlapping at the context of utterance a sea battle takes place at t_2 doesn't depend, according to the supervaluationist, on the point of view from which we are assessing the truth of u.

9.2.3 Truth-relativism

According to MacFarlane, it is the *absoluteness* of utterance-truth which determines the failure of Thomason's supervaluationism with respect to DETERMINACY. His solution is consequently to reject utterance-truth absolutism in favour of a truth-relativist approach according to which utterance-truth is relativized to a *context of assessment*. The leap from the standard supervaluationist framework is surprisingly small: the only modification needed is the introduction of the context of assessment in the postsemantics, along the following lines:

(7) A sentence Φ is true/false at a context of use c from the point of view of a context of assessment c' iff Φ is true/false at every point of evaluation $\langle c, w \rangle$, where w is a world overlapping both at c and c'.[4]

---

[4]To avoid useless complications – given the aim of this paper – I will assume as admissible <context of use, context of assessment> pairs only those, such that the set of worlds overlapping at both contexts is non-empty. See MacFarlane (forthcoming, p. 13).

Otherwise, Φ is from the point of view of c' neither true nor false at c.

From which, utterance-truth is defined as follows:

(8) An utterance u of a sentence Φ is true/false from the point of view of a context of assessment c iff Φ is true/false at every point of evaluation $\langle c_u, w \rangle$, where c_u is the context in which u is uttered and w is a world overlapping both at c_u and c. Otherwise, u is from the point of view of c neither true nor false.

The latter definition of utterance-truth allows for a simple and straightforward account of both DETERMINACY and INDETERMINACY:

(RI) From the point of view of the context in which it was uttered, u is neither true nor false since only in some worlds overlapping both at the context of use and the context of assessment of u a sea battle is taking place at t_2.

(RD) From the point of view of the context in which a sea battle has effectively taken place at t_2, u is to be assessed as true since in every world overlapping both at the context of use and the context of assessment of u is a sea battle taking place at t_2.

It thus seems that a proper accommodation of our intuitions about future contingents renders necessary the relativization of utterance-truth to a context of assessment as invoked by the relativist.

9.3 Retrospective assessments, propositions and actuality

9.3.1 Utterance truth and proposition "Truth"

MacFarlane (forthcoming) has recently criticized his earlier approach to the puzzle of future contingents. In his latest paper on the subject, "Truth in the Garden of Forking Paths", he compares two different ways of presenting his earlier argument from retrospective assessments:

(U) Yesterday I uttered the sentence "It will be sunny tomorrow". It is sunny today.
_____
∴ My utterance was true.

(P)   Yesterday I asserted that it would be sunny today.
        It is sunny today.
        ─────────────────
        ∴ What I asserted was true.[5]

The difference is that in (U), truth is predicated of an utterance of a sentence, while in (P), truth is predicated of "what I asserted" – a proposition. The kind of truth-relativism advocated in "Future contingents and relative truth" (2003) relied implicitly on (U).

However, MacFarlane (forthcoming) now acknowledges that our intuitions about retrospective assessments are not driven by considerations about the technical notion of "utterance-truth", but rather by reflections upon the truth of what has been said by our assertions. We should then reformulate INDETERMINACY and DETERMINACY as follows:

INDETERMINACY-P: At t_1, when it is still objectively unsettled whether a sea battle will occur the next day, what I say by uttering U is neither true nor false.

DETERMINACY-P: At t_2, once a sea battle has in fact taken place, it is true that what I have said by uttering U was true.

Can supervaluationism cope with DETERMINACY-P despite its failure with respect to DETERMINACY?

According to MacFarlane (forthcoming), in most cases the supervaluationist has the resources to vindicate both these intuitions. What she needs is only to introduce the following truth-predicate for propositions in the object-language:

(T)   "True" applies to x at a point of evaluation $\langle c, w \rangle$ iff x is a proposition and x is true at w.

Notice that this definition has two immediate consequences: (i) the absence of an argument place for a time in "True" deprives tenses associated with it of any semantic significance; our use of "was True" instead of "is True", for instance, is determined only by grammatical reasons; (ii) the following *disquotational schema* is true at every point of evaluation:

(D) $\forall x((x = \text{the proposition that } S) \supset (\text{True}(x) \equiv S))$,[6]

With the truth-predicate envisaged by MacFarlane at her disposal, the supervaluationist appears to be able to vindicate DETERMINACY-P, at least when sentences like (4) are concerned:

─────────────
[5] See MacFarlane (forthcoming, p. 14-15).
[6] See MacFarlane (forthcoming, p. 17).

ARGUMENT-A

(A1)	Yesterday you uttered the sentence "There will be a sea battle tomorrow".	[premiss]
(A2)	Yesterday you said that a sea battle would take place today.	[from (A1) and the semantics of "tomorrow" and "yesterday"]
(A3)	A sea battle is taking place today.	[premiss]
(A4)	What you said yesterday was True.	[from (A2),(A3),(D)]

Nevertheless, MacFarlane (forthcoming) claims that, even with this truth-predicate in play, the appeal to contexts of assessment is still required for a full accommodation of our intuitions about retrospective assessments, the reason being that the supervaluationist doesn't seem to have the resources to account for DETERMINACY-P when the operator "actually" is involved.

9.3.2 Adding "actually"

In a standard (non-branching) framework, "actually" works as follows:

(9) ⌜$Actually$:Φ⌝ is true at $\langle c, w \rangle$, iff Φ is true at $\langle c, w_c \rangle$, where w_c is the world of the context c.

(9) respects an important constraint which MacFarlane dubs *Initial Redundancy*:

(10) An operator ★ is *initial-redundant* just in case for all sentences S , ⌜★S⌝ is true at exactly the same contexts of use (and assessment) as S (equivalently: each is a logical consequence of the other).[7]

In standard, non-branching semantics, in order to respect (10) the actuality operator returns the world of evaluation to the world of the context of use. In a branching framework, however, there is no such thing as *the* world of the context of use, since for every context c we have a non-empty set of worlds overlapping at c. To accommodate the constraint of Initial Redundancy the following seem therefore to be the appropriate defining clauses for "actually" in a supervaluationist and in a relativist framework, respectively:

---
[7]See MacFarlane (forthcoming, p. 20).

(11) ⌜$Actually{:}\Phi$⌝ is true at $\langle c, w\rangle$ iff Φ is true at every point of evaluation $\langle c, w'\rangle$, where w' is a world overlapping at c.

(12) ⌜$Actually{:}\Phi$⌝ is true at $\langle c_u, c_a, w\rangle$ (where c_u is the context of use and c_a the context of assessment) iff Φ is true at every point of evaluation $\langle c_u, c_a, w'\rangle$, where w' is a world overlapping both at c_u and c_a.[8]

Suppose then that yesterday I uttered both:

(4) There will be a sea battle tomorrow

and

(13) There will actually be a sea battle tomorrow.

Call what I said by means of these utterances, respectively, my "first claim" and my "second claim". According to the relativist, from the point of view of today (continuing to suppose that a sea battle is occurring today), both my claims are true, since in both cases the worlds we have to look at are the worlds that overlap both at the context of use and the context of assessment and in any such world a sea battle is occurring at t_2.

What about the supervaluationist? We have seen above that she rightly predicts my first claim to be True. Nevertheless, MacFarlane (forthcoming) claims that the semantics for "actually" given in (11) compels the supervaluationist to assess my second claim as False. Why? MacFarlane is not fully explicit on this point, but it seems clear enough that what justifies his negative answer must be something along the following lines:

> For the standard supervaluationist, no matter how deeply embedded we are, no matter how far the world of evaluation has been shifted, the actuality operator returns it to the worlds overlapping at the context of use.[9]

In what follows I will argue against MacFarlane's novel criticism of standard supervaluationism. Firstly, I will show that the supervaluationist can choose to give a "non-indexical" reading of the actuality operator defined in (11). Secondly, I will prove that, under such a reading, MacFarlane's truth-predicate can be used to accommodate

---

[8]See (MacFarlane, forthcoming, p. 21).

[9]This is nothing but the obvious adaptation to a branching framework of MacFarlane's comment on the behaviour of "actually" in standard semantics: "No matter how deeply embedded we are, no matter how far the world of evaluation has been shifted, the actuality operator returns it to the world of the context of use. Of course, this only works if there *is* a unique world of the context of use – as there is not when worlds can overlap and branch" (MacFarlane, forthcoming, p. 20).

DETERMINACY-P even when sentences containing "actually" are concerned, rendering therefore truth-relativism an unnecessary departure from standard semantics.

9.4 Actuality in the open future
9.4.1 Indexical vs Non-indexical
Recall the supervaluationist definition of "actually":

(11)   ⌜$Actually{:}\Phi$⌝ is true at $\langle c, w \rangle$ iff Φ is true at every point of evaluation $\langle c, w' \rangle$, where w' is a world overlapping at c.

From (11) we can gather that "actually" is, in a broad sense, a *context-sensitive* operator. Given a sentence S which expresses the same proposition in any context, ⌜$Actually{:} S$⌝ may – according to (11)– have different truth-values with respect to points of evaluation which differ only in the context-parameter.[10] The fundamental question pertaining to the truth of MacFarlane's criticism is therefore how the context of use determines this potential difference in truth-value. Drawing on the distinction put forward by MacFarlane (2008) between "indexical" and "non-indexical" contextualism, we can distinguish two main construals of the actuality-operator as defined in (11):

(14)   "*Actually:*" is an *indexical* operator iff for some pair of contexts c and c' and pair of sentences Φ and Ψ, such that the proposition expressed by Φ in c is the same as the proposition expressed by Ψ in c', ⌜$Actually{:}\Phi$⌝ in c expresses a different proposition from the one expressed by ⌜$Actually{:}\Psi$⌝ in c'.

(15)   "*Actually:*" is a *nonindexical* operator iff, for every pair of contexts c and c' and pair of sentences Φ and Ψ such that the proposition expressed by Φ in c is the same as the proposition expressed by Ψ in c', ⌜$Actually{:}\Phi$⌝ in c expresses the same proposition as ⌜$Actually{:}\Psi$⌝ in c'.

It follows directly from (14) that the contribute of "actually" to the proposition expressed by a sentence featuring it is determined by the context of use. In this case, therefore, "actually" behaves similarly to other indexicals, like "I", "here", "now". On the other hand, the definition given in (11) tells us that the way in which the context of use affects the truth conditions of a sentence containing the actuality operator is by determining a set of worlds (*i.e.* the set of worlds overlapping

---
[10] In our case, letting "c_1" denote the context before a sea battle and "c_2" the context in which a sea battle takes place (for any world w) the sentence "There will actually be a sea battle tomorrow" is true with respect to the point of evaluation $\langle c_1, w \rangle$ but false with respect to $\langle c_2, w \rangle$.

at the context of use). A possible way to make sense of the indexical profile of "actually" is represented, for instance, by the view according to which the proposition expressed by a sentence containing an occurrence of "actually" has the *set* of worlds overlapping at the context of use as a proper constituent.[11] This kind of view is advocated (in a non-branching framework) by Scott Soames (2007):

> [...] the sentence "Actually Kaplan wrote *Demonstratives*", used by anyone at the actual world-state, @, expresses the proposition *that Kaplan wrote 'Demonstratives' at* @, while the same sentence used by a speaker at a world-state w expresses the proposition *that Kaplan wrote 'Demonstratives' at w*. In this way, actually stands for the world-state c_w of the context in a manner analogous to the way in which "now" stands for the time, and "I" stands for the agent, of the context. When p is the proposition expressed by S in c, "Actually S" expresses the proposition that p is true at c_w. (Soames, 2007, pp. 252-253.)

On the other hand, an example of a non indexicalist stance on "actually" is given by Philip Percival (1989):

> Suppose Thatcher said: "Actually, Reagan is a great president." I will never assert this type. But, intuitively, if I had asserted it, I would have non-actually asserted exactly the same proposition we supposed Thatcher to have asserted. So the proposition expressed by the type "Actually, Reagan is a great president" does not vary according to its world of utterance." (Percival, 1989, p. 191.)

According to the non indexicalist, the role of the context of use with respect to "actually" is only to determine the world at which the proposition expressed by the sentence it embeds is to be evaluated. It doesn't affect the way in which "actually" contributes to the proposition expressed by the sentence in which it features.

Both positions seem equally plausible and compatible with the clause given in (11). What ensues is that the supervaluationist theory, as proposed by MacFarlane (forthcoming), can be construed in two different directions, corresponding to the two interpretations of the nature of the actuality operator delineated in (14) and (15). However, if this is

---

[11] I am not claiming that MacFarlane, or anyone who accepts the indexical treatment of "actually", should think that the proposition expressed by an actuality-sentence contains the set of worlds as proper constituent. My aim is just to point to a way of making sense of the (possible) indexical profile of the actuality operator in order to show (see ARGUMENT-C below) that (at least) under such an interpretation it is indeed true – as MacFarlane claims – that the supervaluationist cannot fully accommodate the determinacy intuition. What I am going to argue is simply that, even granted this point to MacFarlane, there is another reading of "actually" available to the supervaluationist, under which she appears perfectly able to vindicate our intuitions about retrospective assessments.

correct then contrary to what MacFarlane says, the supervaluationist has the resources to accommodate DETERMINACY-P by means of the monadic truth-predicate for propositions defined in (T).

9.4.2 Non indexical actuality and retrospective assessments

In order to be able to account for DETERMINACY-P it is sufficient for the supervaluationist to embrace a non indexical reading of the actuality operator. As a matter of fact, if "actually" doesn't contribute indexically to the proposition expressed yesterday by my utterance of "There will actually be a sea battle tomorrow", then there is nothing in this proposition which determines which set of worlds is relevant to assess its truth-value today. It is therefore my current context, and not yesterday's, which determines the worlds at which the proposition in question has to be evaluated as true, in order for my current utterance of "what I said yesterday was True" to be true.

The gist of these lines of reasoning can be made more perspicuous by means of the following argument:

ARGUMENT-B

(B1) Yesterday you uttered the sentence "There will actually be a sea battle tomorrow". [premiss]

(B2) Yesterday you said that a sea battle would actually take place today. [from (B1) and (15) by the semantics of "tomorrow" and "yesterday"]

(B3) A sea battle is actually taking place today. [premiss]

(B4) What you said yesterday was True. [from (B2),(B3),(D)]

As a matter of fact, dubbing "c_1" the context before the sea battle and "c_2" the context—one day later—in which a sea battle occurs, it ensues from (15) (and the semantics of "tomorrow" and "yesterday") that the proposition expressed by (13) in c_1 is the same as the proposition expressed by

(16)   A sea battle is actually taking place today

in c_2. Since (16) is true in c_2 (as a sea battle is indeed taking place in c_2) so it is true that what I said yesterday uttering (13) was True.

MacFarlane's claim about the inability of the supervaluationist to cope with DETERMINACY-P seems therefore implicitly to rely on an indexical treatment of the actuality operator, according to which – as we have seen above – the set of worlds overlapping at the context of use of "actually" enters into the very proposition expressed by a sentence like (13). If, for simplicity's sake, we let an utterance of (13) in c_1 express the same proposition as an utterance of

(17)   A sea battle is taking place at t_2 in every world overlapping at c_1,

it is possible to prove the supervaluationist' failure with respect to DE-TERMINACY-P when "actually" is treated as an indexical operator as follows:

ARGUMENT-C

(C1)   Yesterday you uttered the sentence "There will actually be a sea battle tomorrow".   [premiss]

(C2)   Yesterday you said that a sea battle takes place at t_2 in every world overlapping at c_1.   [from (C1), (14) and the semantics of "tomorrow"]

(C3)   Only in some worlds overlapping at c_1 is a sea battle taking place at t_2.   [premiss]

(C4)   What you said yesterday wasn't True.   [from (C2),(C3),(D)]

Nevertheless, as we have seen above, the supervaluationist is by no means compelled by the clause for the actuality operator stated in (11) to embrace an indexical treatment of "actually".

I conclude, therefore, that if the supervaluationist is allowed to make use of the monadic truth-predicate envisaged by MacFarlane, than she can perfectly cope both with INDETERMINACY-P and DETERMINACY-P, thus rendering truth-relativism an unnecessary departure from standard semantics.[12]

---

[12] An earlier version of this paper has been presented at the *Arché* Contextualism and Relativism seminar in St Andrews in July 2007. I am very grateful to the *Arché* research centre for having elicited my interest on truth-relativism and for having provided such a wonderful academic environment. I wish to thank John MacFarlane and Sebastiano Moruzzi for their helpful comments on earlier drafts of this paper. Special thanks go to: Patrick Greenough, Philip Percival, Stefano Predelli and Crispin Wright.

References

Kaplan, D. 1989. Demonstratives. In J. Almog, J. Perry, and H. Wettstein, eds., *Themes from Kaplan*, pages 483–563. Oxford: Oxford University Press.

Lewis, D. 1996. Index, Context and Content. In S. Kanger and S. Ohman, eds., *Philosophy and Grammar*, pages 79–100. Dordrecht: Reidel.

MacFarlane, J. 2003. Future Contingents and Relative Truth. *The Philosophical Quarterly* 53(212):321–336.

MacFarlane, J. 2008. Nonindexical Contextualism. *Synthese* doi: 10.1007/s11229-007-9286-2.

MacFarlane, J. forthcoming. Truth in the Garden of Forking Paths. In M. Kolbel and M. García-Carpintero, eds., *Relative Truth*. Oxford: Oxford University Press. http://sophos.berkeley.edu/macfarlane/garden.pdf.

Percival, P. 1989. Indices of Truth and Temporal Propositions. *The Philosophical Quarterly* 39(155):190–199.

Soames, S. 2007. Actually. *Proceedings of the Aristotelian Society Supplementary Volume* LXXXI:251–277.

Thomason, R. H. 1970. Indeterminist Time and Truth-Value Gaps. *Theoria* 36:264–81.

10
A Linguistic Analysis of the Omnipotence Puzzle
NAZIF MUHTAROGLU

The omnipotence puzzle is a complex problem and has different aspects. Typically, philosophers analyse this puzzle by focusing on its metaphysical aspect. In this paper, I will argue that the metaphysical aspect of this puzzle is insufficient to grasp its depth and will introduce an additional aspect which I call "the linguisitic analysis" of the omnipotence puzzle.

10.1 Introduction

Can God create a stone too heavy for him to lift or can He make Himself nonexistent or can He behave unjustly or lie? It is possible to increase the number of these questions, but I will restrict my discussion in this paper only to two types of question involving cases of the following two kinds of contradiction. First, the cases that include contradictions stemming from the relations between the meanings of the terms such as "round square" or arising from negating and affirming something under the same conditions such as "colourful and non-colourful house". Let us call them "logico-semantic" contradictions. So a typical question for this category is whether God can create a round square or not. The second type of case includes contradictions stemming from the nature of God such as God's lying or behaving unjustly. All of the cases specified in the entrance-questions are in fact in this class. These cases can be

Language, Knowledge, and Metaphysics.
Massimiliano Carrara and Vittorio Morato (eds.)
College Pubblication, London, 2008.

considered to be included in the "metaphysical contradictions" with respect to the nature of God.

If we assume omnipotence, being all-powerful, as an essential attribute of God, these questions seem to be puzzling. If the answer to such questions is *yes*, then we allowed accepting that God can kill Himself. But if He can kill Himself, then He is not an eternal being, so not truly God. If the answer is *no*, it seems that He does not have enough power to perform the tasks in question. And this seems to be a defect in His power which implies an imperfection in Him. So again He is not truly God. In any case, the answers to such questions produce a difficulty in terms of the coherence of the traditional notion of God.

On the basis of such puzzles, one can reject the existence of God as an absolutely perfect, omnipotent and eternal being because the notion of such a being seems to be incoherent, thus it has no real referent. However, there are various theistic views that try to make sense of such puzzles by preserving omnipotence as an essential property of God. The crucial point in their proposal is the concept of divine power. And there are two main aspects of the analysis of divine power. The first aspect is the debate over what actually falls under the scope of divine power. The theistic views with respect to the omnipotence puzzle differ according to the positions they take in relation to this issue. With respect to the two types of contradictions, we can postulate two main positions. First, the view that allows them under the scope of divine power. Hence, in this view, God can perform tasks involving two types of contradictions: He can create round squares; He can kill Himself, etc. This view can be associated with some historical figures such as Peter Damian[1] and Descartes.[2]

---

[1] Peter Damian claimed that God has the power to make a past event as though it had not occurred. Not only can He make a woman a virgin after defloration but also He could make the defloration never to have occurred (Damian, 1943, pp. 402–406). So this is a case where God is capable of causing an event to have occurred and not occurred at the same time, which implies a logical contradiction.

[2] Descartes is famous for his doctrine of the Creation of Eternal Truths whose simplest formulation is that eternal truths are freely created by God and dependent upon His will. Dan Kaufman identifies four types of eternal truths created by God according to Descartes: strictly logical truths such as "it is impossible for the same thing to be and not to be at the same time", conceptual truths such as "he who thinks cannot exist while he thinks", and synthetic *a priori* truths such as "nothing comes from nothing" and mathematical truths (Kaufman, 2005, p. 1). There are different interpretations of Descartes on whether any eternal truth depends on God's will or not. According to Harry Frankfurt's interpretation of Descartes, there is nothing God could not have done (Frankfurt, 1977, p. 43). According to Martial Gueroult's interpretation, some contradictions are not within God's power, namely the denial of essential truths about His own nature. The tasks implying the denial of His omnipotence, goodness, *etc.* are impossible for God (Gueroult, 1953, vol. II,

The second view we can postulate does not allow the two types of contradictions under the scope of divine power. This view can be related to the orthodox view in the Middle Ages with respect to the puzzle of omnipotence whose main proponent is Thomas Aquinas[3]. As it is seen, the first aspect of the analysis of the omnipotence puzzle deals with determining whether a certain case falls under the scope of divine power. Let me call it "the metaphysical aspect of the analysis of the omnipotence puzzle". The metaphysical analysis of this puzzle is not my concern here; I will focus on the other aspect in this paper.

The second aspect of the analysis is related to expressing the position taken in terms of the first aspect which I call "the linguistic aspect of the analysis of the omnipotence puzzle". How can we express the intuition behind the first option taken in terms of the metaphysical analysis of the omnipotence puzzle, for example? If a round square falls under the scope of divine power, should we say that "God can create it" or "God could have created it?" Some may say that God can do it any time, since there is no limit on His power at any time. Some may say that He cannot change a square once He decided it to be so. Cartesian philosophers can go in this direction because God's will is immutable according to Descartes[4] and does not change after a certain decree. So God could have made a round square but He decided to make a square as it is now by His own will and cannot change it after that. This is how the debate over the linguistic analysis of the first metaphysical option may develop.

However, I will not consider this part of the linguistic analysis but deal with the linguistic analysis of the second metaphysical option of the omnipotence puzzle in this paper.

In this paper, I will assume that the second metaphysical option is correct, namely that the two types of contradictions do not fall under the scope of divine power. And I will discuss how to express this option better than the traditional way of expressing it by considering mainly Aquinas's remarks on this issue. The orthodox way of expressing the intuition behind the second metaphysical option is uttering sentences such as "God cannot perform such tasks". But this form of expression linguistically implies that there is a defect in the divine power. Instead, I will argue that sentences beginning with "God cannot" suffer from category mistakes and suggest that "Divine power is not applicable to

---

pp. 26–29). The discussion on which interpretation is right is beyond the scope of this paper. But it is useful to point out the different interpretations of Descartes's doctrine of the creation of eternal truths.

[3]I will examine Aquinas's view on this issue in detail later.
[4]Letter to Mersenne, 15 April 1630 (Descartes, 1998, p. 23).

such cases" is a better way of expressing the same metaphysical option.

10.2 Aquinas's Position with respect to the Omnipotence Puzzle

Aquinas is probably the classical figure in the West who defends the second metaphysical option with respect to the omnipotence puzzle. According to the Thomas Gilby translation, Aquinas expresses his position by saying that "Whatever does not involve a contradiction is in that realm of possible with respect to which God is called omnipotent (*Ea vero contradictionem implicant sub divina omnipotentia non continentur, quia non possunt habere possibilium rationem.*)".[5] He gives examples of logical contradictions and some metaphysical contradictions related to the nature of God as cases that do not fall under the scope of divine power. However, what is interesting in his way of expressing this intuition is that he uses the modal verb "cannot" with the subject term "God" in most cases. Let's examine some of his remarks:

> God cannot make yes and no to be true at the same time not through lack of power, but through lack of possibility, such things are intrinsically impossible. (*Et ideo non potest facere qoud affirmatio et negatio sint simul vera, nec aliquod eorum in quibus hoc impossibile includitur. Nec hoc dicitur non posse facere propter defectum suae potentiae.*) (Aquinas, 1952, I-18, 19)

> Now, sin is a lapse from divine goodness: wherefore God cannot will to sin. Therefore we must grant absolutely that God cannot sin. (*Peccatum autem est defectus quidam a divina bontitate: unde Deus non potest velle peccare. Et ideo absolute concencendum est, quod Deus peccare non potest.* (Aquinas, 1952, I-35)

To Aquinas, God cannot perform certain tasks which include different kinds of contradictions as specified above. However, he tries to preserve the doctrine of omnipotence by claiming that this fact does not put a limitation on divine power. The intuition behind this move is that the scope of divine power excludes such impossible things. In other words, contradictions as stated above are not genuine objects of power, so divine power does not apply to them. This is not a lack of power, but a lack of possibility. In contemporary literature, Norman Kretzman emphasizes the point that logical contradictions do not fall under the scope of divine power in Aquinas's account and presents this

---

[5] See Aquinas (1964–1973, Q. 25, art.3, p. 165). Another possible translation can be given as follows: "Indeed, whatever implies contradiction does not fall under divine omnipotence, because it does not have the 'ratio' of the possible." "Ratio" is one of those elusive terms translatable in many ways in different contexts. Here *possibilium rationem* means something like "the character of the possible".

intuition by focusing on Aquinas's remarks that God cannot create or make them happen.[6]

Aquinas expresses the intuition that contradictions do not fall under the scope of divine power in a different way as well. Again according to Gilby translation, he says that "Better, however, to say that it cannot be done, rather than God cannot do it". (*Unde convenientus dicitur quod ea non possunt fieri quam quod Deus ea non possit facere.*)[7] The term "convenientus" can be translated as "approriate" as well in this context. From this remark, we see that he finds the other expressions not so appropriate. George Mavrodes also repeats Aquinas's formulation of inappropriateness of using "cannot" as a modal verb in a sentence whose subject is "God" and claims that the puzzling questions do not pose a real difficulty for divine omnipotence because they are not about real objects of power.[8] He carefully does not use the linguistic expressions which begin with "God cannot" in formulating Aquinas's position. Unfortunately, however, he does not suggest any reason why this formulation is more appropriate than the others or try to answer the question of what are the possible interpretations of the term "appropriateness" which is not so clear in the context where Aquinas used it.

Before I discuss Aquinas's formulations, I will introduce the key concept of category mistakes that I will make use of in my analysis.

10.3 Category Mistakes

In *The Concept of Mind*, Gilbert Ryle points out an important mistake that occurs in using language. When an expression systematically misleads us because of category confusion in representing a certain fact, then it is a "category mistake".[9] For example treating colleges, libraries, museums and scientific departments in the same category with the university is a category mistake. The university is not a member of the class of which the listed units are members but it is rather the way in which all of them are organized.[10] We can give more examples. Predicating colours of numbers is another category mistake. For example, "Number 2 is yellow" is a sentence asserted as a result of category confusion.

The notion of category mistakes depends on the notion of category which should be clarified in some degree. Fred Sommers proposes that a

---

[6]See Kretzman (1998, p. 117 and p. 118).
[7]See Aquinas (1964–1973, Q. 25, art. 3, p. 165).
[8]See Mavrodes (1963, pp. 221–223).
[9]See Ryle (1949, p. 16).
[10]See Ryle (1949, p. 16).

category can be defined in two different ways: The first one comes from Russell. For Russell, a type is a set of things or relations spanned by a given predicate. In this view, a predicate ranges over things, objects or relations. Sommers gives the following example for Russell's categories: Socrates and Julius Caesar are in the set spanned by the predicate "is a philosopher" but the Industrial Revolution is not in this set.[11]

The second category belongs to Ryle. Ryle's type is a set of expressions which span some given things.[12] In this view, a category includes expressions instead of things. For instance, the predicates "is blue," "is heavy" and "is tough" are in the same set if they span to a stone. As a result, there is a certain scope of things or expressions for each category. Things or expressions which are not in the scope of a certain category lead to a category mistake if they are associated with this category. The issue of how the exact range of a scope of a notion is determined is a matter of metaphysical analysis which is not considered in this paper.[13]

What I am dealing with in this paper are cases rather than objects (things) or expressions. However, cases are closer to objects than to expressions. Both cases and objects are extra linguistic entities, but expressions are not. Let's modify Russell's notion of type (or category) by adding cases to it. Thus, the notion of type or category that I will use in this paper is a set of cases as well as of objects or relations.

Another important point relevant to category mistakes which I have presented so far is that they are semantic issues. A category mistake is not a pragmatic matter relevant to the person who utters a sentence involving such a mistake. The statement "The Empire State building is a philosopher" constitutes a category mistake for any person who utters it. There are opposing views on the semantic status of category mistakes and there seem to be three main views.

According to the first view, category mistakes are meaningless. This view is derived from Russell's intuitions about type confusions. Russell considers all type confusions leading to a paradox to be meaningless.[14] For instance, if you claim that a set is a member of itself, then your assertion is meaningless according to Russell and consequently neither true nor false. So in Russell's logic, there is a range of significance for each predicate as Arthur Pap points out.[15] "x is green" becomes

---

[11] See Sommers (1963, p. 328).
[12] See Sommers (1963, p. 329).
[13] As I said, I do not deal with the metaphysical aspect of the omnipotence puzzle in this paper but focus on just the linguistic aspect. For Ryle's discussion about how a category mistake is identified, see his "Categories" (Ryle, 1971) and "Systematically Misleading Expressions" (Ryle, 1932).
[14] See Russell and Whitehead (1960, p. 37).
[15] See Pap (1960, p. 42).

meaningless if x is 2 which is not in the range of significance of the predicate "is green".

In the second view, category mistakes are meaningful but they lack a truth value. So they are neither true nor false but not nonsensical. This is Gilbert Ryle's position. He considers them to be absurd and clearly differentiates absurdity from nonsensicalness or meaninglessness.[16] Thus for Ryle, "2 is green" is a meaningful sentence but lacks a truth value.

According to the third view, category mistakes have a truth value, namely they are false. Quine[17] and Arthur Pap are in this camp. Pap characterizes the falsehood here as synthetic *a priori* falsehood. His reason for this result is as follows: "Whatever is red, is extended" expresses a synthetic *a priori* truth which is necessary without being formally analytic. If so, its negation "Some entity which is not extended is red" should express an *a priori* falsehood without being formally contradictory.[18] Pap suggests a trichotomous classification of falsehood: formal contradictions, empirical falsehood and synthetic *a priori* falsehood.[19] In order to express synthetic *a priori* falsehood, Pap distinguishes two senses of the operator "not" or the value "false". There are two kinds of negation: limited and unlimited negation. If not-(S is P) is interpreted as (S is non-P) where non-P is the disjunction of all the other members of the predicate family to which P belongs, then the negation in question is limited, it is within a limited genus.[20] Under this interpretation, the denial of "x is green" is that x has a colour other than green. So "This stone is green" is limitedly false; it is not in fact green but colourful. On the other hand, the denial of "2 is green" does not imply that 2 is colourful even though it is not green. The negation here is unlimited and under this interpretation of the negation operator, we do not presuppose that 2 belongs to the category of being colorful which includes green objects in its scope, when we deny that 2 is green. In this case, "2 is green" is unlimitedly false.[21] After the presentation of the key concepts that are necessary for my linguistic analysis of the omnipotence puzzle, let me go on to discuss Aquinas's position.

---

[16] See Ryle (1971, p. 180).

[17] Quine considers type mistakes "false by meaning." See his *Word and Object* (Quine, 1976, p. 229).

[18] See Pap (1960, p. 53).

[19] *Ibid.*

[20] See Pap (1960, p. 54).

[21] See Pap (1960, p. 54).

10.4 Evaluation of Aquinas's linguistic formulation

Aquinas's first kind of formulations which begin with the phrase "God cannot" suffer from category mistakes. It is clear from his other remarks that the two types of contradiction do not fall under the scope of divine power. So what God cannot do is in fact not a genuine possible case and because of that there is no defect in divine power according to Aquinas. However, the term "cannot" in this context semantically suggests that God has not enough power to do certain things, not that certain things are not objects of divine power. The semantics or meaning of the term "can" or "cannot" includes the idea of ability or inability to do something, which is closely linked to the notion of power. The sentence "God cannot do x" or its reformulation as "x cannot be done by God" includes category mistakes if x is an instance of the two types of contradiction. In other words, x is not included in the extension to which divine power is applicable.

Aquinas's other formulation[22] can be interpreted in different ways. Gilby translated the passage "*ea non possunt fieri*" as "it cannot be done." This translation presents the sentence in the passive form whose agent is missing. The agent is implicit in this passive sentence and he is God. So it (a contradictory case) cannot be done by God. According to this translation, even though Aquinas seems to try to avoid using the phrase "God cannot do", what he says actually implies it. Saying that such things cannot be done does not change the fact that such things cannot be done by God. Again here there is a category mistake as mentioned before. Here, what differentiates saying "it cannot be done" from "God cannot do it" cannot be a semantic matter. However, it may be a pragmatic one which makes us interpret the appropriateness in question not semantically but by a reference to the speaker and the context of the saying. The utterance of sentences beginning with "God cannot" may be inappropriate according to the social-cultural standards of a society or according to the religio-psychological norms of somebody. A pious person may consider the phrase "God cannot do something" to be a rude expression, although he may believe that God cannot create a round square. In addition, in a religious society, people uttering such expressions may face difficulties. However, all of these considerations are related to the pragmatic conditions of these formulations. It is a pragmatic matter[23] whether such a formulation is appropriate or not

---

[22] "Better (more appropriate), however, to say that it cannot be done, rather than God cannot do it." (*Unde convenientus dicitur quod ea non possunt fieri quam quod Deus ea non possit facere.*) (Aquinas, 1964–1973, Q. 25, art. 3, p. 165).

[23] By the term "pragmatics" or its derivative phrases such as "pragmatic matter" or "pragmatic conditions," I do not refer to the pragmatic elements which are closely

under this interpretation. Let's call this interpretation the "pragmatic interpretation".

One of the common usages of term "fieri" in Latin is its usage as the passive form of the verb "facere" which means to make something. In this usage, the translation of "*ea non possunt fieri*" can be given as "it cannot be done or made." My pragmatic interpretation given above depends on this translation. However, there is another usage of this term: it is a verb in the infinitive form which means to happen. In this usage, the translation of the mentioned Latin sentence would be "It could not happen."[24] So the translation that it could not happen does not imply any passive case which is affected by an agent. It depicts a case in which contradictions could not possibly happen. The difference between the two translations may be understood better by the *de re-de dicto* distinction. *De re* simply means "about the object," *de dicto* is "about the statement." Let us consider the sentences that "the number of U. S. states (50) is possibly even" and that "it is possible that the number of U.S. states is even." The first sentence says that the number 50, which is the object in the sentence is possibly even. It is in the *de re* mode. However, 50 is not possibly but necessarily an even number. The sentence in *de re* mode is false. The second sentence states that the number of the U.S. States is even is a possible truth. It is about the whole sentence, not about the number 50. It is in the *de dicto* mode. Since U.S. might have had more or less than 50 states it is true.[25] Aquinas was well aware of the distinction between *de re* and *de dicto*, and used it in many contexts. So it is quite plausible to interpret the sentence "*ea non possunt fieri*" in a *de dicto* mode. If so, the focus of the sentence is not contradictory cases (objects-*re*) which cannot be done but the whole idea that they could not happen. Let me call this, "semantical interpretation" of appropriateness. This interpreation makes sense in terms of dealing with category mistakes. A category mistake is a semantic inappropriateness independently of the pragmatic elements as mentioned above. The issue of determining the exact sense of the semantic inappropriateness in question is related to the three main views on the semantic status of sentences including category mistakes. Let's consider this issue now.

---

linked to the semantics of the terms. A scientific community may introduce a certain scientific term by convention and play a role in determining its meaning. This is a pragmatic fact which is closely related to the semantics. This is not what I mean in this context by "pragmatics."

[24] I would like to thank the participants of the Marquette 2008 conference on "The Philosophy in the Abrahamic traditions" for their help in seeing the possibility of this different translation.

[25] See Lepore (1999, p. 211).

10.5 Inappropriateness of Category Mistakes

It is unclear what Aquinas means by "more appropriate" in saying that "It is more appropriate to say that such things cannot be done, than that God cannot do them".[26] From that sentence, we see that his distinction between two types of formulations is not exactly a semantic one even though it seems to be so. To say passively that such things cannot be done also implies that God cannot do them. So the appropriateness he mentions is not a semantic kind of appropriateness or inappropriateness.

A more plausible interpretation is to link appropriateness not to a semantic category but to a pragmatic one, namely to the speaker. The utterance of sentences beginning with "God cannot" may be inappropriate according to the social-cultural standards of a society or according to the religio-psychological norms of somebody. A pious person may consider the phrase "God cannot do something" to be a rude expression, although he may believe that God cannot create a round square. In addition, in a religious society, people uttering such expressions may face difficulties. However, all of these considerations are related to the pragmatic conditions of these formulations. It is a pragmatic matter[27] whether such a formulation is appropriate or not under this interpretation. Let us call this interpretation the "pragmatic interpretation." It seems that Aquinas's remarks on appropriateness have a pragmatic aspect rather than a semantic one. However, this is not the case. In my analysis, the inappropriateness of sentences beginning with "God cannot" which assume the applicability of divine power to the two types of contradiction stem from the category mistakes such sentences involve. It is a semantic inappropriateness independent of the pragmatic elements as mentioned above. The issue of determining the exact sense of the semantic inappropriateness in question is related to the three main views on the semantic status of sentences including category mistakes. Let us consider this issue now.

---

[26] See Aquinas (1964–1973, Q. 25, art. 3, p. 165).

[27] By the term "pragmatics" or its derivative phrases such as "pragmatic matter" or "pragmatic conditions" I do not intend to refer to the pragmatic elements which are closely linked to the semantics of the terms. A scientific community may introduce a certain scientific term by convention and play a role in determining its meaning. This is a pragmatic fact which is closely related to the semantics. This is not what I mean in this context by "pragmatics".

10.6 The Semantic Status of the Sentences involving Category Mistakes

As I mentioned before, there are three main views on the semantic status of sentences including category mistakes. In principle, I do not want to commit myself to one of them but some of them must be assumed with respect to certain presuppositions. So I want to point out the different directions resulting in different views on the basis of different presuppositions in this section.

According to our analysis of category mistakes, to say that God cannot do x where x is an instance of the two types of contradiction is semantically inappropriate as well as to say that God can do x. Both sentences involve a category mistake because divine power is not applicable to x. However these two sentences seem to be contradictory. If we deny both of them together, it seems that we violate the principle of excluded middle. This is a problem that must be taken into consideration. The force of this objection depends on what we understand from the notion of negation. If "God cannot do x" is the logical negation of "God can do x", then these two sentences are contradictory. But it is not clear why we should treat the negation here as a logical one. Let us remember Arthur Pap's distinction between limited and unlimited negation. The limited negation of the sentence "This stone is not green" is that this stone has a colour other than green, namely it is not green but colourful. The unlimited negation of the sentence "2 is green" does not imply that 2 is a colorful object. If logical negation is unlimited negation, there is no threat to the principle of excluded middle. The logical negation of the sentence "God can do x" is then the sentence "It is not the case that God can do x" but not the sentence "God cannot do x". So the sentences "God can do x" and "God cannot do x" are not logically contradictory pairs under this interpretation. However, if the logical negation is accepted to be limited negation, then these sentences must be assumed to be a logically contradictory pair which implies the violation of the principle of excluded middle under our analysis of category mistakes. Then under the interpretation that the logical negation is limited negation, we have two options in front of us: either we reject the principle of excluded middle as a universally valid principle of logic or try to make sense of our claim by preserving its universal validity. As far as the first option is concerned, we do not mean that the principle of excluded middle is rejected altogether. It is not applicable to the case of category mistakes but may be applied to some other cases. However, this option seems to rule out this principle as a principle of logic because logical principles are traditionally assumed to be applicable to any case. If we reject the universal validity of this principle, then we are not forced to commit ourselves to one of the views regarding the semantic status of the sentences involving category mistakes. They may be meaningless or meaningful but truth valueless or they have the truth value false.

If we want to preserve the principle of excluded middle as a logical law, then we cannot accept the third view which ascribes the truth value "false" to the sentences involving category mistakes. If the sentence "God cannot do x" is false, then "God can do x" is false as well according to this view. But one of the sentences must be true if the principle of excluded middle is presupposed. The second view which maintains that the sentences involving category mistakes are meaningful but truth-valueless does not seem to be open for this option either. If two propositions are meaningful and are the negation of each other they must have opposite truth values according to the principle of excluded middle. So the only view that remains open to this option is the first one. Sentences that involve category mistakes are meaningless and so no logical principle is applicable to them. They do not express genuine propositions which are in the domain of logic. We can understand such sentences, they are meaningful in this sense, but the meaningfulness in this context is assumed to be different from being understandable. We can understand the sentence "Tom school flies". However, it does not express a genuine proposition; it is simply ill-formed. In that sense, sentences involving category mistakes are meaningless and do not express genuine propositions. Since the principle of excluded middle is not applicable to pseudo-propositions, there is no conflict in assuming that sentences involving category mistakes are meaningless and truth valueless by presupposing the logical principle of excluded middle.

10.7 Conclusion

The puzzle of omnipotence is complex. To analyse it, I suggested distinguishing between metaphysical and linguistic aspects of the puzzle. The notion of divine power is at the centre of the omnipotence puzzle. Previous thinkers have been interested in this puzzle from the metaphysical point of view. They have concentrated on what the exact scope of divine power is. However, it is also important to figure out how to express correctly the intuition presupposed by a particular metaphysical position of this puzzle. In this paper, I assumed that the two types of contradictions, namely semantic-logical, and metaphysical contradictions regarding the nature of God, do not fall under the scope of divine power and dealt with the linguistic aspect of this assumption. I argued that Aquinas's most formulations as well as the pragmatic interpretation of the appropriateness of the Latin sentence "*ea non possunt fieri*" are problematic on the basis that they include category mistakes. Instead, I offered a semantical interpretation of the appropriateness of the mentioned Latin sentence and proposed the following formulation: divine is not applicable to the two types of contradiction.[28]

References

Aquinas, Thomas. 1952. *On the Power of God (Quaestiones disputatae de potentia Dei)*. Westminster, MD: The Newman Press. Translated by Lawrence Shapcote.

Aquinas, Thomas. 1964–1973. *Summa Theologiae*. London: Eyre and Spottiswoode. Translated by Thomas Gilby *et al*.

Damian, Peter. 1943. *De Divina Omnipotentia*. Firenze: Vallecchi. Edited by Paolo Brezzi.

Descartes, Renè. 1998. *The Philosophical Writings of Descartes*, vol. III. Cambridge: Cambridge University Press. Translated by John Cottingham, Robert Stoothoff, Dugald Murdoch and Anthony Kenny.

Frankfurt, Harry. 1977. Descartes on the creation of eternal truths. *Philosophical Review* 86(1):36–57.

Gueroult, Martial. 1953. *Descartes selon l'ordre des raisons*, vol. II. Paris: Aubier.

Kaufman, Dan. 2005. God's immutability and the necessity of Descartes's eternal truths. *Journal of the History of Philosophy* 43(1):1–19.

Kretzman, Norman. 1998. *The Metaphysics of Creation: Aquinas's Natural Theology in* Summa Contra Gentiles *II*, vol. II. Oxford: Clarendon Press.

Lepore, Ernest. 1999. *De Dicto*. In R. Audi, ed., *Cambridge Dictionary of Philosophy*. Cambridge: Cambridge University Press.

Mavrodes, George. 1963. Some puzzles concerning omnipotence. *Philosophical Review* 72(2):221–223.

Pap, Arthur. 1960. Types and meaninglessness. *Mind* 69(273):41–54.

Quine, Willard van Orman. 1976. *Word and Object*. Cambridge MA: MIT Press.

Rorty, Richard, ed. 1992. *The Linguistic Turn*. Chicago: University of Chicago Press.

Russell, Bertrand and Alfred N. Whitehead. 1960. *Principia Mathematica*, vol. I. Cambridge: Cambridge University Press.

---

[28]Earlier drafts of this paper were presented in the following conferences: "Knowledge, Language and Metaphysics" in Padua University in 2007 and "Philosophy in the Abrahamic Tradition" in Marquette University in 2008. I would like to thank the audiences in general and Oliver Leaman, David Bradshaw, David Burrell, David Hunter, Gerald J. Massey, Sanford Goldberg, Clare Batty and Alan Perreiah in particular for their valuable comments.

Ryle, Gilbert. 1932. Systematically misleading expressions. *Proceedings of the Aristotelian Society* 32:139–170. Reprinted in (Rorty, 1992, pp. 85–100).

Ryle, Gilbert. 1949. *The concept of mind*. London: Taylor and Francis.

Ryle, Gilbert. 1971. *Collected Papers*, vol. II. London: Hutchinson Publisher.

Sommers, Fred. 1963. Types and ontology. *Philosophical Review* 72(3):327–363.

11
Relative Truth and the Metaphysics of Tense

GIULIANO TORRENGO

11.1 Introduction

Truth relativism is, roughly, the idea that in order to assess certain kinds of statements (such as evaluative claims concerning artworks or taste, and tensed claims), we resort to an *irreducibly relativized notion of truth*. The idea of relative truth is suggested by the following two platitudes:

- claims concerning aesthetic, taste and ethic issues, along with epistemic modals and knowledge attributions, seem to be true or false *only* with respect to certain canons or "perspectives";
- sentences containing tensed expressions may have different truth-values depending on when they are uttered.

All such cases have been lately seen as *prima facie* plausible candidates for relative truths. The thought behind the idea of considering the notion of truth as irreducibly relative[1] is that once we have interpreted someone S claiming (1) in a certain context,

(1) Roasted snails are delicious

it is still open with respect to what "canon of taste" (or "taste perspective") we should assess the attribution of deliciousness to roasted snails (and analogously for similar cases).

---
[1] See MacFarlane (2003), MacFarlane (2008), and Kölbel (2008b). See also Wright (2008).

Now, truth relativism is a stronger thesis than the claim (which may be labelled "vanilla relativism") that *sentences* containing certain "perspectival" expressions, such as tensed verbs and evaluation predicates (*e.g.* moral, or aesthetic predicates such as "good" or "beautiful") are context sensitive, namely are differently evaluated depending on the context of utterance. In particular, truth relativism has to be distinguished from forms of vanilla relativism that treat the claims at issue as possessing indexical elements – either "hidden" in the underlying syntactic form or provided pragmatically by the context.[2] Indexicalists maintain that tokens of the same *sentence* type containing perspectival expressions express different contents – namely different *propositions* – depending on their context of utterance. According to the contextualists, tensed verbs and evaluation adjectives work roughly as "I" or "this": they pick up different semantic values in different contexts of use. The notion of relative truth that the indexicalists resort to, thus, boils down to the familiar idea of a (indexical) sentence requiring contextual parameters to be fully interpreted. A truth value can be associated to a sentence S only relative to a certain set of contextual parameters, but once the semantic values of all the sub-sentential expressions of S are contextually settled, a proposition is thereby determined, which is not true or false relative to a further parameter – but true or false *simpliciter*. Therefore, as far as propositions are concerned, indexicalists endorse an absolute notion of truth. On the contrary, "genuine" relativists maintain that what is irreducibly relative is not only the truth of the various occurrences of a sentence, rather, it is the truth of the very *same content* (*i.e.* the proposition) expressed.

Genuine relativists have marshaled many arguments against the "vanilla" treatment of assessment sensitivity advanced by the indexicalists. I will not review them here.[3] Rather, I will focus on John MacFarlane's argument to the effect that *future contingent claims* provide the clearest example of assessment-sensitivity that requires us to employ a notion of relative truth (in a later article MacFarlane has acknowledged that traditional semantics fares better than he first diagnosed, but this will not touch on my main point here).[4] The general idea is that *retrospective assessment* of utterances can lead to differences in evaluation of the proposition expressed by a sentence in a context, and this requires us to make the interpretation and evaluation of an utterance relative both to a *context of use* (C_u) and a *context of assessment*

---

[2] An example of the fist kind of indexicalism is Stanley (2005). For the second kind see Recanati (2007).
[3] See, for instance, Kölbel (2008a).
[4] See MacFarlane (2003) and MacFarlane (2005).

(C_a). If I say today that tomorrow it will be sunny, my utterance, as assessed from the viewpoint of the present context, is undetermined (neither true nor false). But if I assess *tomorrow* the utterance that I have made in yesterday's context, I end up with a definite truth-value: my utterance was true if the sun shines, false otherwise.

In what follows I will first look at the semantic treatment of tenses proposed by the "double context relativists" (as we may dub them), and argue that truth relativism thus understood forces us to a construal of propositions as *tensed* propositions. Then, I argue that understanding the role of *tensed* proposition in a double time reference framework requires us to flash out a certain picture of the link between language and reality: *perspectival realism*. Finally, I conclude that truth relativism with respect to tensed expressions – once fully articulated and clearly distinguished from its indexicalist cognate – boils down to a form of perspectival realism, viz. tense realism: the idea that reality is composed at different times by different (tensed) facts.

11.2 Parameters and Propositions

Apart for contexts of assessment, MacFarlane's semantic framework is standard: what proposition a sentence S expresses in a context of utterance C_u depends on certain parameters, which are linked to the context C_u (such as the agent, the time, the world, and so on). In a standard framework, there are two roles that contextual parameters may play in the interpretation and evaluation of a sentence in a context.

(ER)   *The evaluation role:* the parameter determines an aspect of the point against which the proposition is evaluated.

This aspect or element does not "enter" into the content expressed (or it is not "represented" in the content – depending on your favourite view of propositions). Possible worlds provide a typical example of parameters playing this role. By evaluating an occurrence of a statement with respect to a world parameter, we do not take the world at issue to be part of the content expressed by the statement. Rather, the world parameter stands for the (part of) reality against which we are evaluating what is expressed: the actual world, say, rather than a hypothetical one.

(CR)   *The completion role:* the parameter determines an element of the content expressed.

This element or aspect is a constituent of (or is "represented in") the proposition expressed. Parameters that enter in the interpretation rules for indexical expressions, such as the agent parameter, provide a typical example of parameters playing the completion role.

Among the contextual parameters of the standard framework, we find a *possible world* parameter and an agent parameter, corresponding – in normal cases – to the world where the utterance takes place and to the speaker:

$C_u = <w, a>$.

Consider, then, the truth-conditions of a simple sentence such as "I am blond", whose interpretation and evaluation is sensitive both to the world and to the agent parameter:

(TC)   "I am blond" is true at $<w, a>$ iff a is bond in w.

While the agent parameter's role is to *complete the interpretation* of an utterance of "I am blond", namely to yield the referent of "I", thereby contributing to the determination of the proposition contextually expressed by such a sentence, the world parameter's role is to "complete" the evaluation of such a proposition, namely to contribute to the *determination of its truth-value*, "once" the propositions expressed have been determined.

11.3 Tensed and Tenseless Propositions

In the case of the temporal parameters these two roles are connected to two different conceptions of proposition to be found in the literature:[5] if time plays the evaluation role, the proposition expressed is a tensed proposition, *i.e.* it has a truth-value only relative to a time; if time plays the completion role, the proposition expressed is *tenseless*, *i.e.* it has a truth-value *simpliciter* (as far as time is concerned).

To illustrate this last point, we can think of tensed propositions as complex entities among whose constituents no time points or lapses show up as "completing" or "saturating" any further constituents. For instance, the tensed proposition expressed by an utterance of

(2)   I am (presently) sitting

(assuming that I am the speaker) may be thought of as an entity composed by me, and the property of *being sit* (or by some sort of representations of such things):

< Giuliano, *Being sit* >.

In order to evaluate whether this proposition is true, namely whether it is the case that I am (presently) sitting, we need to relativize the evaluation of the proposition to a time point. In a present tense sentence such as (2) the time relative to which the tensed proposition expressed

---
[5]See Richard (1981), and King (2007).

is to be evaluated is identical to the contextual time t.[6] In other words, tensed propositions are propositions that bear a truth-value, and thus can be evaluated, only *with respect* to a temporal parameter.

Contrariwise, tenseless propositions are propositions which bear a truth-value, and thus are evaluated, *simpliciter* (as far as temporal factors are concerned). The proposition expressed by an utterance of the sentences (2) – again assuming that I am the speaker – at a time t, may be thought of as a complex entity encompassing me, the property of being sit and a certain time instant or lapse t:

$<$ Giuliano, *Being sit*, $t >$.

The time focus here enters into the content expressed by the utterance, and the proposition is evaluated *simpliciter*, rather than with respect to such a parameter. Note that the indexicalist, by treating all context sensitivity as a form of indexicality, is bound to construe the content expressed by a tensed sentence in a context as a tenseless proposition. This is why she does not resort to a notion of a relativized (to times) propositional truth.

11.4 Contexts of Assessment

What makes MacFarlane's framework *non*-standard is the indexing of the assessment of utterances to a context of assessment C_a, along with a context of utterance C_u. Although, as in the standard framework, the context of utterance C_u contains all the parameters which are relevant for determining the proposition expressed by the utterance (namely all the parameters playing the completion role that we need in order to interpret the utterance), MacFarlane claims that the evaluation of an utterance will require also parameters *which are not contained in the context of utterance* (at least in certain cases). Such parameters are to be found in the context of assessment C_a. The evaluation of future contingent claims, as hinted at before, provides a case in which a context of an assessment is called for. Consider the following sentence:

(3) It will be sunny tomorrow.

Suppose that (3) has been uttered in a context C_u, occurring on a certain day d – let us say today – which for simplicity we may take as the time parameter of C_u. In the standard framework, tensed expressions are interpreted and evaluated only with respect to such a parameter d. If evaluated with respect to d, (3) is *indeterminate*.[7] However, con-

---

[6] At least in "normal" situations. There are also "shifting" contexts, see Predelli (2005).

[7] We are here granting an indeterministic framework to the truth relativist. Obviously, in a deterministic framework the whole case for truth relativism as applied to

trary to what one would expect from the point of view of the standard framework, the truth-value of an utterance of (3) in a context C_u does not seem to be absolute (*i.e.* settled once for all). If we consider the very same utterance at a later time d' – let us say sometime tomorrow – it looks like we should assess (3) either as true, if the weather is fine, or as false, in case of overcast – but *not* as indeterminate.

Consider what happens in figure 1, where A is the day of utterance of (3), and B and C are two "alternative tomorrows" to A – in which it rains and it is sunny respectively.

"It will be sunny tomorrow"

FIGURE 1

It is easy to see that while (3) is indeterminate if $C_u = C_a$, namely with respect to $C_u = A$ and $C_a = A$, it can differ in truth value when $C_u \neq C_a$. In particular, (3) is true in case $C_u = A$ and $C_a = C$, and it is false in case $C_u = A$ and $C_a = B$.

Note that it is the presence of a context of assessment in the formal framework what makes MacFarlane's semantics a form of *truth* relativism. In the standard framework, the completion parameters of the context of utterance determine a proposition, and such a proposition is evaluated *with respect to* the evaluation parameters – usually the world of the utterance, and in certain frameworks a world *and* a time (in such cases we have tensed propositions). Therefore, a form of relativized propositional truth is part and parcel also of the traditional framework. However, the traditional framework is not thereby relativistic, since the context of utterance yields all the parameters needed to *absolutely* settle the truth-value of the proposition expressed – in particular, all the evaluation parameters too. Thus, although propositions in the standard framework are true or false only with respect to possible worlds (and, in certain frameworks, to couples of worlds and times),

---

tense expressions will not even arise. Moreover, the fact that d is the only temporal parameter relevant for the standard framework does not imply that it is the only time involved in the evaluation and interpretation of (3). Indeed, future and past tense will involve reference to future and past moments in time.

an utterance will be *absolutely* true (or false) if and only if it is true (or false) with respect to the world (and, in certain frameworks, the time) of the context[8].

11.5 MacFarlane and Tensed Propositions

The context of assessment contains parameters that are required for assessing the truth-value of an utterance of a sentence such as (3). Do such parameters play the evaluation or the completion role? Since it is the presence of a context of assessment what makes MacFarlane's framework a relativistic one, and this is but a formal feature of the framework, we might be tempted to answer that a relativist makes do either way, and a choice is not forced upon her. Indeed, MacFarlane seems to think that way, at least in the case of tense. Although MacFarlane is well aware of the difference between tensed and tenseless propositions, he maintains that understanding assessment-sensitivity, and thus relative truth, does not require us to choose between those two options. At first sight, from such a stance it follows that the parameters in the context of assessment may either be completion or evaluation parameters. In other words, it seems to follow that *one may uphold an irreducibly notion of truth even where she takes an indexicalist bent in her semantics.* Or, at least, this can be done when we are dealing with tense, and truth relativism elicited by tensed expressions.

Relativists usually have independent reasons for rejecting contextualism in areas of discourse such as aesthetics, taste and ethics. For instance, they appeal to the intuition that two persons disagreeing on the truth value of a claim such as (1) contradict each other, namely ascribe and refuse to ascribe the very same property (deliciousness) to the very same thing (roasted snails). Since contextualists maintain that (1) contains a hidden indexical referring to the standard of taste of the speaker (or the standard of taste relevant in the context), they are bound to deny that the two parties are actually contradicting each other. Rather, they simply express different, but compatible, properties (delicious according to my taste *vs.* delicious according to your taste) and attribute it to roasted snails. However, the case of tense seems to be slightly different (and closer to the case of epistemic modals and knowledge attributions), since if two persons assess the same utterance from different points in time, nothing suggests that they are contradicting each other, or that they disagree over anything. What is relevant for retrospective assessment is to take into account a further context

---

[8]And analogously for frameworks, in which truth is defined as true at each or every evaluation parameter.

C_a beside the context of utterance C_u, and to allow the truth-value of the utterance to vary with the temporal parameter we find there.

Now, we have to be clear on what exactly mixing relativism with a tenseless view of propositions amounts to, and more generally about the costs of endorsing truth relativism*cum* a neutral stance toward the semantic of tense. Although tense relativism cannot appeal to the intuitions concerning disagreement, an account of *retrospective assessment* that involves an irreducibly relativized notion of truth requires that the *very same proposition* expressed in an utterance may be evaluated differently – depending on whether we assess it at the time of utterance or at a some later time. Otherwise, if we let the same utterance express different propositions with respect to different contexts of assessment, the difference in assessment would be parasitic on the difference in *interpretation*. And, as we have seen, sentential truth relativism is utterly compatible with an absolute notion of truth; it is at best a form of vanilla relativism. What is peculiar about the relativist's retrospective assessment is the fact that the content (*i.e.* the *proposition*) expressed by an utterance can *change* its truth-value as times goes by.

But then, in which sense can a relativist be neutral with respect to the kind of content expressed by tensed talk – *i.e.* can endorse either a tensed or a tenseless view of propositions? Surely not in the sense that the parameters in the context of assessment are completion parameters playing the role they play in a standard framework. A tenseless proposition that a standard interpretive system associates to a sentence and a set of completion parameters is a proposition whose "temporal slots" are all already "saturated" (by times or quantification over times), and thus it has a truth-value *simpliciter* (modulo sensitivity to other parameters). If a tenseless proposition is indeterminate, it is not possible that at a later time this *very same proposition* is assessed with a *determinate* truth-value. In the standard reading, tenseless propositions are time *insensitive*, and thus cannot be differently assessed with respect to different times. What should a change in truth-value depend on, then, given that all the time-sensitive elements of the proposition have been made insensitive by saturation? The sentence expressing them can have its content differently completed with respect to different parameters, but once its content is settled with respect to time, nothing (temporal) can alter its evaluation. Either the former proposition changes some of its temporal constituents, but then it will be a *different* proposition (which undermines the core of MacFarlane's position), or it will be assessed as indeterminate at a later time too.

It might be argued that MacFarlane here is appealing to an essentially relativistic notion of assessment, which differs from the standard notion of evaluation. Thus, while tenseless propositions are barred from any sensitivity to temporal parameters with respect to the traditional idea of evaluation, they are still sensitive to temporal parameters with respect to such a relativistic notion of assessment. Now, even if we take such a notion as a primitive, we should at least be in a position to gesture something toward its meaning, and the standard understanding of tenseless propositions as entities "saturated" with respect to all their temporal constituents definitely seems of no help here. However, maybe my worry about tenseless propositions is misplaced, not because such a non-standard understanding of tenseless propositions is indeed viable, but because the problem is even more general – one arising regardless of whether we have tenseless or tensed propositions in our framework. Suppose we consider the proposition expressed in an utterance of (3) on a day d, a tensed proposition. In a double time reference semantics, the context of utterance $C_u = d$ is not enough to settle the utterance's truth-value; we need to resort to a context of assessment $C_a = d'$ (with possibly $d = d'$). Does this mean that we should take the day d' of the context of assessment as the time of evaluation of the tensed proposition expressed by the utterance of (3) on d? No. MacFarlane explicitly maintains that, in retrospective assessment, propositional truth has not to be taken as time-relative,[9] we have rather to consider the time of evaluation as an independent parameter. The time of evaluation *is* given by the context of utterance, or – rather – by the interaction of the tense and the context of utterance. Roughly, a future tensed claim expresses an ascription that has to be evaluated with respect to a future time (*i.e.* a time coming after that of utterance), a past tensed claim expresses an ascription that has to be evaluated with respect to a past time (*i.e.* a time coming before that of utterance), and a present tensed claim expresses an ascription that has to be evaluated with respect to the time of utterance. Therefore, considering the content of a tensed sentence a tensed proposition *simply* seems to be tantamount to misconstruing double context relativism. What truth relativism claims is that evaluating an ascription *with respect to a given time* can lead to different results depending on a further temporal parameter, *i.e.* the time of assessment we are considering.

This puts the relativist in an impasse: taking the proposition expressed as a tenseless proposition makes relativization to a further time of assessment meaningless, or at least difficult to informally capture, while taking the proposition expressed as tensed amounts to misinterpreting the double context framework. I suggest that we dissolve the

---

[9] See MacFarlane (2005).

impasse by focusing on the second horn. Obviously, the simple fact of taking the proposition expressed by a tensed sentence as a tensed proposition does not boil down to misconstruing MacFarlane's proposal – given the proposal itself is allegedly neutral with respect to the two options. Rather, the point here is that according to double context relativism for tense, an utterance of (3) on d is evaluated with respect to a certain time (depending on the tense in it), but what is the result of such an evaluation depends on the context from which we consider it – that is to say that a further temporal factor, a context of assessment, is called for. Today, it is undetermined whether we should evaluate as true my utterance that it will be sunny tomorrow, because it is (still) undetermined what will happen at the time targeted by my utterance. Tomorrow, when amongst many possible futures only one has turned out to be actual, it is determined whether the tensed proposition expressed by my past utterance has to be evaluated, relative to the very same day, true or false.

It may be thought that double context relativism, rather than being neutral with respect to tenseless and tensed proposition, is actually resorting to an *intermediate* kind of propositions, one that is saturated with respect to the time targeted by the occurrence of a tense in a context, but it is still tensed by being sensitive to temporal factors – *e.g.* the passage of time. Intuitively, we can easily grasp what such a proposition would look like if we think of the fact that changes in truth-value of *sentences* may occur even when we explicitly express a time of evaluation. For instance if someone says on December 31st 2008

(4) There will be a sea battle on January 1st 2009

assuming an indeterministic view of time, it seems that the utterance has an indeterminate truth-value. But on January 1st that very same utterance would have acquired a determinate truth-value (either true or false). We can take (4) as expressing a proposition that includes an explicit (and thereby fixed through contexts) temporal reference, but which nevertheless changes its truth-value as time goes by. Such propositions (which have been advanced as a kind of tensed propositions by John Tooley and by William Lane Craig[10]) are certainly compatible with the relativistic framework of MacFarlane. However, I think it is a mistake to consider them – in a double time reference framework – an intermediate kind of propositions, they are rather a kind of *tensed* proposition. This is not, as it might seem at first sight, just a matter of labels. Besides the terminological point (utterly irrelevant here) there is a substantial one. The point is that (as I argue in the next paragraph)

---

[10]See Tooley (1997), and Craig (2003).

understanding retrospective evaluation (and more generally evaluation *cum* assessment) in a double reference semantics requires us to use the standard notion of tensed proposition. And this latter fact hides an even more important one, as we will see in the last paragraph.

11.6 Evaluation, Assessment, and Kernel Propositions

The neutral stance of double time reference relativism suggests that we have relativism once we take into account assessment factors, along with evaluation factors, in order to establish the truth-value of an utterance of a sentence such as (3). In the tenseless case, as we have seen, it is not clear how the assessment factor should work – given that the standard understanding of tenseless propositions has them utterly time *insensitive*. However, we won't do any better by resorting to tensed propositions – or so it seemed. Understanding assessment of tensed propositions in a double time reference pushed us towards a non-standard reading of them. But if either way we need to go nonstandard, then, at the end of the day, the framework is indeed neutral. Or at least, it elicits a middle way position, which can be seen either as an expansion of tenseless standard semantics, or as an expansion of tensed standard semantics. I am about to show that this is not the case. The alternative is rather between endorsing a non-standard (and difficult to catch) notion of tenseless proposition, and endorsing the standard notion of tensed proposition and evaluation thereof, within a different framework. Thus, truth relativism with respect to tense is not neutral between tenseless and tensed propositions.

To see this last point, we need to distinguish between kernel propositions and *embedded* propositions. Simplifying a bit, I will analyze "simple" past and future tensed sentences in terms of past and future tense operators operating on present tense sentences falling within their scope. For instance, a future tense sentence will have the following form:

(F) $\mathcal{F}\alpha$.

Namely, it will be analysed as a future tense operator '$\mathcal{F}$' applied to a present tense kernel α. The tense of a sentence along with the context of utterance C_u allows the semantic rules to individuate a time. I will call such a time, the time focus of an utterance of a sentence S in a context C_u. For instance, the time focus of an utterance of (3) on a day d, is the day d' immediately following d. Now, in a standard framework, it is the kernel sentence α, rather than the whole embedded sentence $\mathcal{F}\alpha$ that is evaluated with respect to d' or completed with respect to d' – depending on the role we let the temporal parameter have. It is easy to see why. If we take tensed sentences to express tensed propositions, whether

(3) is true, false or indeterminate on day d depends on whether the proposition expressed by the *kernel* sentence of (3), namely the kernel proposition *that it is sunny* is true, false or indeterminate on d'. It obviously does not depend on whether the whole embedded proposition *that it will be sunny (tomorrow)* is true, false or indeterminate on d', namely tomorrow; and *mutatis mutandis* if we take tensed sentences to express tenseless propositions.

In a double time reference framework, if we take the time focus as having the completion role, the sensitivity of the evaluation of the tenseless proposition expressed will suffer from the problems we have seen before. Consider figure 2.

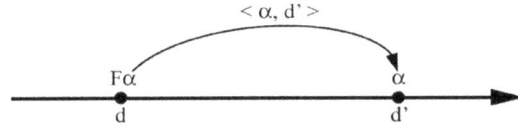

FIGURE 2

An utterance on day d of a sentence of the form $F\alpha$ – for instance, (3) – is completed with respect to the time focus d', thereby yielding the tenseless proposition $<\alpha, d'>$. This proposition is assessed with respect to a context of assessment, and, assuming that on day d' it is indeed sunny, the assessment will yield the following results:

(R1) $\quad T[<\alpha, d'>, d]$ = indeterminate

(R2) $\quad T[<\alpha, d'>, d']$ = true

That is, true tomorrow (on day d'), and indeterminate today (on day d). However, given that tenseless propositions, in the standard reading, are time insensitive the notion of sensitiveness to assessment the relativist is applying here cannot be sustained by an informal grasp of the notion of tenseless proposition. Consider now the tensed case and figure 3.

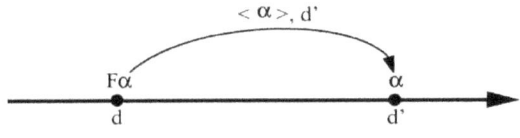

FIGURE 3

An utterance of a sentence of the form (F) – again, take (3) as an example – expresses a tensed proposition whose kernel (namely the proposition $<\alpha>$ expressed by its kernel sentence α) is to be evaluated with respect to the time focus d'. However, given that we are in a double reference framework, such evaluation will yields different results depending on whether the time of assessment is d or d'. Again:

(R3) $T[<\alpha>, d', d]$ = indeterminate

(R4) $T[<\alpha>, d', d']$ = true

Now, surely the idea of a tensed proposition that gets differently evaluated with respect to the same time focus, depending on further temporal factors, is non-standard. Still, what is completely standard here is how the *evaluation* of the tensed proposition comes about: it is simply a kernel proposition which gets evaluated with respect to a time parameter, *i.e.* the time focus of the utterance. The assessment factor somehow influences the result of the evaluation (and this is the non-standard bit of the story), but in order to allow such an influence we do not need to resort to a change in content expressed. Rather the assessment factor changes the reality we are confronting the expressed content with. Contrariwise, in the tenseless case, the assessment factor cannot change the content – which by assumption is not changing through assessment contexts – but neither can it stand for a change in the reality we are confronting the tenseless proposition with; this is not the role of completion parameters. Thus, it seems like we are forced to endorse a hybrid notion of content which purports to be both tenseless and yet sensitive to temporal factors, or alternatively a non-standard notion of evaluation – *simpliciter* and yet sensitive to temporal parameters.

Note, moreover, that there is a difference between tensed kernel propositions and tenseless propositional kernels. On the one hand, kernel tensed propositions represent present tensed facts, exactly as embedded tensed propositions represent past or future tensed facts. On the other hand, tenseless proposition kernels do not represent tenseless facts, they need to be completed (into full-fledged propositions) by a time focus to do so. Therefore, while a tensed proposition may correctly represent a tensed fact (in case it is true) or incorrectly represent it (in case it is false), depending on time, a tenseless proposition can represent a tenseless fact only eternally – if it is a correct representation (namely if it is true).

11.7 Perspectival Realism

Now, in a relativistic "tensed" framework, the evaluation of a tensed proposition with respect to a time focus is sensitive to a context of assessment. Still, what does it mean that a tensed proposition evaluated with respect to the *same* point in time may lead to different results, depending on the time of assessment of the evaluation? As far as tenses are concerned, truth relativism can give an answer to this question by endorsing a specific metaphysic of time – indeed a metaphysics that goes hand in hand with tensed propositions, as it were. The idea behind such a metaphysics is that reality is composed of different facts at different times. Therefore, by shifting from a time of assessment to a different one, we may happen to find different facts in the world and thus to evaluate differently a proposition, even with respect to the same point in time – since both past and future facts may change their status as time goes by. This idea is grounded in what I will call "perspectival realism".

Let me explain what I mean by *perspectival realism*. Perspectival realism is a form of realism that does not concern what entities exist, but rather what properties things have, or more generally what facts compose reality. As Kit Fine has it, it doesn't concern *what* there is, but rather *how* things are.[11] According to perspectival realism, prima facie *perspectival properties* of a certain kind are properties that things have independently of the perspective they are in, and thus they are not *merely* perspectival properties. In other words, perspectival realism concerns the reality of what looks like a perspective of a certain kind – such as the perspective from the present time, the first-person perspective, or the perspective from a certain ethical or aesthetic canon. Consequently, disputes concerning a form of perspectival realism must not be confused with disputes concerning the *existence* of the centre A of a perspective (a person, a time, ...). What is at issue in the latter disputes is whether the perspective π is a *feature of reality*, or not. Therefore, whether our semantic theory quantifies over items of the context or not (for instance, the centres of the different kinds of perspective) is not relevant. What is relevant is the role the parameter a (the centre of a perspective π) plays in the evaluation and interpretation of a sentence S sensitive to π. If π is a feature of reality, a change in the centre of the perspective will correspond to a change in the circumstances against which we are evaluating the proposition expressed (other things being equal); consequently, a is treated as an evaluation parameter; whereas if π is not a feature of reality, a change of perspective will not correspond to a change of circumstances (other things being equal). But S is sensitive to π (by assumption), thus a change in perspective must correspond to a change in the proposition expressed; consequently, a is treated as a completion parameter.

---

[11] See Fine (2005).

The relativist can be seen as a perspectival *realist* towards certain perspectival properties, namely the properties that are sensitive to the parameter to which she is relativizing truth. In other words, certain perspectival expressions (for instance tensed predicates) express genuine properties, and thus are not differently interpreted with respect to parameters they are sensitive to; rather, they lead to different evaluations with respect to such parameters. Thus, the relativist is a realist toward the perspectival feature she is considering truth *relative* to: a change in the parameter to which truth is sensitive to is tantamount to a change in how things stand. The indexicalist, on the other hand, may be seen as a perspectival anti-realist. According to the indexicalist perspectival expression reflects *merely* the perspective we are in. Therefore, the indexicalist does not relativize truth to parameters that reflect this kind of sensitivity, it is rather the *interpretation* of perspectival expressions (*i.e.* what content they express) that has to be relativized to such parameters.

Perspectival realism concerning temporal perspectives is a well-known kind of realism, which is often called *tense realism*.[12] A philosopher maintaining that tenses are real (namely that time "really" flows), will take tensed sentences as expressing propositions evaluated with respect to evaluation parameters: when the temporal perspective changes something in *reality* changes. Therefore, an utterance of a tensed sentence expresses a *tensed proposition*, namely a proposition that is not true or false *simpliciter* (modulo other parameters) but only with respect to a time. A philosopher maintaining that tenses are not real (namely that the "passage" of time is just a matter of our position in time) will take tensed sentences as expressing propositions (partly) determined by the temporal perspective of the context; in particular, the propositions will have all their "temporal slots" saturated by time-parameters. Therefore, the proposition expressed will be a tenseless proposition, namely a proposition that has a truth-value simpliciter, rather than with respect to a time.

A context of assessment, thus, is just a temporal perspective – in the realist's sense - *i.e.* a class of facts characterized by tensed properties, and a context of utterance is just a means to fix the "place" *within a perspective* that the tense of a sentence (uttered in that context) makes relevant for the evaluation of the kernel proposition expressed. Now, in the case of a retrospective assessment, what changes is not the context of utterance, and thus the reference to a certain point in time, but the perspective on such a point in time: different facts now com-

---

[12]See, for instance, Zimmerman (2005).

pose reality – possibly also concerning *that* point of time. On the day d of utterance of (3) the facts composing the world are such that it is undetermined whether day d' will be sunny or not; as a consequence, (3) will have an indeterminate truth-value.[13] But on day d' the facts will be changed, and indeed it will be determined whether that very day d' is sunny or not. Consequently, also the truth-value of (3) will be determinate. Being true with respect to a context of assessment, thus, boils down to correctly representing the facts in a certain perspective, and whether the representation is correct or not depends (beside on the tensed proposition and its time of evaluation, which do not change through change of perspectives) on the perspective we are considering. But this sort of dependence is utterly trivial. Since a tensed proposition purports to represent facts *in a certain perspective*; whether the representation is correct or not will obviously depend on the perspective considered. Whether a representation of x is correct or not obviously depends (among other things) on x. Relativity, then, is a matter of what facts compose reality, rather than of *truth* in the first place. Indeed, *tense realism* is what is left of truth relativism concerning tense once we tidy up the conceptual room around it.

References

Broad, Charles D. 1938. *Examination of McTaggart's philosophy*. Cambridge: Cambridge University Press.

Craig, William L. 2003. In defense of presentism. In A. Jokic and Q. Smith, eds., *Time, Tense and Reference*, chap. 12, pages 391–408. Cambridge MA: MIT Press.

Fine, Kit. 2005. Tense and reality. In *Modality and Tense*, chap. 8, pages 261–320. Oxford: Oxford University Press.

King, Jeffrey. 2007. *The Nature and Structure of Content*. Oxford: Oxford University Press.

Kölbel, Max. 2008a. How to spell out genuine relativism and how to defend indexical relativism. *International Journal of Philosophical Studies* forthcoming.

Kölbel, Max. 2008b. Motivations for relativism. In M. G. Carpintero and M. Kölbel, eds., *Relative Truth*, chap. 1. Oxford: Oxford University Press. forthcoming.

MacFarlane, John. 2003. Future contingents and relative truth. *Philosophical Quarterly* 53(212):321–336.

MacFarlane, John. 2005. Making sense of relative truth. *Proceedings of the Aristotelian Society* 105(1):305–325.

---

[13]This may be because facts concerning d' do not yet exist (as in Tooley (1997), who takes inspiration from Broad (1938)), but we do not need to endorse this further thesis.

MacFarlane, John. 2008. Truth in the garden of forking paths. In M. G. Carpintero and M. Kölbel, eds., *Relative Truth*, chap. 4. Oxford: Oxford University Press. forthcoming.

Predelli, Stefano. 2005. *Context*. Oxford: Oxford University Press.

Recanati, Francois. 2007. *Perspectival Thoughts*. Oxford: Oxford University Press.

Richard, Mark. 1981. Temporalism and eternalism. *Philosophical Studies* 39(1):1–13.

Stanley, Jason. 2005. *Knowledge and Practical Interest*. Oxford: Oxford University Press.

Tooley, Richard. 1997. *Time, Tense and Causation*. Oxford: Oxford University Press.

Wright, Crispin. 2008. Relativism about truth itself: Haphazard thoughts about the very idea. In M. G. Carpintero and M. Kölbel, eds., *Relative Truth*, chap. 7. Oxford: Oxford University Press.

Zimmerman, David. 2005. The a-theory of time, the b-theory of time, and 'taking tense seriously'. *Dialectica* 59(4):401–404.

12

The Contingent *A Priori*: Metaphysical and "Rational" Modality

PAUL WINSTANLEY

12.1 Introduction

Philosophy, as traditionally conceived (at least the core elements of metaphysics, epistemology, logic, semantics and ethics, for example), is a largely *a priori* discipline; philosophers often seek to argue from "p is justified *a priori*" to "p is necessarily true" or from "p is conceivable (*i.e. a priori* possible)" to "p is possible". This being the case, Kripke's necessary *a posteriori* and contingent *a priori* are very interesting (alleged) phenomena, since if there are necessary a posteriori truths, conceivability does not entail possibility and if there are contingent a priori truths, apriority does not entail necessity. In my thesis,[1] I argue for strong connections between the metaphysical modal and the "rational" domains; p is conceivable only if it is metaphysically possible and p is a priori (or "rationally necessary") only if it is meta-

---

[1]This is a heavily amended version of the paper presented at the SIFA conference. At the conference I attempted to defend the thesis that (5) (or its equivalent) was contingent and *a priori*. After questions from Tim Williamson and several other commentators (and much further reflection), I have now retracted this thesis and argue that (given that (5) was the only version of the contingent *a priori* I was willing to endorse), there are, strictly no contingent *a priori* propositions. I am heavily indebted to Williamson and to other commentators for making me go through the "much further reflection"!

Language, Knowledge, and Metaphysics.
Massimiliano Carrara and Vittorio Morato (eds.)
College Pubblication, London, 2008.

physically so². In this paper I wish to focus on the contingent *a priori* and, specifically, on the putative example,

(1) I exist.

I shall use this target sentence to illustrate a wider claim; that in alleged cases of the contingent *a priori*, the putative example sentences express two (or more) propositions; one asserting contingent circumstances only knowable on an *a posteriori* basis; and another asserting necessary circumstances only knowable *a priori*.³

In section 12.2 I discuss briefly the Kripkean background and introduce the main example, arguing, as above, that it is either contingent and *a posteriori*, or *a priori* and necessary. In section 12.3 I consider a "neo-Evansian" objection to such claims, discussing (1) as expressing an *a priori* knowable indexical proposition, which is more than just "superficially" necessary. In response to this I argue that this would then be necessarily true as opposed to contingently so. I conclude (section 12.4) that all putative cases of the contingent *a priori* suffer a similar fate; there are no genuine contingent *a priori* propositions.

12.2 The Kripkean background

Kant aside, almost all philosophers prior to Kripke had (more or less) identified two related notions of necessity; apriority and (logical) necessity. In *Naming and Necessity*,⁴ Kripke draws a clear distinction between the epistemic and metaphysical domains; apriority cannot be identical to or co-extensive with ("logical", or better, metaphysical) necessity, since the former is an epistemic notion, concerning how a proposition is justified or known, whereas the latter a metaphysical issue concerning a proposition's modal truth.⁵ Further supporting this claim, Kripke also argues for the existence of contingent *a priori* statements, such as

(2) Neptune is the planet causing disturbances in the orbit of Uranus⁶

(at least as uttered by Leverrier⁷ – the astronomer who first postulated the existence of Neptune). The point here being that if names

---

²See Winstanley (2008).

³In my thesis, Winstanley (2008), I argue for similar conclusions with respect to the necessary *a posteriori*.

⁴Kripke (1980).

⁵Or, perhaps better, concerning the modal obtaining of relations between the relevant objects and attributes.

⁶See Kripke (1980, p. 79, n. 33). Not a quotation from Kripke but a statement or sentence reconstructed from the text.

⁷This apparent "subjectivity" of "*a priori* propositions" is, of course, interesting.

can be introduced so as to fix their references by description, then the introducer of such a name (allegedly) knows statements such as (2) *a priori*, yet they assert contingent circumstances; although Leverrier knows *a priori* that "Neptune" is the name of the relevant object, that object *could have been* destroyed by an asteroid many millennia ago, for example (*i.e.* it is metaphysically possible that there is no such object).

In short, I reject this example, since it is not at all clear that one (even Leverrier) can have *substantive* knowledge of the *object Neptune*, simply in virtue of introducing the name "Neptune" – the name (as per Kripke's example) might be entirely empty; there might be no such object. By way of fleshing out this claim, imagine that I introduce the name "Bob" to fix the reference of the uppermost pebble on Mount Everest at t_0. Having so introduced the designator "Bob", I then know *a priori* that

(3) Bob is the uppermost pebble on Mount Everest at t_0

expresses some proposition p, but, having never climbed Everest, *I do not know what proposition that is* (and even whether it is true); strictly, I don't know what p says about the world. The point here very much turns on a three-way distinction I rely on in the remainder of this paper; that of a sentence expressing a proposition that is about, or *asserts*, a circumstance (*i.e.* an arrangement of objects and (or just) attributes). My claim is that where a subject s "knows *a priori*" that a sentence expresses a proposition p, given that apriority is an epistemic notion, it operates at the propositional (and circumstantial) level(s) first and only derivatively at the sentential. For s to know precisely which propositions he is expressing, he must know the nature of the circumstance that proposition concerns; he must know what arrangement of objects and attributes the proposition asserts. So if s does not know what circumstance p asserts, s does not know (*a priori* or *a posteriori*) that p. Thus, whilst a given p might assert a contingent circumstance such as a (possibly non-existent) pebble's being so high, in failing to grasp the relevant circumstance the subject fails to have contingent *a priori* knowledge of p; he fails to express a contingent *a priori* proposition.

Now, there is a large debate here between the likes of Plantinga and Donnellan, on the one side, and defenders of Kripke, on the other[8] – but I ignore this for present purposes, as there is a further example, which I think helps to settle the issue in favour of the opponents of the contingent *a priori*, namely (1).

---

[8]See Plantinga (1974, pp. 8–9, n. 1) and Donnellan (1977). The most recent (and forceful) defender would be Jeshion (2001) and Jeshion (2002).

As with the "Neptune" and "Bob" cases, my claim is that the apparent contingent *a priori* status of (1) turns on the nature of the proposition(s) and/or ultimately the circumstance(s) it asserts.

Let us look at the metaphysical, modal aspects first. In terms of contingency, (1) certainly appears to be a saying something contingent about the world. Assuming that the sentence (or thought) has not been uttered[9] by a necessarily existing being, it certainly seems to express a contingent proposition or circumstance. Given that I am certainly not a necessary being, my existence is a very contingent circumstance. The problem with (1) however is that if it is read as asserting a metaphysically contingent circumstance, it is also fairly clearly rationally contingent, *i.e. a posteriori*. The point being, the negation ("I do not exist") is rationally possible (*i.e. conceivable*), since I might (well) not have existed; so (1) cannot be rationally necessary or *a priori*. In addition, without tying the proposition to the time of its utterance or grasping, its asserting a contingent circumstance means that more detailed empirical information is required to ascertain when it is true and when it is false; its being tenseless, I need to know particular pieces of information at particular times in order to know whether or not it is true. So, simply read (as the tenseless) (1), "I exist" cannot be an example of the contingent *a priori*.

There are however two further relevant, candidate, contingent *a priori* propositions that the English "I exist" can be taken to express:

(4) ⌜I exist at the time of uttering "I exist"⌝

(5) ⌜I exist at t_0⌝

Fairly clearly, (4) is so deeply self-referential that it is, presumably metaphysically necessary, as well as being *a priori* (or "rationally necessary"). This leaves (5) as the only relevant, potential candidate contingent *a priori* proposition. Thus, we need to understand whether this can steer a course between the contingent and a posteriori (1), and the a priori but necessary (4).

In terms of contingency, initially, (5) appears to be much closer to (1) than to (4). That ⌜I exist at t_0⌝ can be seen possibly not to have obtained strongly suggests that it is not (or does not assert) a metaphysical necessity. In addition, and perhaps more to the point, my not being a contingent object certainly seems to suggest that (5) is contingent; surely I might not have existed at t_0. If however the negation of (5) is metaphysically possible (and (5) is contingent), I would argue,

---

[9] As throughout, I use "utter" here widely, to cover sentences, thoughts and anything else that might express a proposition. I insert "(or thought ...)" tacitly from here on.

as before, that ¬ (5) is *rationally* possible, *i.e.* (5) is not rationally necessary, not *a priori*.

Alvin Plantinga offers something like (5) as a contingent *a priori* proposition, arguing that "I know *a priori* that I believe that I exist; I also know *a priori* that if I believe that I exist, then indeed I do exist".[10] Thus, the defender of the contingent *a priori* might argue that (5) is just such a proposition; in virtue of ascribing the contingent property of existence to its utterer u, and in virtue of u's uttering and thereby grasping (5), it is rationally necessary and so *a priori*, and therefore independent of experience. The main problem with such a line however is usually taken to concern the nature of introspection.[11] The point being, introspection is an experiential or *a posteriori* mode of knowing; (5) is essentially justified via introspection, thus it is contingent but *a posteriori* rather than *a priori*.

Having said this, there are two potential objections to this line of argument, one concerning introspection, and another involving indexicality. In effect, both objections aim to preserve the contingency of (5) whilst arguing that it is, after all, knowable on an *a priori* basis. I discuss introspection, very briefly, in the remainder of this section and indexicality, in more detail, in the following.

Making a similar point, Bonjour claims that introspection is *a posteriori* since it consists in a causal-perceptual "awareness of temporally located contingent facts."[12] So whilst "I exist as a thinking thing" is "automatically justified for anyone who understands"[13] it, since it is based on introspection *qua* causal-perceptual awareness of a contingent fact, it is justified a posteriori rather than *a priori*. My additional argument for this claim is reasonably straightforward. Ultimately, if rational modality is to be an interesting, useful and genuine modality, then it must be "grounded in" the metaphysical; it must be something akin to metaphysical necessity (or possibility) in virtue of rationality – what it is necessary (or possible) to think. In particular, it must be (as I go on to argue both in what follows) distinct from "epistemic necessity". This being the case, if a proposition ((5) for example) expresses a metaphysically contingent circumstance (my tenseless, or temporal but non-indexicalised, existence), Ei, the very possibility of $\neg Ei$ re-

---

[10] See Plantinga (1974, p. 8).

[11] Pryor (2006), for example argues that (his version of) (5) is straightforwardly *a posteriori*, since it relies on occurrent experience.

[12] BonJour (2005, p. 99). See Pryor (2006, p. 333f). Briefly, Pryor argues that ⌜I am uttering a sentence⌝, whilst being "hyper-reliable" (or true in virtue of being thought), is not thereby justified *a priori*.

[13] See BonJour (1998, p. 10).

quires that ¬ (5) be rationally possible (or *conceivable*). Clearly then, if both (5) and ¬ (5) are rationally possible, then (5) must be rationally contingent; it must be knowable on an *a posteriori*, rather than an *a priori*, basis. So, if (5) is metaphysically contingent, I claim, (if it is at all knowable) then it is rationally contingent, or *a posteriori*, as well.

As mentioned above however, there is another potential objection to the claim that (5) is (or expresses) a contingent but *a posteriori* proposition. This involves indexicality, to the effect that (5) might be contingent but still knowable on an *a priori* basis. I now discuss this issue; indexicality and Evansian "superficial" contingency.

12.3 Apriority, indexicality and Evansian, "superficial" contingency

In "Reference and Contingency", Gareth Evans attempts to defuse Kripke's contingent *a priori* by arguing that the alleged cases are effectively equivalent to those involving descriptive or "Fregean" names. The point being, whilst (*de re*) *a priori* knowledge is possible for the introducer of such names, the propositions asserted are "superficially" contingent. That is, there are many cases of the contingent *a priori*, but they are fairly trivial; they are neither "interesting" nor "scary".[14] Consider, for example, the following examples from Kripke, Donnellan and Evans:

(6) 'Jack the Ripper' is the man, whoever he is, who actually committed all these murders[15]

(7) Provided the murderer exists, let "Vladimir is the murderer" express a contingent truth[16]

(8) Let us use "Julius" to refer to whoever invented the zip

(9) If anyone uniquely invented the zip, Julius invented the zip.[17]

For what it is worth, I think (6), (7) and (9) are fairly similar to Kripke's original examples, the "actually" being tacitly assumed in the original, and, importantly, *not a genuine predicate*; that is, *not designating a genuine property*.[18] Thus, I claim, the Evansian cases are not

---

[14] See Evans (1979). The "interesting" and "scary" are from Donnellan (1977, p. 23).
[15] Amended slightly from the original Kripkean version.
[16] Donnellan (1977, p. 20) (my numbering).
[17] See Evans (1979, p. 163 and 171) (my numbering). Evans also mentions Kripke's use of "Jack the Ripper" at p. 163.
[18] The point being, "actually" is either a rhetorical term or a genuine predicate. And if it is intended as a predicate, it requires a substantive (and wrong-headed) metaphysics of possible, and especially of the actual, world(s), understood on a very realist interpretation. I argue against all of in my thesis (Winstanley (2008)).

cases of (*a priori* or otherwise) knowledge. Interestingly concerning (7), Donnellan claims that a detective, stipulating "Vladimir" as the name of the murderer, does not thereby come to "know [*a priori* or not] the existence of any state of affairs". Hence my use of the Kripkean (6); after "naming" "Jack the Ripper", I do not think Scotland Yard's work was complete.

That said, Evans spends much of "Reference and Contingency" arguing that (9) is *a priori* and contingent, but only "superficially" so, because of the indexicality of the tacit reference to actual circumstances given the introduction of "Julius" via (8). Now, as much as Evans argues that (9) is only "superficially" contingent (and "deeply" necessary or *a priori*) we need to understand whether (9) is sufficiently distinct from (6), so as to provide a basis for a response to the foregoing objections to the Kripkean contingent *a priori* such that, in fact (9) is a genuinely *a priori* but contingent proposition. In what follows then, I present Evans's arguments for the "superficial" contingent *a priori*, but in a "non-Evansian" light; I aim to see whether the "superficiality" can be removed from "Julius"-type examples, whilst preserving the contingency.

Evans's argument in "Reference and Contingency" very much turns on Donnellan's distinction (discussed again in my terms here) between knowing that a sentence expresses some proposition and knowing what circumstance (or "wide" proposition) that proposition asserts. His main point *contra* Donnellan is that the latter assumes that for an utterer u to understand what circumstance the relevant sentence asserts (via the relevant proposition-(9) in this case), u must have causal or *a posteriori* knowledge of the referent of the relevant name used therein. That is, according to Evans, Donnellan rules out any possibility of knowledge of the meaning of (9) and the like, in the absence of *a posteriori* knowledge of (8) and the like.[19] In short, according to Evans, Donnellan rules out the possibility of 'Fregean' or descriptive names. As he goes on to claim however, in cases such as "Julius", where we have such a descriptive, indexical or Fregean name, we just can have such *a priori* knowledge of meaning. This is because, allegedly, the form of (9) is very similar (or even equivalent)[20] to that of

(10) $\forall x(Fx \rightarrow \mathcal{A}(Fx))$

---

[19] Evans (1979, p. 172). Evans's presentation in what follows (pp. 172-186) is quite dense and difficult to follow. I can only hope that I have done justice to his argument.

[20] I explain why below.

where $\mathcal{A}$ is an "actually" operator; for example, "If anything is red it is actually red".[21] (The uniqueness-universality difference between (9) and (10) would be taken care of by the assumption that F is the predicate "the unique inventor of the zip" or similar, in (10).) Now, according to Evans, because (9) operates like (10), we can understand ⌜If anyone uniquely invented the zip, Julius invented the zip⌝, in the same way we can understand ⌜If anything is red it is actually red⌝; that is, on an *a priori* rather than *a posteriori* basis. So, where Fx is contingent, we can know (10) and, by extension, (9), *a priori*; they are "perfectly innocent, if rather uninteresting, examples of the contingent *a priori*".[22] With respect to (5) then, the "non-Evansian" allegation would be that this is a similarly indexical but clearly an *interesting* case of the contingent *a priori*.

There are two main points of objection in the foregoing argument, concerning (i) the possibility of *a priori* knowledge of descriptive or Fregean names (based on "actually" operators), and (ii) the "superficial" contingency (*i.e.* necessity) or otherwise of (5). I now qualify these in turn, focussing on (i) where (against Evans and the non-Evansian objection), I deny the possibility of substantive *a priori* knowledge of contingencies based on descriptive names. I then discuss (ii) briefly, arguing (with and beyond Evans) that if (5) can be rendered knowable on an *a priori* basis via some essential indexicality, this also renders it "very superficially contingently" (*i.e.* necessarily) true.

The first qualification is twofold and disjunctive; either (a) (9) is not equivalent to (10) and so fails along with the other Kripkean examples – including (6) – or, (b) (something like) (9) is equivalent to (10) but (partially agreeing with Evans), it is a purely semantic, insubstantive and ultimately artificial example of the contingent *a priori*. Turning to (a) first, on a simple parsing of (9) into,

(11) $\forall x(Fx \rightarrow Fj)$

it is difficult to see immediately how this is equivalent to (10). Of course, one might insist that since Julius is a descriptive, Fregean name, (9) *should* be parsed as (10) but the immediate, apparent non-equivalence (epistemically) of (11) and (10) would appear to suggest that significant argument is required to show that (9) should be parsed as (10) *i.e.* that (9) is epistemically, propositionally equivalent to (10). Evans spends much of pages 173 to 182 of "Reference and Contingency" arguing that (9) and (10) are equivalent; in very brief detail, the argument is as follows. Sentences are associated with functions from

---
[21] Evans (1979, p. 184).
[22] Evans (1979, p. 186).

possible worlds to truth values, which Evans calls propositions (and I call "wide" propositions or "circumstances"), but such functions are not the same as a sentence's "content, or what it says".[23]

According to Evans, when two sentences with the same content (*i.e.* what I would call a "narrow" proposition) are believed, "then what is believed by one who understands ... the one sentence ... is the same as what is believed by one who understands ... the other sentence" (p. 176). So, for Evans, content is the epistemic notion, whereas a proposition (*i.e.* a "wide" proposition or "circumstance") is an "external" item more akin to a state of affairs. This is the terminological background, but the key argument that (9) and (10) are propositionally (or content-wise for Evans) equivalent, essentially boils down to the following claim; given (8), although propositions (9) and (10) assert different circumstances-because "Julius" is stipulated to be the actual inventor of the zip and there are possible worlds where "Julius" might not have invented the zip-they are, allegedly the *same proposition*; they say the same thing.

Now, on the face of it, this argument seems to work. However, its force very much hinges on the possibility of substantive knowledge of contingencies based on descriptive or Fregean names (f-names hereafter). What I mean here is that there is a sense in which f-names are "names", but in reality, I claim, f-names cannot do the work they are being expected to do here; there remains a strong sense in which we cannot have genuine, substantive knowledge of contingent circumstances on the basis of f-names. (This being the case, I suggest that the "f" in f-names should stand for "fictional", as opposed to "Fregean" – and that perhaps f-names should be pronounced "phnames"). What I mean by all of this is that whilst it might be "a presupposition of free logic that there exist Fregean names",[24] to argue that we can have substantive knowledge based thereupon is to reverse the sensible order of explanation.

That is, Evans is arguing from the possibility of some logico-semantic entity to the existence of a significant epistemic state (and presumably beyond, *i.e.* to the existence of an object-however fictional-designated by such a name). In short, Evans is doing epistemology (and arguably metaphysics) on the basis of semantics.

In response to this, I would argue that this is precisely the wrong order of explanation. Instead, we should insist that where there is no object or, at least, potentially no object (i.e. metaphysics), we cannot

---

[23] Evans (1979, p. 176).
[24] Evans (1979, p. 173).

have genuine, substantive knowledge of that object (epistemology), and so, any "name" supposedly 'designating' such an object (which does not exist) is not a genuine name. That is, f-names, in virtue of the very possible empty reference, are not really names; they are fictional names.[25] All of this being the case, I would insist that however contingent (9) or (10) might be, subtly they are not equivalent, since (10) is a general condition ranging over possible objects, which is *trivially*, logically or semantically *a priori* (as I admit below), whereas (9) is subtly, particular involving where, importantly, there may well be no particular to quantify over – **Julius** (the "object") might well not exist. Thus, in the absence of compelling argument that (9) is equivalent to (10), whilst the latter is *a priori* (in some sense), it is very unclear that the former is so justified.

To add rhetorical force to the claim that (9) does not offer substantive *a priori* – or any-knowledge, note that a Scotland Yard press conference announcement of ⌜If anyone killed all those women, "Jack the Ripper" killed all those women⌝ would not result in the closing of the case and the re-assignment of the relevant detectives. Clearly there might have been no such "object" (the women might have died of natural causes), or there might have been more than one such "object" (two or more "Jacks").

Having said this, Evans's argument is complicated, so assuming I have missed an essential point, let us turn to the second disjunct, (b). *Assuming* that (9) (given (8)) is equivalent to (10), I would agree in large part with Evans that (9) appears to be a "contingent" and *a priori* proposition, but its contingency is trivial, superficial and insubstantive.

So why might (9) and (10) be trivial? In short (going beyond Evans somewhat), to 'drum up' a substantive *metaphysical* contingency from an indexical "actually" operator is an illegitimate *manoeuvre*; following Salmon's criticism of Kripkean essentialism,[26] this is akin to pulling a metaphysical rabbit from a semantic hat. Again, even assuming (6), (9) and (10) are effectively equivalent, ⌜If anyone killed all those women, "Jack the Ripper" killed all those women⌝ is not going to result in any arrests.

That is, such a case is superficially contingent in virtue of being trivially *a priori*. Even if (6) is *a priori* it does not provide an example of interesting, substantive knowledge; it does not say anything about the world – it does not assert a clearly *de re* circumstance.

---

[25] The difference with genuine names would be based on the latter being causally or baptismally introduced with relevant causal-historical chains preserving reference, and so, *de re* knowledge.

[26] See Salmon (1982).

Of course, one might object here that (8), in being a universal generalisation, would generate interesting instances of the contingent *a priori* upon particular instantiation, *à la*

(12) $Fa \to \mathcal{A}(Fa)$.

Against this, I would suggest two considerations. First, very much as before, even whilst the proposition appears to be contingent and *a priori*, any substantive, contingent, existential claim such as Fa itself, either involves an f-name (with the same foregoing considerations concerning the lack of substantive knowledge) or it requires empirical justification, since it asserts the contingent existence of a named object. Thus if any such conditional is contingently existentially committing, in relying on an *a posteriori* antecedent, it would be, as a whole, a posteriori. And second (again as suggested above), to generate contingent circumstances via a proposition involving an actually operator is to semanticise substantive, metaphysical conclusions.

By way of a brief summary of the foregoing, on both counts, I claim that the "non-Evansian" objection[27] is reversing the sensible order of explanation. Either (b) it uses an indexical "actually" operator to semanticise a (false) substantive metaphysical contingency, or (as I think is the preferable interpretation) (a) it uses an f-name to generate illegitimately, substantive *a priori* knowledge. On both approaches, we move from semantics to epistemology (and metaphysics). I contend that, on the contrary, we should move in the opposite direction. Either (b) the "contingency" is superficial *qua* not genuine, not metaphysical, or (as I prefer) (a) given the very strong possibility of there being no relevant, actual object, we cannot have genuine knowledge of 'objects' so introduced; f-names are not genuine names; f-names cannot generate substantive knowledge of contingent propositions and circumstances.[28]

In my second, brief qualification of the Evansian argument (as promised several paragraphs above), I claim that this failure to introduce additional, substantive examples of the contingent a priori

---

[27] *I.e.* the attempt to show that Evans's cases are significantly contingent *a priori*.

[28] In the final section of "Reference and Contingency", Evans provides (p. 182) a non-indexical variant of his earlier examples:

(j) John is as tall as John

The problem with (j) is parallel to that of the "Julius" case discussed in the main body. Either there is an object (**John**) who has the property of being **as tall as John** in all worlds in which he exists (so (j) is an *a priori* but necessary proposition; *i.e.* j asserts that **John** has the property of being **as tall as himself**), or, the second "John" merely serves as an f-name, whereby (j) would be contingent but not substantively *a priori*, given the fictionality of the f-name (and the emptiness of the reference).

carries over to (5) and the like, and for similar reasons as before. The key point is as follows. Either (5) asserts the contingent circumstance Ei (my existence), in which case it is both metaphysically and rationally contingent (*a posteriori*), or the 't_0' is so constitutionally tied to the time of utterance of (5) that it is a rationally necessary proposition asserting a metaphysically necessary circumstance; it is *a priori* but necessary. In slightly more argumentative detail, if (5) is asserting a contingent circumstance such as Ei (my timeless existence), then given that it is metaphysically and so surely rationally possible that $\neg Ei$, (5) turns out to be the rationally contingent (*i.e.*, *a posteriori*) proposition asserted by (1); *i.e.* contingent but *a posteriori*. If on the other hand (5) is *a priori*, this is in virtue of the fact that the 't_0' is so constitutionally tied to the time of utterance that (5) expresses a rationally necessary proposition to the effect that "if I am uttering e at t_0 then I exist", which is *a priori* but metaphysically necessary as well.[29]

In summary of the foregoing then, examples such as (5) (and I would very much extend these arguments to include the likes of ⌜I am thinking at t_0⌝ and ⌜I know/believe that (rationally necessary p) at t_0⌝ are either *a priori* in virtue of an essential indexicality, whereby such propositions assert metaphysically necessary circumstances, or they are closer to the original (1) in being contingent but requiring causal, *a posteriori* justification to generate substantive knowledge.

12.4 Conclusion

In summary of the foregoing then, examples such as (5) (and I would very much extend these arguments to include the likes of ⌜I am thinking at t_0⌝ and ⌜I know/believe that (rationally necessary p) at t_0⌝ are either *a priori* in virtue of an essential indexicality, whereby such propositions assert metaphysically necessary circumstances, or they are closer to the original (3) in being contingent but requiring causal, *a pos-*

---

[29] I am indebted here to Tim Williamson (and others), who raised the question of indexicality in my paper at the SIFA graduate conference in Padova. In addition, it would perhaps be remiss to write about indexicality without mentioning the work of Kaplan (Kaplan (1978) and Kaplan (1989b), Kaplan (1989a) in particular). Very briefly, in "Demonstratives", Kaplan proposes that words such as "he", "she", "it" and "that" are "demonstrative indexicals", requiring some "presentation of a local object" in order to determine reference (Kaplan, 1989b, p. 490); "dthat" being paradigmatic ("dthat" is discussed in the eponymous article of 1978). Terms like "I", "now" and "here" (usually – if I am pointing to a map than it is demonstrative) are "pure indexicals", requiring no such demonstration, such that the "linguistic rules which govern their use fully determine the referent for each context" (Kaplan, 1989b, p. 491). This is precisely the kind of account whereby (5) would be "contingent" and *a priori*, but trivially so because of an essential indexicality; the linguistic rules governing "I" making (5) *a priori* but superficially contingent.

teriori justification to generate substantive knowledge.[30]

In short, I claim there is there is an unresolved tension between knowing *a priori* that a certain sentence expresses such a proposition and knowing this proposition *a priori*; *i.e.* alleged contingent *a priori* sentences generally express (at least) two propositions; one contingent but requiring *a posteriori* justification to generate substantive (*de re*) knowledge of contingent circumstances; and another knowable *a priori* but asserting a necessary circumstance.

A key corollary (that I argue for in more detail elsewhere)[31] is that rational modality is grounded in the metaphysical; if p asserts a metaphysically contingent circumstance, p must (if knowable), ultimately, be a rationally contingent (or *a posteriori*) proposition. There can, therefore, be no contingent *a priori* propositions.

That said, the contingent *a priori* is no philosophical dead-end, since a genuine understanding begins to suggest several important theses (which I argue for above or elsewhere); (i) that there is a three-way, sentence-proposition-circumstance relationship; (ii) that sentences are only derivatively *a priori* or *a posteriori*, since propositions are the bearers of rational modality (which is, in turn, dependent on the metaphysical); whereas (iii) circumstances (or arrangements of objects and (or just) attributes) and then propositions are what is metaphysically

---

[30]Williamson (1986) argues that p, "There is at least one believer" is contingent and *a priori* on the basis of substitution into the *a priori* and "absolutely reliable method for forming true beliefs ... (M) Given a valid deduction from the premise that someone believes that p to the conclusion that p, believe that p (pp. 114-5). According to Williamson, p does not rely on any indexicals whatsoever, since, allegedly, (M) simply requires a valid deduction from Bxp to p. The problem with this, is that if p is so embedded in (M) then we would seem to have "if x believes that p is valid then p, which is surely *a priori* and necessary. Alternatively (and very much as with (5)), if someone needs to believe p', ⌜I am a believer (in virtue of believing this belief)⌝ (or similar), in order to believe p, then the latter must be *a priori* and necessary in virtue of the deep self-referentiality of p'. If, on the other hand someone needs to believe p'', ⌜I am a believer (tenseless)⌝ (or similar), then p would have to be contingent and a posteriori in virtue of the (metaphysical and) rational possibility of $\neg p$. Hawthorne (2002, pp. 250-251), expresses related doubts about Williamson's (M) and p.

On a separate but related note, Williamson introduces the notion of "hyper-reliability" as a sufficient condition of apriority, such that if "it is impossible [for subject s] to believe falsely that p" (p. 117), then s knows that p *a priori*. Against this, I urge that this is a confusion of something akin to epistemic necessity for rational necessity. If s knows "I exist", there is a strong sense in which this is hyper-reliable (or epistemically necessary?), but $\neg$ (5) is surely metaphysically and rationally possible, hence (5) cannot be rationally necessary and *a priori*. Pryor (2006) expresses similar thoughts as to the hyper-reliability, but non-apriority, of "I exist", "I am thinking" and similar.

[31]See Winstanley (2008).

necessary and contingent in the first instance; sentences are only very derivatively so.

As should be apparent then, I view the contingent a priori as very "interesting", in virtue of, at least, its contribution to understanding the distinction between apriority and necessity; it is perhaps not so "scary", since, as I argue throughout, there are no genuine contingent *a priori* propositions. So, whilst I dispute the existence of any genuine, substantive examples of the phenomenon, I do think that the a correct understanding of the relevant modalities strongly supports (a) a clear bifurcation of rational and metaphysical necessity, and (b) the need for a clear distinction between sentences, propositions and circumstances. Indeed, even the failure of Kripke's examples, is as much due to the latter as to the former distinction; the baptiser knowing *a priori* that a sentence expresses a certain proposition, on the one hand, but failing to know what circumstance that proposition asserts, on the other-the circumstance itself (and so the proposition), however, being clearly, metaphysically contingent.

References

BonJour, Laurence. 1998. *In Defense of Pure Reason*. Cambridge: Cambridge University Press.

BonJour, Laurence. 2005. In defense of the *a priori*. In M. Steup and E. Sosa, eds., *Contemporary Debates in Epistemology*, chap. 4, pages 98–105. Oxford: Blackwell.

Davidson, Donald and Gilbert. Harman, eds. 1972. *Semantics of Natural Language*. Synthese Library. Dordercht: Reidel.

Donnellan, Keith. 1977. The contingent *a priori* and rigid designators. *Midwest Studies in Philosophy* 2:12–27.

Evans, Gareth. 1979. Reference and contingency. *The Monist* 69:161–189. Reprinted in Evans (1985, pp. 179–213).

Evans, Gareth. 1985. *Collected Papers*. Oxford: Clarendon Press.

Hawthorne, John. 2002. Deeply contingent *a priori* knowledge. *Philosophy and Phenomenological Research* 65(2):247–269.

Jeshion, Robin. 2001. Donnellan on neptune. *Philosophy and Phenomenological Research* 63(1):111–135.

Jeshion, Robin. 2002. Acquaintanceless *de re* belief. In J. K. Campbell, O. Michael, and D. Shler, eds., *Meaning and Truth: Investigations in Philosophical Semantics*, pages 53–78. New York: Seven Bridges Press.

Kaplan, David. 1978. Dthat. In P. Cole, ed., *Syntax and Semantics: Pragmatics*, vol. 9, pages 383–400. New York: Academic Press.

Kaplan, David. 1989a. Afterthoughts. In J. Almog, J. Perry, and H. Wettstein, eds., *Themes from Kaplan*, chap. 18, pages 565–614. Oxford: Oxford University Press.

Kaplan, David. 1989b. Demonstratives. In J. Almog, J. Perry, and H. Wettstein, eds., *Themes from Kaplan*, chap. 17, pages 481–563. Oxford: Oxford University Press.

Kripke, Saul A. 1980. *Naming and Necessity*. Cambridge MA: Harvard University Press. Originally pubblished in Davidson and Harman (1972, pp. 253–355).

Plantinga, Alvin. 1974. *The Nature of Necessity*. Oxford: Clarendon Press.

Pryor, Jim. 2006. Hyper-reliability and apriority. *Proceedings of the Aristotelian Society* 106(3):327–344.

Salmon, Nathan. 1982. *Reference and Essence*. Princeton: Princeton University Press.

Williamson, Timothy. 1986. The contingent *a priori*: has anything to do with indexicals? *Analysis* 46(3):113–117.

Winstanley, Paul. 2008. *Rationality and Modality*. Ph.D. thesis, Durham University, Durham. Forthcoming.

Index

a priori knowledge, 147–164
Ackerman, F., 115
actuality operator, 184, 189–192, 194
analyticity, 147–164
Asher, N., 65–93

Barcan-Marcus, R., 115
Bayesian strategy, 129, 130
Boghossian, P., 155–160, 162
BonJour, L., 151–152, 233, 233n
Boolos, G., 111
brain in a vat hypothesis, 127, 134
Broad, C., 226n
Brueckner, A., 131, 132
Burgess, J., 111

Carnapian
  epistemic arithmetic, 111–114
  epistemic logic, 111–114
  modal arithmetic, 104–111
  modal logic, 97–104
  Peano arithmetic, 106, 108
Carroll, L., 134
Cartwright, N., 172, 176, 177
causal theory of reference, 150
causality, 167, 168, 172, 174–176, 178, 180
Chisholm, R., 175, 177
coercion, 70, 79, 83, 90, 91
conceptual scheme, 23–25, 27, 29
conditional probability, 133

Conee, E., 139n
context
  of assessment, 183, 186, 187, 189, 190, 212, 213, 215, 217–220, 222, 225, 226
  of use, 185, 186n, 187, 189–191, 194, 212
  of utterance, 186, 212, 213, 215, 218, 219, 221, 225
contextualism, 4, 13, 13n, 16, 191, 194, 217
  content-contextualism, 13
  truth-contextualism, 15–16
contradictions, 133, 197, 198, 200, 205
  formal contradictions, 203n
  logical contradictions, 200
  metaphysical contradictions, 198
  semantic-logical contradictions, 208
Convention T, 29, 30, 37, 38
Copi, I., 125n
copredication, 70, 71, 77, 78
counterfactual dependence, 175, 181
counterfactuals, 169–171
  as stage-one-facts, 170, 172
  backtracking counterfactuals, 169n
  non-backtracking counterfactuals, 170

Craig, W., 220
Cresswell, M., 100
Crowell, R., 154n

Damian, P., 198
Davidson, D., 23–40
definitely operator, 18
denotation, 73, 80–82
Descartes, R., 198, 199
discourse semantics, 68n
dogmatism, 129
Donnellan, K., 231n, 234n, 235

epistemicism, 3, 4, 12
essentialism, 238
   obstinate essentialism, 53n, 60n
   persistent essentialism, 53n, 60n
   weak essentialism, 53
essentiality
   e-obstinate essentiality, 61n
   e-persistent essentiality, 61n
   e-weak essentiality, 44, 54, 61
   obstinate essentiality, 61n
   persistent essentiality, 61n
   weak essentiality, 53
Evans, G., 43, 46–51, 230, 234–239
events, 78, 79, 82, 83, 87, 169, 171, 173n, 174, 175, 180, 198
externalism, 80–82, 92, 147–164

fallibility, 135–141
Fara, D., 5–7
Feldman, R., 139n
Fine, K., 10n, 224
Follesdal, D., 107
Fox, R., 154n
Frankfurt, H., 198n

gap-principles, 5–20
Ghilardi, R., 115
Gilby, T., 200, 204
Gillies, D., 176
Goldberg, S., 157n
Goldman, A., 134, 139n

Gomez Torrente, M., 8n, 44, 53, 56
Gueroult, M., 198n

Haack, S., 140n
Hacker, P., 27n
Hackey, P., 28
higher-order vagueness, 3–20
   Fara's paradox of, 5, 7
Hitchcock, C., 168–172, 175–180
Horsten, L., 111, 118n
Huemer, M., 123, 126, 131, 135
Hughes, G., 100
Humber, J., 167
Hume, D., 167

induction
   over the set of wwf, 14
   sorites induction premise, 13
   strong principle of induction, 98, 105, 109, 111
   weak principle of induction, 97, 105, 106, 108–110, 113
inference to the best explanation, 124, 134
intertranslatability, 25–26, 33, 34, 37

Jackson, F., 63n
Jeffrey, R., 111
Jeshion, R., 231n
justification, 151, 152, 159, 162, 239–241
   defeasible justification, 123–145
   infallible justification, 124, 126
   inferential justification, 127–129, 140
   perceptual justification, 126, 129, 143
   propositional justification, 132
   synchronic justification, 139

Kölbel, M., 211, 212n
Kamp, H., 13n, 69n
Kant, I., 143, 230
Kaplan, D., 63n, 183–185, 240n
Kaufman, D., 198n

Keefe, R., 10n
King, J., 214n
knowability, 98
  knowability operator, 117
knowledge operator, 117
Kremer, M., 101
Kretzman, N., 200
Kripke, S., 44, 47n, 50, 51, 53,
  54, 55n, 56, 81, 147, 153–154,
  229, 230n, 231, 234, 242

law of nature, 171
least number principle, 111
Lepore, E., 205n
Lewis, D., 62, 63n, 171, 172,
  183–185
lexical meaning, 66, 68, 69, 71,
  83, 84, 89
logical form, 66, 69, 74, 75,
  80–84, 86, 92, 93, 149, 157,
  158

MacFarlane, J., 183–194, 211–220
Marti, G., 101
Mavrodes, G., 201
McDermott, M., 169
memory, 129, 156
Montague's Logical Grammar,
  66, 72–74, 85
Montague, R., 66, 72–74
Moore's proof, 124, 125, 125n,
  141, 143, 144
Moore, G., 123–145

names
  descriptive names, 43, 46–51,
    53n, 54, 62, 234, 235, 235n,
    236, 237
  empty names, 43, 44, 56, 56,
    57n
    empty descriptive names, 44,
      47, 55, 57, 58, 60, 62
negation
  limited vs unlimited, 203
non-acquaintance, 50

Olson, E., 168, 174–180

omnipotence, 198, 200, 201

Pap, A., 202, 203n, 207
Parfit, D., 168–181
Partee, B., 67n
Peacocke, C., 160, 162
personal identity, 168
personal identity, 167, 168, 172,
  178, 180
  reductionist view of, 173
Plantinga, A., 231n, 233
possible world, 47, 48, 48n, 53,
  55, 55n, 56–61, 72, 108, 112,
  147, 153, 171, 172, 184, 213,
  214, 237
Predelli, S., 88n, 215n
Principle of Compositionality,
  65–67, 67n, 82–86
Principle of Excluded Middle,
  207, 208
Pritchard, D., 134
probabilistic correlations, 169,
  170, 176, 180
propositions, 48, 77, 126, 127,
  130, 131, 133, 137, 138, 159,
  183–185, 187, 188, 191–194,
  208, 212–214, 216, 231, 232,
  240, 241
  contingent a posteriori
    propositions, 234
  contingent a priori
    propositions, 229, 230, 233,
    238
  indexical propositions, 230
  kernel propositions, 221–223,
    225
  narrow propositions, 237
  pseudo-propositions, 208
  rationally contingent a
    posteriori propositions, 241
  superficially contingent
    propositions, 234
  tensed propositions, 213–215,
    217–221, 226
  true at a world, 184
  wide propositions, 237

Pryor, J., 125n, 129n, 143n, 144, 233, 233n
Psillos, S., 172
publicity, 51
Pustejovsky, J., 66, 68, 76n
Putnam, H., 45

Quine, W., 154, 203

radical interpretation, 35, 38
Rafman, D., 13n
realism
  about propositions, 159
  perspectival realism, 213, 223–226
  tense realism, 225, 226
Recanati, F., 212n
Reed, B., 140n
reference, 43, 48, 49, 49n, 50, 54, 57, 62, 150, 153, 154, 156, 157, 204, 216, 220, 225, 231, 235, 238, 239
referential theoretical terms, 44–46
Reimer, M., 63n
relativism, 16, 218, 221
  context relativism, 219, 220
  double time reference relativism, 221
  tense relativism, 218
  truth relativism, 186–187, 191, 194, 211–213, 215n, 216–218, 221, 224, 226
  vanilla relativism, 212, 218
Richard, M., 214n
rigid designation, 43, 44, 47–48, 50, 51, 53–61
  e-weak rigidity, 44, 54, 57
  obstinate *e*-rigidity, 58n
  obstinate rigidity, 53n
  persistent *e*-rigidity, 58n
  persistent rigidity, 53n
  rigidified descriptions, 48
  weakly rigid designator, 56
Russell, B., 126, 202
Ryle, G., 201, 202, 202, 203n

S5 modal system, 10, 100
Sainsbury, R., 50n
Salmon, N., 53n, 55n, 60n, 63n
Salmon, W., 170
Sankey, H., 24n
scepticism, 123–125, 141
Schiffer, S., 156n
self-predication principles, 97, 98, 101–104, 114, 119, 120
semantic incommensurability, 23, 25, 31
Shapiro, S., 16n, 154n
Soames, S., 13n, 48n, 50, 51, 53n, 192
Sommers, F., 201, 202n
Sorensen, R., 8n
Stanley, J., 212n
subvaluationism, 4, 15
supervaluationism, 4, 9–12, 15, 18, 183–186, 188–190, 192, 192n, 193, 194
Swinburne, R., 139n
synthetic a priori, 198, 203
Szabó, Z., 85n, 88n

Tappenden, J., 13n
Tarski, A., 38
testimony, 129, 162
Thomason, R., 183, 185, 186
Tooley, R., 220, 226n
Twin-Earth, 147–149, 155, 157, 160, 161
Type Driven Theory, 65, 68–86
types
  Associating Types, 77
  Dependent Types, 77–79
  Dot Types, 77–79, 92
  Dynamic Types, 78

validity, 4, 31, 112, 120, 156, 159, 160, 207, 208
  global validity, 4, 10, 10n, 11, 13, 16, 17
  local validity, 5, 11, 13–16, 20
  regional validity, 10–12
  relative-stateless validity, 18–20

stateless validity, 5, 15–17, 20
Varzi, A., 10n

Whitehead, A., 202n
Williamson, T., 8n, 10, 12, 12n, 15n, 127n, 138n, 241n
Wittgenstein, L., 138, 144
Woodward, J., 178
Wright, C., 6n, 125n, 143n, 211n

Zimmermann, D., 225n

www.ingramcontent.com/pod-product-compliance
Lightning Source LLC
Chambersburg PA
CBHW071227170426
43191CB00032B/1071